Books by Nicolas Nabokov

Bagázh   (*1975*)
Old Friends and New Music   (*1951*)

Bagázh

BAGÁZH

Memoirs of a
Russian Cosmopolitan

Nicolas Nabokov

Atheneum   *New York*

1975

Portions of this book originally appeared in the November 1975 issue of *Vogue*.

To Dominique,
with love and gratitude

Foreword

T HIS IS NOT, properly speaking, a book of memoirs. It is
a story-teller's and a story-maker's book. When the reader
has read the first four or five chapters of "Russia . . . then,"
he will discover the reason for my warning. Since the age of five I
have been a compulsive story-teller and some of my stories have
turned out to be personally prophetic.

Nor are the stories I tell in this book concerned with my own
self. In one way or another, I am hiding behind each one of them,
but the chronicles included in the book are concerned primarily
with the life around me, with people I have met, with events that
took place during my life, and with my life's vagrant itineraries.
Thus, for instance, I do not impose upon the reader my repetitive
experiences of matrimony and of their component part, divorce. Nor
do I discuss my love or other personal affairs. They are private
matters that have no place here.

Though I am by profession a composer of music, this is not a
composer's book. For better or for worse, I have had many other
interests and occupations in life besides making music.

The stories I tell are arranged in chronological order, except that
sometimes—as for instance when I attempt to draw a person's portrait, or describe the making of a ballet or of an opera—a particular
chapter or section of the book acquires its own chronological sequence.

In a way, this is a book about memory. Or rather about memory's
capacity to remember—its achievements and failings.

I have never kept a diary, never taken notes, I destroy most of
my private correspondence, and I possess no archives to speak of. I

did not consult anyone while writing this book, especially not the hawkish memories of relatives. I know that they would be the first ones to contest my way of remembering. Only once in a while did I scan the pages of an encyclopedia to find a date or the spelling of a name. All the rest—the meat of the matter—I left to my memory. I tested, so to speak, its capacity for being truthful, for not distorting or embellishing what it keeps. While doing so I tried to be a faithful "free agent" of my own memory. When, for example, I re-invented dialogues and adorned them with quotes, I tried to follow memory's advice. I cannot swear, of course, that in conversations that took place a long time ago precisely these words were used, but the meaning, the spirit of the dialogue is the one that memory has retained. And as a story-teller I prefer to use the dialogistic form rather than the strictly narrative one.

This book has many lapses and gaps in time. I could not possibly tell in one volume *all* that I remember and all that might be of public interest. Maybe, sometime in the future, I will be able in another volume to fill in those gaps.

A small part of the material in this book, now revised and transformed, appeared twenty-five years ago in a book called *Old Friends and New Music*. Though by now *that* music has grown "old" and the friends are, I hope, in paradise, it seemed essential to use the material once again in this new and different context.

To me, personally, this book is something quite different from the stories it tells: It is a book about friendship and about friends. My life has been a *hortus deliciorum* of friendships. When I think back, I believe more in friendship among humans than in anything else. I have had the enormous luck of having throughout my long life a host of delicious and dedicated friends. Hence this witness to the faithfulness of some of them. Alas, not to all.

In fact, I owe this book to friendship—to the help and encouragement of so many friends that I could not possibly name them all. Some of them, like my wife and my publishers, helped me with advice and with their enormous patience during the long years of birth pangs and incubation. Others, like Elizabeth Hardwick and Saul Bellow, by reading my manuscript and giving me their counsel and stating their frank opinions. Others again by providing financial aid and hospitality to enable me to write this book. To all of them, collectively, I express my devoted gratitude.

One last warning: I do not pretend to be a writer, especially not in what to me still remains a foreign tongue. I tried to do my best and hope that at least to a certain degree I have succeeded. And, as Ariel says, my wish was and is "to please." Nothing more, but perhaps just a tiny bit of that.

1

Russia . . . Then

E YDTKUHNEN WAS THE German border station on the main line from Berlin to St. Petersburg. Eydtkuhnen's Russian counterpart was Verjbolovo. Here the narrow tracks of Western railroads stopped and the wide gauge of the Northwest Railroad of Russia began. Between the two lay a traveler's inferno: a double passport check, the German customs and the Russian customs, screeching children who had lost their parents, throngs of varied nationalities and social classes, and, above all, majestic mounds of luggage being shifted from one train to another.

Through this inferno, on an early summer morning of 1908, and in the direction of Russia, passed the three Nabokov children, in the company of harried Aunt Caroline, Fräulein Abzieher, and a few other melancholy members of the household staff—a mademoiselle; Nyanya Lyuba, my Russian nurse; and perhaps a manservant. Tired and grimy, but full of cheer, we children left the narrow compartments and corridors of the soot-covered German *wagon-lit* and burst into yelps of enthusiasm at the sight of the broader and more commodious first-and-second-class carriage, the *vagon mikst* of the Imperial Russian railroads.

While Aunt Caroline and the *Kinderpersonal* were checking and counting the luggage in the racks, my sister Onya and brother Mitya went about inspecting corridors, compartments, WCs, the samovar in the attendant's cubicle, the copper lanterns with their short, squat candlesticks, and the special way to open and close doors and windows.

I sat in a seat by the window, lost in a kind of reverie, waiting for the train to start. I was five and a half years old. The object of my reverie was not the change of track nor the improvement in comfort nor even the frightening transition from the world of Germany to the unknown world of Russia. I had left Russia in 1905, at the age of two, in the wake of my mother's divorce from my father, and was returning to Russia for the first time. To me, the great discovery of the day, which left me in amazement, was simply a new word: *Bagázh*. Not "luggage," mind you, but *Bagázh*—a Russian term (as I learned in due time) of French origin, covering a far greater range of possibilities than its limited English equivalent. It was at Verjbolovo that, for me, Russia began, and with it *bagázh*—from that day on, the most permanent and faithful companion of my peripatetic life. When I recall my childhood, sentences like *"Faites vos bagages? Qui a oublié ses bagages?"* and *"On a perdu les bagages!"* reverberate in my mind, and I see *bagázh* in entrance halls, in train racks, behind landaus, inside *dormeuses* and Benz motorcars, or forming a tarpaulin-covered mountain in the huge cart that followed us across the steppes of southern Russia between the years 1908 and 1917.

Pre-eminent among the various species of *bagazh* in use at that time was the *porte-plaid*. I rather think it was a product of Victorian England. The native Russian, lower- and middle-class *baool* (a twice-transplanted Turkish word meaning "bundle" which came from Italy by way of Odessa) was similar in form and function. The *porte-plaid* consisted of personal belongings wrapped in a Stuart or Mackintosh tartan, or in a handsomely bordered brown cloth, held together by leather straps and carried with a comfortable handle. It looked like a huge, fat envelope. The *baool* was the same kind of thing minus the Scotch plaid or bordered cloth (anything from a blanket to an old rag would do) and held together—often precariously—by whatever came to hand or was available in the household at the time of the packing. However, the *porte-plaid* moved determinedly to the position of the dominant piece of luggage in the feudal society of the period, while the *baool* simply continued to proliferate among the lower and middle classes of the Russian population. The *porte-plaid* was found not only in Russia but also among the upper classes all over Europe. The *baool* was very scarce in the West, abundant in Russia, and probably endemic in the Middle East and most of Asia.

Both species have become rare nowadays. During the Second World War a hybrid of the *porte-plaid* was to be seen at military

4

airports. It was usually carried by a squat-bottomed American colonel, and instead of being a neat envelope it looked like a sausage. Like its carrier, it was khaki in color and thus he and it melted into one unicolored Christian object, a cross, a vertical-and-horizontal sausage. Soon after the end of the war this degenerate *porte-plaid* was replaced by the standardized and Sanforized Scotch-plaid luggage of Madison Avenue. In the Soviet Union the *chemodán* (from a Tartar word meaning "travel case"), which in my childhood was limited to the upper and middle classes and ranged in composition from calf hide to cotton fiber, has, I am told, completely squeezed the *baool* out of existence.

Next in importance to the *porte-plaid* and the *baool* of my youth were the white and brown species of wicker basket. These came (and still do) in all shapes and sizes. There was the small one, longish and flat, held together by a stick (usually lost), and used for carrying the traveler's picnic (cold chicken, hard-boiled eggs, and battered fruit). Then there was the middle-sized one, often wrapped or sewed up in cloth. Those who couldn't afford a trunk carried in one or two such blankets all their belongings when going from one household to another. Finally, there was the huge, deep one with an iron rod and a large black lock. It was used mostly for linens and children's shoes, and on rare occasions for cut-up corpses.

The most capacious of our household's heavy luggage was the *kofr* (from the German *Koffer*). Every member of the family had his own *kofr*. The word sounded like an anagram of Korff, my Grandmother Nabokov's maiden name. The thing itself had about it an air of Baltic bourgeois dignity. It existed both in metal and in fiber hybrids and was, I believe, in use all over the world. But at the time of my childhood it had not yet developed the faculty of standing upright. It lay flat on the floor. "Upright *korfs*," or steamer trunks, were virtually unknown in Russia at the time. There were only rumors of their existence. Persons who, like our Fräulein Abzieher, had crossed the Atlantic Ocean and had visited or lived in the fairy-tale land of millionaires were said actually to have seen them.

In 1934, at the end of my first visit to America, I bought myself just such a highly advanced traveling convenience at a cut-rate luggage store on Sixth Avenue. It was shiny and glossy, with hangers and drawers and a huge metal safety lock. I felt very grand disembarking with it from the boat train in Paris, and soon word spread about that N.N. had returned from America *"couvert de dollars."* Alas, that upright *kofr* did not last long. It fell apart after its second Atlantic crossing and ended its short life on a junk heap.

Hatboxes were of varied sizes, shapes, and types. The standard ones were ladies' hatboxes. They were as they are now—cylindrical sections made of thin leather, oilcloth, or simply cardboard. On the top of the cardboard variety one could read names like Lucy or Georgette or Mme. Iris, which seemed to promise more than merely a lady's hat.

All ladies' hatboxes, regardless of construction, were delicate and fragile, and hence objects of great concern at the time of departure, when the *bagázh* was being collected in the antechambers. (*"Voyons! Vous voyez bien que c'est le carton à chapeau de votre mère! Pourquoi fourrez vous dessus vot' porte-plaid? Faites donc attention pour une fois!"*)

Gentlemen's hatboxes were more substantial, but they also varied in size and shape. My stepfather's hatboxes consisted of: (1) the hatbox for a top hat or bowler, (2) the hatbox for a military-style cap, and (3) the hatbox for a large, square fur hat. All of them were truly Platonic objects in that their outward form was an emanation of their inner one.

The third and last type of hatbox that accompanied our family's peregrinations had little to do with headgear. In fact, they weren't really hatboxes at all. They were made of light wooden veneer, usually yellowish in color, and bore on the cover an inscription in black, such as Nika or Lida or T.C. (Tante Caroline). These contained enameled night pots.

And, finally, the queen of *bagázh*, the rarest, most inbred, and yet most beautiful species: the lady's *nécessaire*.

I knew only one such object—my mother's. All others, in comparison, would seem rustic and bleak, But that one was custom-made by a mysterious foreign magician. It was perfection of its kind.

It was made of dark-red saffian leather and had two small gilded locks on top that opened smoothly and noiselessly at the turn of a tiny key. From its creases and cracks came an aroma connecting it with its owner: a blend of well-tanned leather and of Trèfle Incarnat—a scent so unwisely discarded by its maker, La Maison Piver. It opened like a ripe fruit, like the loins of a goddess, the two halves of its cover falling gently apart and offering its enchantments to the gaze of the onlooker. The four inner walls of the receptacle were of quilted doeskin. Three of those walls were lined with crystal and gold: small and large cream pots, cologne and scent bottles, toothbrush tubes, a soapbox (gold-covered, with engraved crowns and crescents). The fourth wall was all ivory, silver, and bristle.

At the bottom of the case, in small boxes of various shapes and sizes, lay the delight and the seduction: *les bijoux*. Rarely, very rarely, only after insistent begging, would my mother consent to show them to me. I would crouch near a table that was covered by a dark velvet cloth and look intently at the beautiful treasure. Then, after the viewing was over, the treasure would be put back in its proper receptacles. The reliquary would be locked up and deposited in the vaults of the Azovsko-Donskoi Bank.

Mother's *nécessaire* was always carried by her or by my step-father. It was never entrusted to the servants or to children. It followed the progress of our lives faithfully—rather like a kind and generous friend, a protector and helper in times of stress and want. Often it had to be hidden, and once it was buried in a garden, but fortunately was retrieved before hostile people had discovered it. It survived the turmoil of the Russian Revolution, the death of my stepfather, and the murder of my grandmother. It was with us in our flight from Russia and stayed with my mother through long years of exile.

As the years went by, it got scratched and battered, but still kept its poise and dignity. Alas, it grew constantly lighter and less miraculous inside. Some of the crystal objects got lost or broken. The little jewel boxes were fewer in number, and those that were left contained much less attractive ornaments. Emeralds and rubies, diamonds and pearls had gradually been exchanged for meat and rent, bread and clothes, till finally the old friend, the helper and protector, the *nécessaire* of my childhood, lost its distinction, its meaning, and its purpose. It became tired and worn.

It must have dissolved somewhere between Lubcza and Berlin, for when I last saw my mother, in 1936, herself stricken by an incurable illness, the faithful companion was not there any more. I did not ask any questions about its departure, respecting what was obviously the last wish of a noble friend.

That summer's morning in 1908 when we finally got off the train we were met by the stationmaster and a flock of manservants.

7

There, sent from Pokrovskoe, waiting for us, were the horses and carriages—two or three victorias, a phaeton, a *kabriolet*—and the *bagázh* was being piled up on a huge cart. The train started moving away before we had time to count our *bagázh*. It disappeared into the forest, leaving a grayish cloud in the blue, blue sky. And a little dog, a mongrel, ran out of the station, barking cheerfully at us and wagging its tail.

And as we jumped around the horses, bursting with excitement, there came from all sides, from the forest, the river, the sky, and the earth, new smells, hot smells, sweet, bitter, and ripe: hay and honey, tar and horse dung, bread and leather, burnt pine and sweat, the smells of Russian summer, like a gift—like a warning.

If you unfold a pre-Revolutionary map of northwestern Russia, you will find at a glance the three main cities of our region: Minsk, the capital of Belorussia; northwest of it, Vilna (presently Vilnius), capital of Lithuania; and farther southwest, Grodno. Through that region curves the river Neman. Looking southward, you will find a smaller but perhaps more famous tributary to the Neman, the Berezina, symbol of Napoleonic disaster.

While the name Neman, like those of most rivers or lakes of European Russia and some of eastern Germany, have pre-Slavonic Ugro-Finnish origins (Volga, Neva, Elbe, Spree, Oder), the name of the other famous river, Berezina (plumed marshals crossing it eastward and deplumed ones recrossing it westward), is derived from Russia's nationally beloved tree, the birch: *beryoza*.

Looking more closely, one discovers to the west of Minsk a kneelike bend in the Neman and—depending on the scale of the map—a place marked Lubcza. Twenty kilometers south of it was our district capital, Novogrudok, famous for its ancient ruins of a Yagellon castle and for being the birthplace of Adam Mickiewicz, Poland's greatest poet, so much admired by Pushkin and by most nineteenth-century Europeans.

Some forty miles south of Novogrudok lay a railroad junction with a small but very busy town attached to it. Marked on every map of European Russia, it linked two of the most important railroad lines, the one from Europe to Moscow, and the one from St. Petersburg to Odessa. It was called Baranovichi, and had the reputation of being one of the best restaurant stops in the region. Trains stopped for thirty to sixty minutes to give the traveler time for a fair amount of vodka, *zakuski,* and one or two courses. I remember cooks in white garb lined up behind silver platters containing woodcock, grouse, partridge, rack of hare, and other Russian game and fowl. In front of them stared the greedy eyes of upper-class epicures of various sizes and degrees of appetite. Between Baranovichi and Novogrudok lay Pokrovskoe, the estate of my stepfather, Nicolas von Peucker.

White Russia, as it used to be known before the Revolution, or Belorussia, as it is now known, was by far the poorest land in European Russia. It cannot compare with the "black-earth belt" of the South (between Kharkov and the isthmus of the Crimea), nor with the fair, well-tilled land of central Russia (around Orel, Kursk, and Moscow), nor even with the happy and gay Malorossia (now called Ukraina) from Poltava westward to Kiev.

At the time of my childhood Belorussia contained large expanses of forest, some of them very ancient. It also contained sweeps of deep and hazardous marshland, The arable soil was poor—gray and sandy, with a tough lime crust some twenty inches below the surface. Despite the improvements in agricultural techniques and the adoption of a rotational field system, our land in Belorussia needed large amounts of manure to make the crops grow. Yet the pasture and meadow land of our region was limited in size and very little of it was of first quality.

There was no village at Pokrovskoe, and the nearby villages were of indescribable filth and poverty. After rainy spells, stagnant water stood in the midst of the village for months, and in it wallowed underfed pigs (their exposed parts usually black with flies), swam broods of meager ducklings, or bathed cross-bred dogs. The peasant houses made of rotting beams were one-storied, very low and close to earth, their thatched roofs green with moss. The peasants and their children looked bedraggled and there was an air of hopelessness about all of it. Little children would run behind our carriages shouting, "Give us a penny, give us a sweet!"

The few places that stood out among this age-old poverty were the whitewashed Russian Orthodox or Roman Catholic churches, the police station, and, if the village contained over five hundred souls, the jail.

Many villages had a Jewish settlement, much neater and better kept than the Russian one. Here houses were painted, roads paved. In the Jewish general stores one could get everything: nails, boots, harness, herring, soap, and Odekolon.

Despite its social and agricultural shortcomings, our Belorussia, especially the part we lived in, was filled with a quiet beauty of its own. One sensed intuitively its mishaps, its precarious existence, and one was, as it were, submerged by its misery. Yet at the same time one felt strongly attracted by its lovable gentleness and its unostentatious charm.

Out of these contrasting feelings grew my lasting love for that land, a very special love, a bit sad, a bit helpless, yet infinitely tender and devoid of bitterness.

I believe that everyone who came to our land, even the toughest member of the foreign *Kinderpersonal*, felt the same way about Belorussia.

As for me, I feel that, whatever happens, I will remain forever a "Beloruss." This is my only way of "belonging" to a patch of earth, however remote and unreachable.

Belorussia, where my mother, my stepfather, and one of my mother's brothers, Uncle Frederick Falz-Fein, owned large estates with comfortable houses, farm land, and forests, was by no means the cradle either of the Nabokovs or of the Falz-Feins, and even less of my stepfather's family, the Peuckers.

According to family tradition, the Nabokovs originally came from Pskov, a town on Lake Ilmen, some two hundred miles south of St. Petersburg. They settled there in the thirteenth and four-teenth centuries, and their name is derived not, as one would expect, from *lech na bok* (to lie down on one's side), which would be plausible, but from old Arabic or Persian (I could not say which, knowing neither), *nab ocq* or *nab ocqe*, which in one of those languages means simply "son of . . ."

At the time of the Tartar Yoke, so the story goes, a Nabokov ancestor, supposedly a relative of the Khan, came to Pskov and settled on its outskirts. There he collected the Khan's tribute from the incoming and outgoing travelers. He or his descendants grew fairly prosperous, married Russian girls or boys, converted themselves to Christianity, and, like so many Tartars, became thoroughly Russianized.

I've always thought that this story was a family myth, and that the ancestral relative of the great Khan, the tribute collector of Pskov, never existed. The family, I thought, must have invented him in the course of the centuries as an excuse for the somewhat indolent connotation of the name. But maybe the tribute collector did exist. Maybe he was a Tartar, maybe he was a Persian, or an Arab, or an Armenian, or a Jew—and maybe he was indeed in the employ of the great Khan. There can always be convenient and inconvenient "maybe's" in matters like ancestry.

At any rate, before us—that is, before my mother and father and their three children—there had been no Nabokovs in the heartland of Lithuania or in Belorussia.

Nor did my mother's family, the Falz-Feins, have anything to do with Lithuania or Belorussia. In 1890 or 1891 two brothers of my mother bought a large "morsel" of land for a very low price. It had belonged to the German branch of the Princes Hohenlohe. Their estates lay in a region called Prilesie (Forest Land), or just a bit northeast of it, and had in the past been part of Russia, or Lithuania, or Poland. It was finally incorporated into Belorussia. Soon the younger brother, Uncle Charles, backed out of the deal and sold his share to Frederick. Thus Uncle Frederick became the sole owner of some 40,000 to 45,000 *desyatinas* (a *desyatina* is slightly more than two acres) of land in Belorussia. They included a huge expanse of primeval forest, in the midst of which lay a somberly quiet lake, Ozero Kroman. It was a mysterious lake. All sorts of legends were told about it, including the familiar one about churchbells ringing from the depths where a village had once stood and had sunk into the water.

Lake Kroman and the little river that flowed from it, the Kromanitza, were in a curious way our local meteorological stations. A colony of beavers had established itself at the outflow of the Kromanitza and had built an impressive dam made of tree trunks, weeds, mud, and juniper twigs. Beavers seem to be endowed with prophetic meterological gifts. They would adjust the height of their dam on the Kromanitza early in the spring in accordance with the amount of rain that would fall in the summer, so as to keep "their" lake, upon whose fish they thrived, at an even level. As a result, my uncle's foresters, who watched the beaver colony and protected it against intruders, knew in advance what kind of summer we were going to have.

My mother, Lydia Falz-Fein, was about to be married to my father at the time her brothers dealt so profitably at the Hohenlohe sale. She visited the castle of Lubcza (which was part of the estate and was the Hohenlohes' residence), loved it, and bought it from her brothers, with some 3,500 *desyatinas* of adjacent land. What she purchased, though doubtless the nicest part of the Hohenlohe "morsel," was about one-tenth of the whole property then owned by her two brothers. But, with shrewd brotherly love, they made her pay for it a very large share of what they had paid to the Hohenlohes.

Sometime between 1905 and 1907 my mother divorced my father and married a neighbor of ours, an upright gentleman and the *maréchal de noblesse* of our district.

Nicolas von Peucker, not quite a baron, was part Balt, part Greek, and only a bit Russian. Yet, like many cross-breeds of foreign extraction (particularly the German ones) born on the vast Slavic plain, he was intensely and patriotically Russian. As one of our governesses used to say, he was *"plus russe que le Pape."*

The Peuckers owned Pokrovskoe, the handsome estate to which we had come in 1908. It lay some thirty miles from my birthplace, Lubcza. Pokrovskoe, with its eighteenth-century house and garden, was to become my earliest and fondest Russian memory.

Nicolas von Peucker was a tall man of conservative outlook (facial, sartorial, and social) and dedicated to all things orderly and proper: high buttoned shoes, stiff collars with upturned corners, a well-groomed, bushy, but not excessively long mustache, dapper clothes or a well-cut uniform of his civilian rank. But also to prompt payment of interest or mortgages (infrequent in upper-class Russia), careful management of my mother's affairs, moderate drinking, eating, and other hedonistic habits, and, of course, a devotion to "Tsar, faith, and motherland," the formula for a healthy body-politic devised by the Tsarist bureaucracy's most conservative wing.

Yet despite all this, or rather in addition to it, Nicolas von Peucker was a patient, kind, and just man, a loved and loving husband. What concerns me more directly, he not only bore the same first name that I do, but he was also my godfather.

We children called him Uncle Koló or simply Koló, and to me, at least until 1909, he appeared as the originator (and profuse user) of Cologne's famous water.

My father, Dimitri Dimitrievich Nabokov, was a tall, flashily handsome man with a well-trimmed, short, pointed beard and ample mustache, whose facial traits looked more Baltic than Russian. He was, I was told, a great charmer, a great hunter, a fun lover and seducer—all of it, I suppose in equal doses. A court chamberlain like his father, and a justice of the peace, he owned the family *mayorát*, an estate in Poland near Cracow given by Alexander II or III to my grandfather, to be passed on to the oldest son of the Nabokov clan.

But my father Nabokov got lost in pre-history and, except for a single very early ornithological snapshot (as a bird in an ostrich-plumed chamberlain's tricorne), he remained unrecorded by my memory until we settled in St. Petersburg in 1911.

Only then started our yearly visits—always awkward and painful—to the Hotel d'Angleterre, where, in a room still penetrated by the sweetish patchouli smell of a female presence, I would sit on his knee and receive with polite indifference an inkwell in the form of a tin bulldog's head, or a plump metal watch with a Swiss chalet engraved on the back, or else a Solingen penknife with nailfile and ear-cleaner attachments. For the latter I had to give my father a *kopeika*, something I rightfully resented.

In any case, by the time my father reappeared on the horizon of my life at the sporadic Hotel d'Angleterre pilgrimages, my confident and loving relations with Koló were firmly and securely established, and to all intents and purposes, until his death in August 1918, he was our real father.

The date, place, and time of my mother's divorce and remarriage were concealed from us children (or at least from me) as a protection from the evils of the grown-up world. Later, much later, I learned that in 1905, when I was two years old, there had been a flight of children and governesses from Lubcza, my birthplace, down the river Neman on our private steamer. While we were fleeing, it appears, my father was hunting bears, elks, or hares and concomitantly courting the forester's wife. When he returned home to the castle, he found it empty. According to tradition, he wept for two days.

Then there was a long and, as I was later told, sordid divorce suit. In the course of it my father, prompted by unscrupulous lawyers, tried to win his case by naming me as the fruit of my mother's adultery.

Toward the end of his life in 1946, when after long years of hardship and illness he escaped with his wife (the former forester's lady and the exuder of patchouli scent) from the Soviet Zone of

13

Germany and lived with me in my occupation billet in Berlin, he denied having ever rejected me as his son. The allegation, he said, had been made not by him but by a mischievous relative with whom he had been accused of having had a love affair. To defend herself against the charge, she tried to blacken my mother's reputation. She did not succeed with the courts, for my mother won her case, but she planted the doubt in me and made me uncertain of my origin.

I think I was ten, or perhaps eleven, when one day a cousin of mine, for no reason at all, smirked at me and called me a bastard. I asked another cousin what he meant and she explained in a secret-mongering whisper that everyone knew I was not Papa Nabokov's son, but that my real father was Koló and that I'd better know about it.

"When you grow up," she said, and several well-wishers followed suit, "you will have to change your name—you will be forced to do so."

It hurt and troubled me in several ways: it cast a shadow upon my mother's and Koló's relations, it made me feel an outcast from the "normal" family circle, and it hurt my pride. Since my earliest childhood I had known that the Nabokovs were an old and distinguished Russian family. It was bitter at such an age to learn that one had nothing to do with this family.

I never could bring myself to question either my mother or my stepfather about my birth, although intermittently it troubled me for a very long time. At one point my mother seemed to want to speak to me about it. This was, I believe, in the middle 1920s. She had come from Poland and I from Paris, and we met midway in Germany at the Lake of Constance. It happened very rarely that I was alone with my mother, and therefore those days remain in my memory as exceptionally happy.

On the evening we parted we sat on a bench near the lake. It was a gray, misty evening. My mother looked paler than usual, worn and aged. We were both sad and at the same time restive to get the parting over with. After a long silence, without looking at me, she said somewhat solemnly but calmly: "Sometime before I die, I must tell you about yourself and your father. . . ."

Then she paused, as if hesitating.

"But not now," she added. "Another time. Yes, later . . . Let us go now to the station. . . ."

"Another time" never came. She never spoke to me about it again.

Though the question was never answered, and hence the ambiguity remains, I firmly believe that the allegation made by the lady relative at the trial was gratuitous and utterly false.

Koló had slipped into my life before I was capable of recording the event. When I awoke to consciousness he was already there, enthroned as my mother's consort and as an essential part of the family.

But in those early years abroad my mother's and his presences in the family were intermittent, meteoric. They came and went, vanishing into nowhere, appearing here for a week, there for a month, at the ever changing stations of our migratory progress. I do not remember even vaguely having traveled or spent any length of time with them. What I do remember is: "Go and say good morning to Mama and Koló" or "Go and say good night—they'll be leaving tomorrow morning."

We children were left in the care of a remote relative whom we called Tyotya Karolya—Aunt Caroline—and of a flock of linguistically heterogeneous and numerically elastic domestics. Among them my memory has recorded only a few names and faces, and even those are vague. There was the German governess, Fräulein Abzieher ("slipcover" in English). She was followed later by various Misses; there was a permanent nurse, Nyanya Lyuba (strictly Russian); and later on there was my mother's lady's maid, Klara (German and broken Russian). And, of course, there were various Mademoiselles.

In all, a fairly large group of people was constantly around us to bathe and clothe us, to take us out for walks, to teach us to read and write in several languages, to protect and pamper us, and to fuss over us in a hundred ways. Those were milk-and-honey days; they now seem even to me like something out of a fairy-tale.

Until 1909 we were three: sister Onya (corrupted from Sonya), the eldest; my brother, Mitya (from Dimitri) in the middle; and I, the third. Only six years later did my mother have another child, with Koló—my half-sister Lydia. Hence, for quite a while I was the youngest, the blondest, the plumpest, and, alas, the most pampered of the lot. Fortunately, as a kind of compensation, I was also the most teased. There were many and very different kinds of teasers around. But teasing on a permanent and professional scale was done by my brother Mitya with Onya's occasional help.

Tyotya Karolya—that is, Aunt Caroline Muller—was a fixture in our household since time immemorial. She was my grandmother's cousin on my mother's side. Early widowed, she had a perpetual middle-aged or, rather, ageless appearance. Only much later, after World War I, did she suddenly age and get sickly. At the time I speak of, she was a kindly, constantly agitated lady, endowed with that special capacity of "hennishness" which is badly needed by children whose parents are frequently absent. Like me, she was plump and highly teasable, and, like me, she used to burst into tears at the slightest provocation. This created between us a damp bond. As a result, I was known in family circles as Aunt Caroline's darling, her Nikooshka or Poompsie, the latter a nickname she invented for me because of my plumpness.

This caravan traveled through Europe: from Nice to Dresden, to Czemin near Pilsen in Bohemia. The chronology of our movements from one of these places to another has vanished, as have most of the physical attributes of those places. Only bits remain, unconnected, incongruous: a chair with a black Moorish crescent that pricked one's back; a dress full of *broderie anglaise* holes; a black celluloid swan that took in water and let out bubbles.

In Nice we lived in a villa near the old port. In Dresden my mother and Aunt Caroline took intermittent cures. Czemin, a fairly large estate, belonged to my mother's brother, Uncle Nicolas Falz-Fein. He bought it, I was told, while his house in southern Russia was being remodeled. Czemin is the first place I remember.

Czemin was full of children. Uncle Nicolas had four of them: two girls, one son, and a newborn baby girl from his second marriage. Both of his wives were German, so the whole brood spoke mostly German with an occasional sprinkling of hesitant Russian. The three Nabokov children brought the number to seven, but there must have been a few more around. In my memory, in any case, there were at least nine or ten children at Czemin and I was the youngest of the lot.

Thus the population of "ancestors," as we soon started to call them, was in a proportion of approximately two to four, whereas the proportion of the *Kinderpersonal* (children's staff) varied *per capita* from one to two to one to three. The linguistic capacities of the total of ancestors plus *Kinderpersonal* covered, in various degrees of perfection and intelligibility, the four main languages of Europe.

At Czemin, the separation of the children and grown-ups into two groups was clear-cut. On one side there was Group I: the hierarchical feudal society of grown-ups, with parents as top caste, *Kinderpersonal* as middle caste, and servants as lower caste. On the other side was Group II: the "egalitarian classless society" of children.

The relations between the groups ranged from peaceful coexistence through subversive activity (all of Group II against all of Group I) to open warfare. Nevertheless, by virtue of its imposing age advantage, Group I remained the permanent upper dog and controlled the unruly community of Group II.

But there was one exception to this intricate sociological structure: me. Being too young for either group, I was left outside both, and so I continued to live my charmed life, protected by Aunt Caroline and Nyanya Lyuba. On occasion, however, I was called upon to perform certain tasks for Group II, and for this reason became a kind of lower-caste appendage of theirs.

At Czemin there was a beautiful shady path leading from the main house to a playhouse for the children. In front of it stood my sand pile. This is where I was usually ordered by Group II to perform the duty of watchman.

The meetings of Group II in the little house took place at irregular intervals and involved full group membership. I would notice at lunch when a "meeting" was being planned. There were whisperings among my cousins, and one of the older boys, their boss, was giving orders by signs and glances. At about five p.m. the children would start converging on the playhouse and I would be ordered to take up my vigil. One by one, they would slip into the little cottage.

"Now you sit here and watch," the boss cousin would say. "If you see someone coming up from there," and he'd point at the shaded path, "you knock at the door. But don't you dare open it! If you do, I'll beat you up—understand?"

At first I tried to pretend not to be interested at what was going on in the cottage. I squatted near the sand pile, dug tunnels, and obediently kept watch. But few grown-ups walked at that time of day. The ancestors played lawn tennis or croquet in another part of the garden, and the governesses left the children to their games and sat in their respective rooms writing sad letters home.

So after the second or third time I began to be less worried about the possibility of being surprised by some member of the *Kinder-*

personal and more interested in what was going on inside the play-house.

The little house would grow silent after the "boss" had closed the door. I couldn't understand it. What were they doing? What kind of games were they playing inside? I got bolder and left my tunnels. I tiptoed to the door and put my ear close to it and listened. But I could hear barely anything at all. All was quiet inside.

I got more and more curious and somewhat excited. Why didn't anyone talk inside, I asked myself, or sing, or shout, or whistle? Why so much silence?

So I stood on my toes and tried to look through the keyhole. But it was too dark inside, and I couldn't distinguish anything. Drowning my fear in curiosity, I pasted my ear to the crack in the door.

After a while, hearing no words, no whispers, shaking and quivering, I reached for the doorknob. As the knob turned, my will grew firmer. Finally the turn of the knob came to an end. Slowly, carefully, silently, I slipped into the playhouse.

All the girls were crouching on all fours on the floor, their skirts turned up. The boys, the small ones and big ones, were bending over the girls' naked bottoms and inspecting them. All of them were utterly serious.

The little boy at the door stood aghast, frozen in amazement.

Then, suddenly, the door blew open with a bang. And a figure, the dread figure of my mother, appeared.

Everyone was punished. From then on the girls sat at a separate table and weren't allowed to speak to the boys. Governesses surrounded them like vultures, and kept a permanent vigil. All play hours were changed into work hours. All sweets were forbidden for two weeks. The ancestors looked stern, granite-hewn, and barely spoke to the children. Some of the mothers and, of course, Aunt Caroline had red eyes for several days. The little house at the end of the shady path was locked up, declared off bounds for everyone.

Thus, for all intents and purposes Group II ceased to function. The only thing that remained was their united rage against me. "Pig," "Informer," "Spy," I heard them whisper as they passed me.

And what made it worse was that, being the youngest and, in the eyes of the grown-ups, the only innocent one, I remained unpunished. I could go about my business as usual, chaperoned by my

Nyanya. I was smiled at, ate pudding and jam and sweets.

But one day I was caught unawares in the park. Nyanya Lyuba had stayed behind. Two of the boys fell upon me, and while one of them held my mouth shut, the other beat me mercilessly, first with a bunch of hard twigs, then with his fists. My bottom bled through my pants and my eyes looked like blue, bloated plums. But in some way I must have felt that the beating was justified. For the first and, I am afraid, the last time in my life, I did not cry or even whimper, and I refused to give the names of those who had beaten me.

But then, soon, very soon, in 1908 we left Czemin, and there was Russia!

How well I remember those horse-drawn trips in Russia! I remember my perennial childhood fears concerning horses, carriages, and roads. The hazards were many. Would the horse manage to draw the carriage up a fairly steep hill near Novogrudok, or would we have to get out and push while the coachman pulled the horses by the bridle? Would the screeching brakes on the wheels hold while going down the same hill on its opposite side? Would a wheel fall off, or an axle break in the mud or the sand? Would the horses take fright, run amok, throw the coachman off his box and spill the rest of the human ballast into a ditch? I distinctly recall the apprehensive tones in Aunt Caroline's voice as she asked the coachman, Anton, before every trip, pointing to the horses: "Are they gentle?" What often happened with the heavier carriages, the landaus, was that they got stuck in the mud, and the children would have to be carried out one by one, on the coachman's back, to a dry place at the edge of the road. There we would sit on spread-out plaids watching the coachman coax, tug, and pull at the horses, screaming: "*Noo! Noo!* Get on!" Then, in exasperation, he would start whipping the beautiful fat bottoms with a crackling long Cossack whip and mutter unprintable curses.

Most of my fears concerning carriages, horses, and roads were justified in the Russia of 1910–15. Axles did break, wheels did fall off and roll away into ditches or fields, horses did run amok. As a result, there were often bleeding noses, bruised eyes, and hopelessly tattered and soiled clothes after such accidents.

So, in this to me rather perilous fashion we made our way from the railroad station, Molchad, to Pokrovskoe. It was only about twenty miles, but the way was so tortuous and sandy that wheels disappeared up to the axle, and sometimes the road looked like a swamp with deep, slippery ruts running through it.

Neither my mother nor my stepfather came to meet us in Molchad. They were waiting for us on Pokrovskoe's white Corinthian portico. We were hugged and embraced and led through the spacious rooms to the terrace overlooking the garden, where tea, coffee, and cocoa were served in Russian style; many kinds of bread—black, gray, sweet-and-sour, a golden brioche-like one with raisins; soft white peppermint cookies; English fruit cake; sour milk or curd with cinnamon and sugar; various cream cheeses; and a large bowl of *macédoine de fruits* made of gooseberries, currants (black, white, and red), raspberries, strawberries, and two types of cherries, the bloody and sour *vishny*, and pinkish blond but sweet *chereshny*.

I remember that the sun was still high and the smell of phlox, heliotrope, tea roses, and tiny white border flowers melted in the warm afternoon. After tea we ran down the main broad *allée* to the pond. We screamed and laughed until Pyotr Sigismundovich, our new tutor, Fräulein Abzieher, and Nyanya Lyuba caught up with us and whisked us to our respective rooms. First into the round metal tub with three inches of tepid water to scrub yourself in and pitchers of somewhat warmer water to wash off the foam. Then quickly to bed.

But, as I remember it now, sleep did not come at once to me that evening. I lay and listened to the noises downstairs. There the grown-ups were chattering loudly in the large, square living room, waiting for the chief butler to announce that supper was ready. Three or four courses had been prepared, to be absorbed by the apparently gargantuan appetites of parents, relatives, governesses, and our tutor. Meanwhile Mitya, with whom I shared the room, tiptoed in his nightgown to the open window. He stood there for a while silently. Then he whispered to me: "Come here, look up there." I got up and stood next to him and looked. The evening was warm and fragrant. Straight in front of me, just above the treetops surrounding Pokrovskoe's large pond, at the end of the garden hung the sickle of the young July moon. The sky was clear and opalescent. The pond glittered. Pokrovskoe, my first really conscious memory of Russia!

Later my mother, followed by Koló, slipped silently into our bedroom. They went from Mitya's bed to mine, and my mother bent over and gave each of us a kiss on the neck, behind the ear. Then she stood for a while near my bed and whispered to Koló: "How tall he has grown. Quite a boy."

The Peuckers had bought Pokrovskoe at a sale that followed the ruin of another Baltic or German fortune. It had belonged to a railroad magnate, a Herr von Meck. The magnate's widow had been for thirteen years Tchaikovsky's patron and the "beloved friend" of a tormented, though securely epistolary, romance.

There remained in the house at Pokrovskoe a faint trace of an elegant Baltic era. Some of the furniture in the rooms was very pretty. It was of that particular brand of charming Nordic Empire (light Karelian birch with thousands of dark, star-like eyelets) that looks tidy and neat and has well-drawn forms. Some of the flowered wallpaper in the bedrooms, the chintzes and the horsehair upholstery of the dining and living rooms added to the interior of Pokrovskoe house an English country-house flavor.

The garden of Pokrovskoe also had a Nordic charm. It was better kept than Russian gardens usually are and was full of roses, alyssum, heliotrope, and other strongly scented flowers and shrubbery, most of which have now been replaced everywhere by begonias, geraniums, and other unsmiling and unsmelling species.

At Pokrovskoe our day began early. We got up at eight and were downstairs for breakfast at eight thirty. In autumn, winter, and early spring, breakfast was served in the somber, brown-papered dining room. We sat sleepy-eyed under two large spirit lamps with flowing white bonnets. All the double windows were tightly shut and sealed with brown paper strips. We drank our cocoa and ate our bread and butter in dreary silence.

But in the summertime, breakfast was a delight. It took place outdoors, on the large semicircular porch that overlooked the garden. The porch was surrounded by six or eight pairs of white columns supporting a balcony outside Mother's boudoir.

After breakfast came the "classes." I was still being babied and had much shorter and fewer classes than my sister and brother. But I did have to go through a daily routine of building words out of syllables in three or four languages and learning short poems in Russian, French, and German by heart, as well as applying myself to simple arithmetic.

All of this took place between nine and twelve. We were passed from Fräulein to Mademoiselle to an English Miss to Pyotr Sigismundovich like inanimate objects, occasionally bumping into each other in corridors or on staircases. Every day I waited with anticipation for the clock to strike noon and end our educational ordeal.

Twice a week we had religion lessons with the local priest. These lessons left me bewildered. It was difficult to understand the *Katekhisis* and equally difficult to take the priest's word for it. I had to memorize in church-Slavonic the Nicene Creed. The meaning of the Slavonic words was not always clear to me. But the priest said: "Just learn it, my boy, and believe in it. The important thing is to recite it."

Promptly at one we would sit down for our midday meal. Mother established a system of quick meals. They never lasted longer than an hour.

After dinner there was an obligatory nap. The grown-ups had coffee on the porch and then disappeared to their respective quarters and grown-up occupations.

It seems to me that the main occupation of the grown-ups of that time was epistolary. Following nineteenth-century custom, everyone wrote letters to everyone else. The letters were about everything and nothing, touching and trivial, charming and pointless. The grown-ups also kept diaries, and we were urged to follow their example. For my seventh birthday Aunt Caroline gave me a pretty leather-bound book with dates and neatly drawn lines. But after putting down in clumsy handwriting: "Today we ate a big carp," I forgot about the book.

Pokrovskoe had a large farm with barns, sheds, haylofts, stables, a pigsty, and a smithy. I liked to go to the smithy and watch the cumbersome procedure of putting fresh shoes on horses' hooves and making brown and smelly glue out of hoof parings.

Autumn, winter, and early spring were seasons for indoor games and occupations. I liked to sew doll's clothes and play checkers. There were two ways of playing checkers in Russia. The regular one was called "hard" checkers, the other one was called "give-in" or "soft" checkers. The point of the first kind was to "eat up" the checkers of one's opponent, the second to lose all of one's own checkers as quickly as possible. I liked the latter type, and acquired a mastery of being "eaten up" quickly.

When there was a holiday, a birth- or name-day, all of us children with our governesses and tutor would put on a show. I remember participating once in a performance of "The Dragonfly and the Ant," a fable by Russia's Aesop-and-Lafontaine, Krylov. I was the dragonfly. I wore a green cape and a huge green headgear representing the insect. Brother Mitya wore a terrier-sized brown monster on his head that looked more like a turtle than an ant. At times Onya or Mitya would scratch a piece of music on a small fiddle.

Usually toward the end of such festivities I would be urged to tell a story. I do not remember when I started to tell stories, but by the time we came to Pokrovskoe I was already known as the family's story-teller. My stories were all of them fairy-tales. As is usual in Russian fairy-tales, my hero and heroine were a Tsarevna and a Tsarevich. They went through all sorts of ordeals—fights with monsters, getting lost in enchanted castles, escaping from evil magicians. But my stories always had a happy ending. "There was a great feast," I would say toward the end of my story, "and it lasted forty days and forty nights. Everyone was reunited—the Tsarevich and the Tsarevna, their father and their mother—and all of them were very happy and the Tsarevich kissed the Tsarevna a hundred times and they were blessed by a priest in a golden chasuble and then they started marrying . . . and they married . . . and married . . . and married all over again."

I never quite understood why everyone laughed at this (maybe by some odd premonition), but I liked to tell stories on every festive occasion, always with the same ending.

There was at Pokrovskoe quite a lot of music in and about the house. One of our governesses was an expert violinist. Mother accompanied her on a quadrangular pianoforte. Unfortunately the old relic (it was supposed to have been "blessed" by Tchaikovsky's fingers) was permanently out of tune. Its dentures were worn and a few strings missing. The governess-violinist was justly exasperated, but my mother seemed to be unaware of the coughs, rattles, and grunts. She liked to play on it, and I liked to watch her play.

Mother played a repertory of salon music, mixing *chansons tristes* with Virgin's prayers in a non-stop medley. The defective digestive system of the ancient pianoforte gave the melancholy medley a certain unity. The same sound holes, gargles, and jangling always surrounded the same notes, and all chords produced the same kitchenware clatter.

Onya and Mitya started to practice, or rather to scratch the catgut of their three-quarter-size violins with the horsehair of their bows. At noon or just before supper, "ill-tempered" violin scales

23

pierced the placid silence of the house and after a while scales gave
way to bits of soured Fibich and Kreisler.

Like most Russian children, we loved to sing together, and soon
learned to sing in parts. Mitya and I sang the tune in unison while
Onya supplied a secure third or sixth below. We sang loudly and
cheerfully, uninhibited by a need for nuances or any expressive
shibboleths. In accordance with our multilingual upbringing, we
sang the current children's repertoire in French, German, English,
and Russian. The French songs, the meaningless "*Malbrouque* [for
Marlborough] *s'en va-t-en guerre*" and the penumbral "*Frère Jacques*" were a bore, and so was the English canonic "Three Blind
Mice." Some of the sweet and tender German tunes, especially one
involving "little roses on a moor," were pretty and pleasant to sing.
But the three of us loved to sing the Russian songs of our repertoire.

The Russian songs we learned had little to do with Russian folklore. Only one or two were even faintly "genuine," and even the
"Volga Boatmen" was of dubious ancestry. The tunes of these songs
had quite obviously come from different lands and passed through
many hands before reaching Russia.

Later on I was taught that what we had sung during those early
childhood years was trash; that one should like those songs that had
sprung out of the "soil, the heart, and the womb" of Matooshka
Rossiya. These were to be found in "reliable" song collections, like
those of Borodin and Balakirev, or in Mussorgsky's and Rimsky's
operas. These "authentic" folk songs, stemming from Russia's soil,
heart, and womb, had been classified by "great scholars" according
to region, custom, ritual, and age. Some of them were very ancient
and therefore must be "true, good, and beautiful." But I could not
help preferring (and still prefer) the hybrid tunes of my childhood,
despite their "un-authentic" origins.

I am happy to see that some of these "pseudo-Russian" songs, like
"The Swallow" (with its Neapolitan lilt), "The Three Maidens" (a
German soldiers' tune), and the "Solitary Little Bell" (straight from
the Jewish Diaspora), are now sung by excellent Soviet choruses
and described in programs as "the Soviet people's folklore."

Another source of music for us was the small whitewashed vil-
lage church at nearby Gorodishche. We went there for Vespers on
Saturdays and for High Mass on Sundays. Onya and Mitya, as far as
I remember, sang in the church choir. I preferred the less crowded

and less festive Vespers to Sunday mass. The service was quieter and the chants simpler. The church was penetrated by delicious smells, a mixture of incense, candle wax, and body warmth. I loved to watch the rays of the evening sun pass through clouds of bluish, scented smoke, scanning the gilt and silvery "coat of mail" of the Iconostasis.

At the end of the service the choir would sing the last evening prayer—sweet, gentle, and unpretentious. It was like the symbol of sabbath repose after a week's labors. We would walk back to Pokrovskoe in the cool of the evening, singing our "bastard" tunes and arousing swarms of rooks and blackbirds that settled for the night in the aspen groves that surrounded Pokrovskoe's ancient park.

Later on, when I grew up, I learned to dislike the kind of music that was used in the Russian church at the time of my childhood. Instead of singing traditional Russian chants, all the choirs of Russia were singing authentic nineteenth-century trash gleaned from secondhand Italian opera. Most Russian so-called "church composers" were imitating lowbrow Western examples. While I have always enjoyed the hybrid pop songs of my childhood, I have resented the use of phony music by church choirs all over Russia. None of these choirs seemed to be aware of the existence of a large body of ancient Russian church chant that was still being sung in remote monasteries, mostly in northern Russia, like Valaam on the Lake Ladoga or at Solovki, which has since become a Communist jail.

At the end of that first year at Pokrovskoe, in 1909, the autumn rains started early. It rained continuously throughout September and the roads became impassable. Visitors stopped coming. Even the priest from Gorodishche had a difficult time reaching us in his old rig. Second frames were put into the windows in October, leaving one square of each window in operative condition. It was called caressingly *fortochka*, from the German *Pförtchen*. The stoves were lit, and like bears we settled in for a long Belorussian winter.

Toward the end of October, Mother got sick. She grew pale, complained about pains and headaches, and her eyes were sad and feverish. Koló and Aunt Caroline whispered together in corners, and I felt that something unexpected was about to take place. One day after snow had made roads passable, Mother and Koló left. I

25

remember standing on the front of the house, tucked into a fur-lined coat, crying and waving goodbye.

A few weeks later we started receiving parcels wrapped in paper and sewed into oilcloth. The porter of the *wagon-lits* of the St. Petersburg–Nice express brought them to Baranovichi and someone fetched them from there. They contained *fruits confits* and tightly compressed bunches of roses, violets, and carnations. We put the flowers into tubs of tepid water, but they died in one or two days, leaving behind them a scent of a faraway, warm, and festive world.

One day at dinner, about a month after Mother's departure, Aunt Caroline, the titular chief of the tribe, announced that we should be leaving Pokrovskoe to spend the rest of the winter at Lubcza. The announcement was greeted with cheers from the children and the glum silence of the *Kinderpersonal*.

"*On vient de s'installer,*" grumbled the Mademoiselle, "*et voici qu'on repart.*" "*Schon wieder weg,*" retorted her German colleague, "*ein wahres Zigeunerleben.*" Even the gentle English Miss looked despondent about the packing that had to be done.

For me, the announcement was something special. It was not so much the adventure of traveling on sleighs in the Russian country-side that made me happy, it was something much more precise. Everyone around me had been talking since my earliest days about the beauty of Lubcza, about the castle surrounded by its deep moat, its ancient towers, the comforts of its house, the river Neman at the foot of its hill. But most important, I was the only one of the brood who had been born at Lubcza.

In the course of the summer the superintendent of Lubcza had come to Pokrovskoe several times and reported on all the improvements that were being made to the castle and its farm. A guest house had just been completed. New parquets or fresh linoleums had been laid everywhere. The furniture was being repaired and redecorated. The garden, especially the fruit and vegetable part of it, was filled with new trees, new shrubbery, new flower beds. At the farm, everything was being restored or newly built; there was a new cow barn, a new hayloft, a new horse stable, and a modernized dairy with an adjacent cheese factory. Even the old steamer that had whisked us out of Lubcza in 1905 had had its machinery modernized and had been covered with a coat of white paint. "Now she looks," said the superintendent, "like an Imperial yacht."

Several days after Aunt Caroline's announcement, the baggage ritual started. From the four corners of Pokrovskoe's house came German, French, English, and Russian voices, snapping at each other in different pitches and states of agitation.

"*Madame Muller, est-ce qu'on prend ça?*" or "*Soll man wirklich all' diese Kinderbücher einpacken?*" or Aunt Caroline's exasperated voice: "*Deti . . . ne . . . shumite . . . perestante orat!*" (Children, stop that noise . . . stop yelling.)

I was given a worn old *kofr* and was occupied packing and repacking it. All kinds of things went in and out of it. Toys, my own "personal" books, and, of course, all those precious trinkets that had been given to me: my silver goblet, a cuckoo clock with its, alas, silent bird, a red piggy-bank with my five-*ruble* goldpiece in it, my fishing equipment, and an inkwell representing Beethoven's head in some sort of pewter-like metal. The real problem was my collection of dolls and fuzzy animals. The *kofr* refused to close. Finally I called my tutor to the rescue, and with his help I got most of my stuff in. The lock being broken and the key lost, we tied it up with a roll of cord.

About a week later, long before dawn, we were awakened. We washed and dressed and hurriedly ran downstairs. There the priest and the sleighs with horses and coachmen were waiting for us. After a brisk breakfast our village priest sang a *Moleben* (Te Deum) for travelers and sprinkled us all with holy water.

Meanwhile a mound of baggage was rising in the front parlor. It was counted over and over again and then was moved to a large cart on sleigh runners, covered with a tarpaulin, and tied tightly with a dozen cords. Four hefty horses pulled it out of the gateway.

By that time the stars were beginning to fade and were being replaced by the bland light of dawn. Although the frost was biting its way down to twenty degrees below zero Centigrade, the air was still and dry and the day promised to be sunny. Following Russian ritual, we all sat down in the living room for a last moment of silence. Then we moved outdoors into the frosty morning. The stars were gone. The horses emitted clouds of steam.

The two first sleighs were high ones of foreign make in which one could sit. The others were Russian *rozvalni*, in which one had to lie between layers of fur and woolen blankets. They were low and flat-bottomed—basically, planks of wood covered with straw or hay. On the top of the straw, like a sandwich, was a furry envelope lined with several Scotch plaids or other woolly stuff. The stuffing for this sandwich was human beings. The whole thing was managed by a coachman wearing so many coats that he looked like a huge stuffed animal on its hind legs. There were either three (a troika) or four horses to each sleigh.

Aunt Caroline, the leader of our Arctic expedition, mounted the first sleigh with sister Onya and the English Miss, all of them in heavy furs. The other two foreign ladies and Nyanya Lyuba squeezed into the second sleigh. Our tutor, my brother, and I were tucked into the largest and furriest of the *rozvalni*. The remaining sleighs gathered up the rest of the migrating tribe.

Aunt Caroline, a fur-clad, dark, ovoid object in a white woolen hood, lifted her muff and gave the coachman the sign to depart. Off we slid upon noiseless roads into the first rays of a cold, rising sun.

The drive in the *rozvalni* turned out to be neither smooth nor cozy. Despite the triple-decker sandwich of straw, fur, and blankets in which we lay, the bumps of the road, covered with layers of dirty ice, hit our backs, buttocks, and heads. The coachman drove the horses at a fast trot, trying to keep pace with the front sleigh, the well-upholstered one on springs with Aunt Caroline in it.

Our native contraption swayed, skidded, and tipped from left to right. The three of us were tossed about like lettuce in a salad basket. The goose grease on my face got hot and sticky. It started to bake my skin. The harsh white sunlight hurt my eyes, and the tinkle of the bells on the horses' harness was exacerbating to my ears.

The only thing I could see from my supine position was the coachman's huge back and beyond that a quartet of horses' bottoms in rhythmic motion, their lobes separated by long, frosted tails.

Soon Mitya and I started to whimper. Our tutor told the coachman to slow down. "Never mind if we are late . . . the children are not accustomed to this kind of thing." The coachman slowed down. Our bodies got a respite. But the heat and the smell of horse sweat and fart, bearskin, and wet wool grew fierce.

Each time I tried to sit up, a whiff of icy air would penetrate into my fuzzy sandwich and my tutor would say testily: "For heaven's sake, lie down and don't move or we shall all get frozen."

He covered my face with a shawl, turned me on my side, and

told me to shut up. "Try to sleep," he said, "it will soon be over." So, for want of anything better, I started dozing.

When I awoke, the heat, the sun, and the light were gone and we were driving in semi-darkness. I removed the shawl and looked up. High above us, I saw the crowns of pine trees covered with a thick layer of snow. Through it, at irregular intervals, darted milky rays of light playing spectral games on the frosted bark of the pines. The ride was now smooth, there were no drops or bumps, and the horses resumed a fast trot.

After a short while we reached a clearing and saw the horses of the leading two sleighs standing unharnessed, tied to trees. Their heads were hooded in sackcloth and they were having their oats picnic. Ours was waiting for us a few yards away near the shores of Lake Svityaz. The coachmen had made two fires and spread plaids between them.

"Where have you been? Why did it take so long? Now we'll never reach Novogrudok by daylight," exclaimed Aunt Caroline.

She rushed us through our *buterbródy* and goblets of tepid cocoa, and after a while, having accomplished our duties to nature knee-deep in snow, we mounted our respective sleighs and our caravan immersed itself anew into the forest. Darkness was falling. The coachmen had lit the lanterns on the front sleighs and now drove at a slow pace. Our *rozvalni* followed them closely. It was two uneventful hours before we arrived at Novogrudok.

When we reached the outskirts of the town, there was still a streak of crimson in the west. A few stars were out, and among them, bright and close, was the crescent of the new moon.

Soon there were lanterns all around us and we were driving uphill on a bumpy street. We passed two churches, a one-storied market building with a white colonnade, and a few two-storied, snowed-in houses. Few windows were lit and there was not a soul outdoors. We turned left, then right, climbed a narrow street, and stopped in front of a small porch leading to a snowed-in house.

All of the windows of the house were gleaming with light. Several people rushed out, having heard the approaching bells of our sleighs. The sleighs stopped one after another and their bells grew silent. We were hustled into the front parlor, where the housekeeper and the servants were waiting for us.

The house had been "lent" to my stepfather by the government, as the residence of the *Predvoditel dvoryanstva,* the head of our district's nobility. We were told that the house was a cultural monument that all Poles regarded with piety: Mickiewicz's birthplace.

The evening that our "caravan" moved into the house the memories of Mickiewicz did not mean much to any of us. What we coveted were the warm tile stoves in all the rooms and the hot dinner with suckling pig and kasha and the fact that one could get off those sticky woolens and the goose grease from our faces, stretch our limbs, jump around, laugh and sing.

The next day we started our drive toward Lubcza long before daybreak. But the weather had changed. Clouds covered the stars and there was a strong wind blowing.

Aunt Caroline squeezed me into her sleigh, or, more precisely, into her lap. It started snowing. Snow was hitting the fur covering of our feet and needling our faces. I hid mine in Aunt Caroline's bosomry and only once in a while turned around to see what was going on.

By daybreak we had somehow managed the hill that descended to the flatlands of the Neman valley and led to Lubcza. The snowfall was growing thicker and the wind was whirling snowdrifts across the road. A blizzard was about to fall upon us. Aunt Caroline told the coachman that we would forgo the midday picnic and he must drive on to Lubcza as fast as the horses could manage.

So we drove and drove, with the sleighs skidding, swaying, and tilting along the invisible road. It seemed endless. The howl of the wind, the whirling snowdrifts, and the gradual darkening of everything around us are all I remember.

Somehow we managed to reach Lubcza just before the full force of the blizzard. There was a sudden rumble of the horses' hooves hitting something hollow—the wooden bridge over the moat, leading to Lubcza's ancient tower and to the castle.

We swung around a circle of snowed-in shrubbery and stopped under a broad portico supported by large pillars. Again the bells grew silent and a door was flung open to receive us. I was carried into the front hall of the castle. Suddenly the world of snow, wind, skidding sleighs, and biting frost vanished. We were home. There was warmth all around us and a lot of friendly, smiling faces. I was unwrapped from my various layers of wool and fur and taken upstairs to my room, where a rubber tub with a jug of warm water was waiting for me.

This, for me, was a homecoming. Even then, at five and a half,

I realized dimly that this house was mine by birthright. Although I had no recollection of Lubcza, it had grown in my child's imagination into a fairy-tale world of beauty and perfection.

Even now, sixty-odd years later, I clearly remember the excitement and exhilaration of that first homecoming at the beginning of December of 1908. I felt a unique and overwhelming happiness, as if a miraculous cornucopia hung over my head, pouring out joy and pleasure in overabundance.

Much of the time I spent at Lubcza between 1908 and 1914 has melted into one indistinguishable whole. Although I do recall separate events, often in vivid detail, I can't fit them into a chronological pattern.

During that first period, while my mother and Koló were away, one of the important people in my life was Moisei Iosifovich. He used to come once a week to what was called the library of the castle, bringing freshly bound books and picking up a few disheveled ones. He would write down the title of each book, the author's name, and the date of publication in a large black account book divided into four parts: Russian, French, German, and English. On the front page of the black book he had drawn in beautiful lettering the word: КАТАЛОГ.

Moisei Iosifovich, whose last name I never knew, was our bookbinder, our librarian, and, on occasion, our reader of Biblical stories. He was a tall, gaunt man with an ample crop of silver hair, a Tolstoyan beard, a parchment face with light blue eyes, and a straight Greek nose. He was, as I later learned, the *Tsadik* ("Elder") of the Hassidic community of our village. He read in a *tenorino* singsong, and when he spoke, his voice was just above a whisper. I remember him in a black redingote, pulling out of his trousers candy with paper wrapping that had about it a faint odor of herring. There was something gentle and saintly about M. I., about his gestures, his smile, his whole demeanor. I grew to like him very much, and looked forward to his weekly visits to the library.

The library lay to the right of the entrance hall of the castle. The hall was a large, two-storied, semicircular room with a glass roof, and a roundabout wooden staircase clung to its walls. All along the walls were stuffed horned trophies—glum-nosed elks, boars' heads, deer and buck, and here and there a *glukhar* (a large wood-grouse) in a state of mating frenzy. At the top of the staircase was a plat-

31

form. There, next to its polished railing (the descent of which on one's bottom or stomach was forbidden, but which nevertheless left an indelible mark on the structure of my nose) stood a life-size stuffed wild boar of unusual dimensions. His nose was black, his mouth pink, and his tusks white. He looked menacing, about to charge. This is why, at nightfall, I would take off my shoes and, with my candle in my hand, slide past the beast as stealthily as I possibly could.

The library was a quadrangular room lined with light-oak bookcases. In the middle stood a green baize table surrounded by chairs and littered with newspapers and magazines. The shelves of the library did not contain anything valuable except perhaps a few illustrated books about hunting and shooting in exotic lands. There were also a few large zoological and ornithological books with colored illustrations, and a few volumes of classics in different languages. The greater part of the library consisted of useless books— books given to someone as presents or forgotten by someone during a visit. The only striking point about them was that, thanks to the labors of M. I., most of the books were beautifully bound, irrespective of value or content.

They were organized on the shelves according to their size and the color of their bindings. I remember that once, as a kind of Christmas gift, M. I. decided to put some order into the library. He pasted signs on top of the bookcases with words like "History," "Travel," "Geography," "Novels," etc., in printed calligraphy. But Aunt Caroline made him take these signs down and rearrange the books according to size and color of binding. She thought it would be prettier that way, as indeed it was.

Moisei Iosifovich spoke good Russian with a very slight Jewish accent, but sometimes Yiddish words, like *mishugene* or *tsimes*, would crop up in his Russian sentences. Often forgetting that he was not in a Jewish home, he would say at the end of a day "*a git'- nocht* instead of *spokoinoi nochi*.

At times I would ask M. I. to read to me something in Hebrew. His face would grow stern, and he would say in an embarrassed but grave voice: "This cannot be done."

Once when he and I were alone in the room he locked the door, pulled out of his vest pocket a tiny scroll, unfolded it, put a little black cap on his head, and read a few sentences very softly. His head bowed, his eyes half closed, and his body swayed backward and forward on the chair. I did not know what he was reading, but I remember that the words sounded heavy, a bit guttural, and awe-inspiring.

On the 24th of December in 1908, not long after we arrived, after a skimpy breakfast of biscuits without marmalade and unsweetened apple tea, we were told to go to the library and not move from there. The house was full of gloom. Aunt Caroline had announced the day before (red face, tears, whining voice) that Mother was in Vilna and was undergoing, or had just undergone, a dangerous operation. The operation involved chloroform (a word that gave me the shivers) and a lot of famous doctors. "The outcome is uncertain," she had said. All three of us children were distressed, particularly when Aunt Caroline added that "Under the circumstances, there is absolutely no question of having any kind of festivities, except of course the religious ones, and there will be no Christmas tree nor presents." She said all this in a tone that excluded any kind of argument.

So we sat in the library in front of the green baize table, fidgeting on our chairs while all kinds of pious stories about the birth of Jesus were read to us. We had been on a fast for several weeks, a Greek Orthodox one which excludes eggs, milk, cream, and butter, and permits fish only on Sundays. On the last day of the fast, Christmas Eve, we were not supposed to eat at all until the appearance of the first star, the star of Bethlehem. We would then be taken to church for a solemn but happy Vesper service. After that, because of Mother's condition, we were to have only the ritual Christmas Eve dishes, a porridge made of butterless and milkless barley and a compote of dried fruit. These dishes were meant as reminders of the Holy Family's flight to Egypt. After that ritual meal we were to go to bed and pray for our mother's health.

The three of us sat from morning until late afternoon in the dreary library listening listlessly to stories in four tongues related to Christmas. We were highly aware of shufflings of feet going to and coming from our large playroom on the second floor. Our tutor and the governesses were called out one by one and came back without saying a word. I thought that it must have something to do with Mother's illness. Snow was falling continuously outdoors and there was no star in sight. The lamp above the library table was lit from eleven in the morning on, and a general mood of apprehension for my mother's health prevailed throughout the long, long day.

33

Toward the end of the afternoon the three of us remained alone with Moisei Iosifovich. The rest of our guardians had left, and I could not help thinking that they were doing something upstairs that we children were not supposed to know about.

M. I. did not read us stories about Jesus. Instead he read psalms and Old Testament tales. I interrupted and asked him: "Is it true that Jesus was born after the star appeared in the sky, or is it just a fairy-tale?"

M. I. answered hesitantly, "Well, this is what your religion teaches you."

"And what does yours teach?" I asked.

M. I. bent this head toward me and replied with his usual gentleness: "You will learn about that later, when you grow up."

"But our *Batyushka* told me," I continued, "that Jesus was born after the star came up and—"

I did not finish my sentence. Aunt Caroline had burst into the room, her face gleaming with joy, her eyes red. She barely could speak. In her hand she held a telegram and waved it at us.

M. I. took the telegram and read it aloud: "Lidochka's operation very successful. She is out of danger. God bless you and the children. Koló."

"We will not go to church," said Aunt Caroline, "it's too late now. The service has started and, besides, it's snowing too hard. But *Batyushka* will come here after Vespers and will celebrate a *Moleben* in the living room. And then we will all have a surprise." Her placid face turned into a moon-sized smile.

"But what about the star?" I asked Aunt Caroline.

"Oh, the Christmas star! It's been out for a long time, but it's hidden by clouds and snow." She smiled again, this time slyly and gaily. "You'll have your star, you'll see, once the *Batyushka* has finished his *Moleben*."

The mood changed instantly. We sat around dear old M. I. and talked and laughed and joked. He gave up reading and joined us in our joyful chatter.

Soon thereafter the *Batyushka* arrived. Prompted no doubt by Aunt Caroline, he sang the *Moleben* at high speed and then we all intoned the *Mnogaya Leta* (a prayer for a long life) for Mother.

Then came Aunt Caroline's surprise. She said, "Now, children, it's time to go . . . Let's all go upstairs." Led by *Batyushka* in his festive robes, his hands holding a bucket of holy water and the bunch of twigs, we followed Aunt Caroline to the second floor.

We passed the horned trophies on the wall, and when we reached the platform of the second floor with its fearsome wild boar, the doors leading to our playroom were flung open and there in the middle of the playroom, bright and glimmering with a hundred candles, stood Aunt Caroline's surprise: a huge Christmas tree.

On its top it had a six-pronged golden star surrounded by candles. By some device, the star revolved, producing a faint tinkling sound of bells. The rest of the tree was covered with silver and golden garlands, snowy fluff, gilded nuts, all kinds of fancy candies and cookies, and tiny tangerines from Nice. Underneath the tree, amid shiny, cottonish snow, lay Jesus' crib, with Joseph, Mary, the shepherds, the Magi, and all those friendly animals around it.

Batyushka intoned a Christmas Vesper prayer. We responded by singing in German *"Stille Nacht"* and *"Oh, du fröhliche"* and the gay and march-like *"Il est né, le divin enfant"* in French. Those were the only Christmas songs we knew. They had surrounded our wanderings abroad, and governesses had seen to it that we should not forget them. Aunt Caroline sat at the harmonium and accompanied our singing as best she could.

And next Christmas the tree stood in the same place in our playroom, and again its branches bent under the weight of garlands, cookies, silvery glitter, shining candles, and the revolving star.

And yet how different everything was!

This time we knew that there would be a Christmas tree, and we also knew that we would go to Christmas Vespers in the village church, and that after Vespers there would be other surprises. But, above all, we knew that Mother and Koló were back home after a long, long absence, and that there was a six-month-old sister, Lida (named after my mother), lying in the same little bed in which I had spent my first years at Lubcza. It stood in a newly whitewashed nursery next to Mother's boudoir.

I do not recall when my mother came back home. It must have been in the late summer or early autumn, but by the time she arrived, my new sister, Lidochka, was a plump pink baby with a crop of dark, curly hair.

So Christmas Eve in 1909 was quite different from the mournful, wake-like day we had spent the year before.

The ritual of the day-long fast was again strictly observed. We were again confined to the library and had to listen to the same

Christmas Eve readings that we had heard a year before. But the day was bright, the sun was shining, and a blanket of crisp snow lay on the ground. This time, I thought, the star must appear. The sky was cloudless and gently blue.

The house was full of noises. There was a lot of coming and going between the first and second floors, and the voices sounded cheerful and gay. Even the stuffed boar at the top of the stairs looked different. Someone had stuck three fat candles into its back, a Christmas cracker between its teeth, and a golden paper crown on its head.

The day moved slowly while my excitement grew. At about four o'clock the library became darker as dusk set in. Moisei Iosifovich went to the window, looked outside, and, pointing to a luminous object in the still luminous sky, said: "There it is." Combing his long sideburns and beard, he added: "There is Venus."

"What do you mean, Venus?" I asked.

"Venus, the evening star," said sister Onya.

"But . . . where's the Bethlehem star? Should it not come first?" I stuttered.

"Well . . . this is what you call the Bethlehem star," answered M. I., still looking at the luminous object and combing his beard, "but it is Venus, and not a star but a planet. See how still its light is—it does not flicker like starlight."

At this point in my first lesson in astronomy I heard the noise of harness bells and horses' hooves hitting the bridge. I rushed to the window. Three large sleighs drew up to the castle's front porch.

The door of the library was flung open and Mother, Koló, Aunt Caroline, and our tutor appeared, dressed in festive coats and hats. Mother wore a dark-burgundy velvet cape with sable lining and a high-standing collar. Her hair was covered with a white shawl and her eyes were smiling.

"Come, children," said Mother, "get dressed, or we shall be late for Vespers."

Her words started a stampede for coats, scarves, felt boots, and hats. Soon, dressed up in wool and fur, the whole household was crowding the entrance hall. Then, under Koló's patient direction, we moved to the three sleighs.

We drove through the tower gate out of the garden and down the main street of the *Mestechko* (the Jewish part of our village) until the three sleighs stopped in front of the church. It was crowded. *Batyushka* had been waiting for us to start the Vesper service.

How clearly I remember those faces bathed by gentle candlelight, exuding joy and warmth. And that powerful mixture of smells: burning wax and damp felt, sweat and leather, but mostly the blue smell of burning incense . . . I stand next to my mother, hatless and coatless, clinging to the lace of her cream-colored dress while she is arranging the silk *lavallière* tie of my sailor suit.

Ceremoniously, Deacon Sergei walks out of the altar through one of its side doors, dressed in festive gold and silver. He walks to the middle of the Iconostasis and stops in front of the Tsar's Gates. First he kneels and bows, touching the floor with his forehead. Then he gets up and, still bowing and crossing himself with a broad golden stole, he starts his incantation, the prayers of supplication. A shudder goes through my spine as I hear the drone of his voice saying the first words of the prayer. He starts it somewhere so low that it seems to be rising from beneath the floor. Slowly, very gradually, his voice slides upward from a soft pianissimo, gathering power and intensity, yet always enunciating each word very clearly. Finally it soars to the utmost limits of the Deacon's lungs. The choir picks up the last tone and thunders back boisterously, a threefold "Lord have mercy upon us"—*"Gospodi pomi-i-ilooy."* The Deacon's drone starts a new series of supplications, again from the depths of his voice upwards, again to its utmost limits, and is again answered by the choir. When the last supplication is over, I am both exhilarated and exhausted. I feel as if I were melting. In my ears swim the names and patronymics of the Tsar, his family, our local Bishop, and the regional Metropolitan, of all of us present, and of "the whole of Christendom."

Suddenly the "Tsar's Gates" are flung open, *Batyushka* comes out in his most glittering festive vestments, and the choir starts its Christmas Vesper chants.

The chants of Russian Christmas Vespers are gloriously jolly. They have always struck me as having been invented by "people on the go," people who had a story to tell while marching. And the story itself is about successive journeys: the journey of the Magi guided by a journeying star, the journey of the shepherds with their flock, and the head-over-heels rush of Herod to destroy that newborn son of Israel on the flight to Egypt.

As we drove home from Vespers, the sky was a black basket filled

37

with stars. Along the road, set in the snow, stood rows of lampions. The castle's gate, its bridge, and the front porch were illuminated by torches.

"Quickly, quickly, children, take off your coats and go to the library," said Koló. "It won't take long, we will fetch you in a few minutes."

So back to the library we went, but this time there were no obligatory readings and every one of the household was with us. Only Mother, Koló, and Aunt Caroline went straight upstairs. Despite our chatter and laughter and the barrage of questions we threw at everyone, we could hear Mother, Koló, and Aunt Caroline going up and down the stairs, and we knew what they were doing, what they were preparing up there in the playroom.

The "few minutes" seemed like eternity. Finally we heard steps coming down the stairs and butler Alexei and coachman Anton in their liveries ceremoniously opened both leaves of the library door. The unruly flock swarmed upward to the second floor and its luminous tree.

Mother, Koló, and Aunt Caroline stood next to it and greeted us with smiles and kisses. All over the room and in the adjoining ones, whose doors were flung ajar, stood tables of various sizes and shapes. Each table was covered with a white cloth and bore a small Christmas tree of its own with a few shining candles. On each table were presents from everyone to everyone.

A cardboard sign with beautiful lettering in red and gold, no doubt the contribution of Moisei Iosifovich, marked the name of each table's prospective possessor: "Carolina Fedorovna" or "Onya" or "Mitya" and gradually downward through the domestic hierarchy of our household and farm workers. No one was forgotten, everyone got his (large or small) share of presents, even the old cross-eyed Avdotya, who came twice a day from the village to feed Djack and Djip and the rest of the brood of dogs that nested in the back yard of the castle. Most of the serving personnel received a piece of cloth and a gold or silver coin, depending on his or her hierarchical position. For the male members there was added a bottle of very sweet, home-brewed cherry brandy, which everyone in Russia liked very much.

Next to my parents, in a new white perambulator, lay my sister Lidoosha, all lace and pink organdy, her eyes staring at the huge luminous object with its hundreds of candles.

38

But before we were allowed to move toward our respective gift tables we had to sing the four or five Franco-German pieces of Christmas trash, to the mute admiration of the non-foreign-language-speaking members of the household. This time we reeled these pieces off loudly, rapidly, and *con scioltezza*. Even "Silent Night" sounded more like a waltz than like the sentimental noodle it is.

I don't exactly remember what presents I received on that particular Christmas Eve. Was it then that my mother gave me an enameled sewing box with needles, thimbles, thread and yarn of many colors, including a set of patterns for dolls' clothes? I remember being moved to tears by one of my presents, so maybe it was that enameled box? Or maybe it was a coveted book or some cloth for dolls' clothes?

It soon dawned on us that there was a rather ominous absence of any present from Koló to the three children. Somebody whispered, "Have you noticed, there is no present from Koló?"

Then Alexei, the butler, said something to my mother, something I couldn't hear. My mother clapped her hands and asked for silence. She announced that we must go downstairs, that the village procession bearing the Christmas star had arrived, and that there was another surprise waiting for us in the front parlor.

We all rushed downstairs. The front door was opened and we stood facing a group of village children and village elders singing in raucous, faulty unison the beautiful Christmas chants we had just heard in the church. The *Starosta*, the elder of the village church, was among them, bearing a large, flickering golden star on a long stick, while the others carried candles protected by paper hoods. Koló gave the *Starosta* an old-fashioned money bag filled with coins, the kind that kings and knights use in Shakespeare plays. The singing grew harsher and louder and lasted for another five or ten minutes. Then the procession departed to the chant of *"Rozhdestvo Tvoye Khriste Bozhe Nash."* It disappeared under the tower and went back to the village.

By that time, as if by magic, the servants had transformed the entrance hall into a theater. Behind our backs they had brought in several rows of chairs and installed a puppet theater in front of the draped, locked door of the library.

I do not remember much of the puppeteers' performance. The day was filled with so many other memorable events. I only remember that I was bored by the show, and that the figures and the props

39

of the minute stage looked unreal and un-alive. Mary and Joseph, not to speak of baby Jesus in his crib, were much too small in proportion to the stage and seemed to be made of plasticine or celluloid.

But fortunately the puppet show did not last long. Soon we were clapping our hands and Koló plunked a coin into the puppeteer's hat.

Then the front door was thrown open again and a wave of icy air entered the front hall. Smiling and wistful, my mother turned to us and said: "Look, children! Look! There's Koló's present for you."

What we saw outside in a cloud of steam were three small, woolly, frosted heads, their nostrils pumping steam like engines. Six tiny hooves stood on the front steps and three young stableboys in festive uniform held the little animals by the bridle.

"Shetland ponies," our English Miss exclaimed ecstatically. "Real Shetland ponies! My God, children, aren't you lucky!"

We rushed first to the little woolen heads and then to Koló and hung all over him, kissing and hugging him. This was certainly the most memorable of all surprises of the day. It was worth the fast, the dull readings in the library, and the boredom of the puppeteers' mystery play.

After everyone present had sufficiently admired Koló's gift, we were called to order. The ponies were taken away. The doors were shut and we marched through the main rooms of the castle, led by *Batyushka* and the deacon. *Batyushka* was sprinkling holy water, bowing, crossing himself and chanting with the deacon, in precarious thirds, the same Christmas chants we had heard in the church.

Finally, when this was over, there was food.

The Christmas meal started as it had the year before with the ritual dishes: the tasteless gruel of barley and a potage of unsweetened dried fruit. It was again served on a table whose snow-white tablecloth hid a thin layer of hay and straw (to remind one of baby Jesus' crib). But the ritual dishes were barely touched by everyone present.

"Don't worry," said Mother to *Batyushka*, "after this there will be a real dinner."

And a real dinner it was! First, cold jellied suckling pig with fresh and creamy horseradish sauce and bogberry jam; then goose with baked apples and buckwheat kasha. At the end of the meal appeared our English Miss's gift to the family: a large round cannonball plum pudding she had received by post from London. It was brought in on a silver plate by Alexei to everybody's applause. It was surrounded by lilac flames and garlands of holly and mistletoe.

Despite a refrain of "Don't eat too much," we ate and ate and ate until we couldn't go on. I was the first to get sleepy, and was carried upstairs to the bedroom I shared with brother Mitya and Nyanya Lyuba.

There in the bedroom, kneeling on my bed, facing the flickering oil lamp in front of St. Nicolas' icon, I said my evening prayers.

I don't remember much about our daily life in Lubcza before my mother and Koló returned and took the marshal's baton out of Aunt Caroline's hands. From then on, the tenor of our life changed. It became more orderly, yet at the same time gayer. It also became more elegant. But "elegant" is perhaps not the proper word. What I mean is that the atmosphere in Lubcza became fresher, more secure, and everything from food to conversation seemed more refined. Koló ran the affairs of the farm and its finances with Greek skill and Baltic vigor. Mother infused into the household her charm and gaiety. But our daily schedule was precise and carefully thought out.

We had to dress for dinner (the midday meal in rural Russia) and were not allowed to fidget at table. We had to keep our hands on the table, not underneath it. The hands were to be in a special position: the two index fingers touching the edges of the plate—"as the Emperor does it," my mother would say. If our elbows waved in the air, we would hear the stern voices of Miss D. or Mademoiselle V. saying: "You are not an airplane" or "Try to be a penguin and not a crow." Infringements of those forms of etiquette were punishable after a few unsuccessful reminders.

An elaborate system of punishments was introduced into our lives. It was strictly hierarchical, as were most of the things that surrounded us:

(a) No dessert;
(b) Same, but for several days or even a week;
(c) To stand from ten minutes to one hour facing the corner of a room;
(d) Same, but on one's knees;
(e) To sit at a separate table and eat a meager meal without dessert;
(f) Bread and water, and to bed at seven p.m. without reading.

41

The most boring and most absurd of all punishments was to have to write one or two hundred times: "I will never again say 'old cow' to Mademoiselle V." or: "I will never again soil my pants, but go to the bathroom in time."

Once while the grown-ups, among them Mademoiselle V., were playing lawn tennis on our bumpy tennis court, I made up a French couplet and sang it loudly to a tune of my own, very proud of my poetic and musical invention:

> "*Venez voir Mademoiselle Verrière,*
> *Frapper par devant, frapper par derrière!*"

I was instantly taken back to the castle and was ordered to write two hundred and fifty times: "*L'insolence est un péché, l'amabilité une vertu.*" The punishment was unjust, for I was only referring to Mademoiselle Verrière's backhand and not to her anatomy.

To compensate for the hierarchy of punishments there was also a hierarchy of pleasures. The simplest and lowest level in this hierarchy was to gather berries or mushrooms in the woods, or rare, scented wild flowers such as lilies of the valley or hyacinths, or to catch butterflies and moths. Fishing in the river or in the adjacent ponds was a degree higher in this hierarchy. Quite high in it were such pleasures as picnics and fireworks.

During the summer months there were many guests at Lubcza. Relatives or friends of the family came. Some of them stayed for weeks or months. When fresh arrivals appeared, there was usually a picnic organized in their honor, or a visit to Uncle Frederick's neighboring hunting lodge.

Highest in the hierarchy of pleasures stood Mother's and Koló's birthdays and saints' days. On those occasions there would be picnics, fireworks and illuminations, followed by protracted festive meals with copious, delicate dishes. A band of Jewish musicians would come and play at the front porch of the castle. During the thanksgiving service the men and women from the farm would join in the choruses, and all of us would sing those cheerful *Moleben* responses wishing Mother and Koló "a happy and long life."

Our daily routine was more or less the same as in Pokrovskoe. There were morning lessons and one or two hours of listening to readings in the languages that we were supposed to know. But soon we obtained from Mother the right to read by ourselves in the presence of our respective governesses or tutor. Only some parts were to be read aloud, the rest was left to our eyes and minds.

Sports, alas, were also added to our schedule. I failed piteously at all of them.

There was riding. Soon after Christmas Koló helped me into the saddle. First I got entangled in the stirrups. Then the pony refused to move. Koló whipped its bottom. Off it galloped straight to the stable with me clinging to its mane yelling: "Help! Help!" After that incident I snubbed the pony and riding in general.

Then there was swimming. Bathing in the Neman was considered healthy. There was a bathing cabin with a promontory to jump from into the deeper parts of the river. Usually I avoided this promontory and played on the Neman's shore near the cabin. But one afternoon I found myself on the promontory in my white sailor suit. Someone slipped up noiselessly behind my back and pushed me into the river. I plunged and hit something sharp in the river's bottom. When I was pulled out of the water, my knee bled. I shed quantities of liquids, mostly from my eyes, and cursed my fate, limping around with a voluminous bandage for several weeks. When the bandage was taken off, I continued limping to avoid further exploration of the Neman's bed. So today I can paddle like a poodle and keep afloat for a while, but I could not possibly swim for more than twenty yards.

Tennis seemed utterly ludicrous to me. I would watch the elders play lawn tennis at Lubcza (a very mild ancestor of today's sport) and could not understand why anyone should be so pleased by hitting with an ovaloid gutted object a ball that had slowly flown over a low string net stretched across a well-kept lawn. It was of course very pretty to see the ladies of our household pop about gracefully in their long white dresses and beribboned straw hats while the gentlemen, their opponents, also in immaculate white and wearing visored caps, attempted to return as gently and politely as possible those infrequent balls that succeeded in reaching their side of the lawn.

Shooting and hunting was another sport beloved for several centuries by the Russian gentry. Koló was an exception, for he never practiced it, but most of my uncles loved it and so did my brother Mitya. I never cared for it.

The sports I liked were milder, quieter ones, unconnected with exertion, hazards, and noise. I liked to play croquet. I also liked rowing alone or in company, not as a sport, rather as a pastime or as

43

a means of getting from one place to another. At Lubcza we all rowed in company on the Neman in a pretty four-oared boat. Often we rowed a mile or two upstream to the woods, moored the boat in a quiet bay, disembarked to pick berries, mushrooms, or hazelnuts, and then drifted back, with our oars down, using the pole to steer.

I cannot recall any other sport or sportly occupation that tempted me either at Pokrovskoe or at Lubcza except perhaps those of any child living close to a farm and taking part in the world of haylofts and barns, stables and cowsheds, and being close to those who work in the fields and forests.

I learned to observe nature in all of its extraordinary abundance. I learned very early to recognize the species of trees, mushrooms, berries, flowers, fish, and birds, and knew the seasons of field harvests and of various pickings in the forests, or the gathering of fruit in our orchards.

If I were to define what in my Russian childhood communion with nature was special and different from what could be experienced by any child living in nature's environment, I think it is the continuous presence of song. Everyone and everything sang, from the men while mowing and the women while milking to the lark in the sky and the thin whisper-like whistle of freshly caught crayfish.

I often ask myself, while writing these pages, whether life at Lubcza was as idyllic as I remember it. It may have been for us, but was it so good for our neighbors who didn't enjoy our privileges? In other words, were there no signs, incidents, forebodings of oncoming troubles that a child's intuitive perception could sense?

I came back to Lubcza from abroad in 1908, at the age of six, and left in 1914. Thus, when I left my birthplace I should have been ripe enough to feel and understand, at least in part, the nature of the world that surrounded us there. The charmed life in our opulent castle with its picnic forays, its sports, pleasures, and distractions, and even the coddled and cozily protected drudgery of our lessons, stood in stark contrast to the squalor and poverty in which our next-door neighbors lived—the Belorussian peasants of Lubcza.

Every Sunday as I stood in church I must have noticed their miserable clothing, their shoddy boots or *lapti,* the native shoes made of birchbark. The women's blouses, washed threadbare and lacking buttons, would show wasted breasts stuck into the mouths of yelping infants bundled in rags. There were rows of beggars—old men, women, and snotty, scrofulous children—lining the path to the church, chanting supplications in sad, nasal voices, while our *Starosta*, the church elder, brushed them aside to make way for the *Kastelyane* (us, the inhabitants of the castle) so that our clothes would not be contaminated by the beggars' multiple sores. What did we do for them except to put a few *kopeikas* in their caps and shyly smile at them?

Were we all, the whole upper crust of Russian society, so totally insensitive, so horribly obtuse, as not to feel that the charmed life we were leading was in itself an injustice and hence could not possibly last?

Yet my mother and, to a lesser degree, my stepfather and surely most of the inhabitants of the castle, especially the children, were not nasty, evil people. And though we were not taught to plow or weave or wear Russian blouses *à la Tolstoy*, a true bond linked us with the peasants of the village, and also with its Jewish population. Our contact with them was natural and humane. We joked and laughed together, and there was no trace of any kind of inhibition in their behavior toward us.

But as I see it now, with the hindsight of over half a century, I seem dimly to recollect having been a witness of several events or incidents that frightened me and implanted in me a feeling of guilt and of apprehension.

The most frequent of these events were village fires. Not a summer would pass without a village burning in the neighborhood of Lubcza. Usually this meant that the whole of the village would burn down. Only in larger villages such as Lubcza itself was there anything resembling a fire brigade—antiquated equipment consisting of two leaky, red-painted barrels with two equally leaky fire hoses. At times the fires were accidental, but often they were the result of peasant exasperation or the work of arsonists.

I remember hearing the local police chief tell my stepfather how they captured a band of "pyro-technicians," as he called them, who had an arsenal of petrol and gunpowder on hand and a list of villages of our region that were to be set afire for "the cause."

After a neighboring village fire, there would be groups of bedraggled peasants with their womenfolk and children coming to the front porch of the superintendent's house and waiting for help. On Mother's orders, clothes, food, and money would be handed out to

45

the victims of fire. Very often they would stay around and camp somewhere near our farm. They would be caught stealing crops, potatoes, fruit, or fowl, sometimes even a pig. One could see them in small groups on the road returning to their burnt-out homesteads. There again they would sit and wait in makeshift huts until the *Zemski Nachalnik*, the land inspector, or some other official, or at times a liberal-minded landowner would provide them with beams and logs to build a new house.

In 1910 or 1911 there was a fire in the Russian part of our village. It was late at night when the churchbell awoke us. We all ran out to watch. Like all fires, it was both beautiful and terrifying. I stared at it in petrified fascination. My stepfather had sent out our stable-boys, coachmen, and farmhands to help put out the fire. A chain of persons passed buckets of water up from the Neman while a hand pump was being worked from an old well, which promptly went dry. Fortunately the fire was stopped before it could do much damage. The wind had turned and the sparks flew toward a potato field.

But besides village fires there were other incidents that occurred during those years in Lubcza.

I remember that one day, while strolling past the horse stables, I heard violent voices coming from inside. I recognized the voice of my stepfather and one of the chief coachmen. My stepfather, usually cool and calm, was shouting and cursing and the coachman was responding in kind. I peered inside and what I saw frightened and horrified me. I had never before seen one grown-up hit another one. Now I saw my stepfather hit the coachman's face hard with a stick. The coachman tried to hit back, but two stableboys got hold of him and twisted his arms. The man's face was bleeding and he shouted curses at my stepfather. I heard what he said and remembered it: "Wait," he yelled, "you will see—you beasts, you bloody pack of dogs!"

Then suddenly my stepfather saw me peering in the door. He turned around and said: "What are you doing here? Go home!"

I started crying.

"Oh, come on, stop it." He took me by the hand and walked me back to the castle.

When I asked him: "Why did you do it?" he looked glum.

"Don't ask," he said. "It's none of your business."

I never heard anything about what caused the incident.

The coachman disappeared. He was dismissed, but one night a

week or two later a larder in the basement of the castle right under the dining room was broken into and pilfered. The police questioned everyone on the farm, but to no avail. No one questioned gave any clues except that a few people admitted having seen the dismissed coachman drunk in a village *traktir*, boasting that he would have his revenge.

A few days later a hayloft and a cowshed on our farm went up in flames. The police could not find the culprit, nor could they find any trace of the dismissed coachman. He had vanished.

I was also sorely aware of the lowly condition of Jews in our part of Russia (after all, it was The Pale). Although we ourselves kept up friendly relations with our Jewish village grocer, our butcher, our contractor, and our sweet Dr. Levin, the dentist from Vilna, it was obvious that the condition of the Jews around us was that of pariahs and that something about it was deeply wrong and inhuman. When I once asked our otherwise gentle farm manager about it, he shrugged his shoulders and replied something to the effect that Jews cannot be trusted and must be treated accordingly.

As I had said before, our life at Lubcza was well regulated and ordered. Among the daily occupations, unquestionably the most boring ones were my piano lessons and supervised piano practices. Fräulein A., who supervised our musical activities at Lubcza, would sit near the piano with a book and at the slightest faltering of my wormlike fingers would bark at me: "Don't play wrong notes. . . . Why don't you keep time? . . . Your fingers are like jelly!"

It surely was not during those tedious ramblings upon the black-and-white dentures of our old upright at Lubcza that I first encountered and fell in love with Euterpe. No, music finds other ways to get into a composer's life and into his bloodstream. Some of these ways are intangible and quite mysterious.

It seems to me that music came into my life as it came into the lives of many other composers: through the illicit communications with that fertile subsoil, that vast underground of life where musical matter of all degrees of beauty and ugliness lives freely and abundantly and is constantly being reinvented, rearranged, transformed, and infused with new meaning by a universe of memories and imaginations.

First of all, music came to me through the large, open window of my early boyhood, the window of my bedroom on the second floor of our home in Belorussia. There, on its broad windowsill I would sit through lingering summer sunsets, watching the gradual recession of yellows, reds, and purples from the glossy surface of the Neman, breathing in the gentle air, filled with the scent of linden and Nicotiana, listening to the resonant knock of an ax falling on the logs of some distant timber raft and forming an ephemeral accompaniment to the "calling songs" of the lumberjacks, those dirge-like evening conversations between the men who floated the rafts down to the German border.

This curious dialogue, or rather antiphon, would fill the shadowy stillness with solitude and desolation. It would rise from afar, from the very edge of the northern horizon where the darkening curves of the Neman were being swallowed up by the forest. It began with a question, intoned in the highest range of a man's voice, plaintively sliding up and down the narrow interval of a minor third, but otherwise remaining quite dispassionate and expressionless. Then, at the end of the question, the voice, as if choking, would break off in a sob-like cadence and again there would be only the total silence of the evening, interrupted by the knock of the hewing ax. A moment, and then another voice, much nearer, quite close, sometimes right under my window, would answer, again turning the last tone into a mournful sob. And from below, in the same plaintive manner but with each word clearly audible, would come the awaited response:

> We're floating five ra-a-fts
> For Merchant Kerneichoo-oo-ook. . . .
> We will take off before dawn. . . .
> And you, when do you start?

This curious responsory would go on far into the evening, until Venus had retired behind the last crimson streaks of the sunset and the farm dogs had begun their nightly roll call.

On early summer mornings the same open window would bring to my bed the voices of peasant women, the haymakers on their way out to the fields. I would slip out of bed and watch them from behind the blinds. They walked in rows, fast and lightly as if dancing, each one carrying a rake on her shoulder, and as they crossed the floating bridge their bare feet splashed in the water. They sang quick, gay songs with short, repetitive phrases. At the end of each stanza they paused. Two or three continued to sing along, and, as if reaching for an utterly unattainable object, their voices would rise in a shrill glissando to the topmost level of their range and there sustain a very loud and a very high tone. Soon the rest of the chorus broke in with the next stanza of the song and with a savage and boisterous onrush toppled over the high note of the soloists. The voices of these women were harsh and strident and the songs they sang were strong and bright.

In the evening the same haymakers returned to the village, but they walked slowly and sang different songs. The evening songs, although sung in much the same manner as the morning ones, differed in mood and texture. They were slow and tired. Their long, wavy melodies lingered endlessly on sustained tones and their harmonies were so clear and so transparent that they gave the impression of constant unison. Here again it seemed as if the women haymakers, trudging homeward after a day's work, were obeying the mimetic laws of nature, fitting their songs into the mood of the evening, into its dying sunlight and its limpid mellowness.

What I liked to listen to through my window were bits of music —jagged dance tunes played by an accordion at a Saturday dance in the village, or snatches of sentimental trivia full of alcoholic loneliness sung by some despondent male on the riverbank, or the gentle, more lyrical songs of the girls who weeded the vegetable garden.

Another memory of Lubcza is that on saints' days and birthdays we hired a Jewish orchestra from our village. The orchestra consisted of a violin, a zither or guitar, sometimes a small upright harp, an accordion, and a contrabass. This combination played an extraordinary variety of music: potpourris of famous operas, military marches, Viennese waltzes, and the ooziest gypsy songs and Jewish dances, rampant with glissandos, tremolos, and tearful vibratos.

I particularly loved the violinists of these orchestras, for I enjoyed their scratchy, edgy tone, their ability to slide all over the bridge of their instrument, and their clumsy, harsh ways of intoning double stops (that Stravinsky so ingeniously copied in his *Histoire du Soldat*). I remember telling my stepfather after one of these teatime performances how much I liked the violin and how much rather I would learn to play it than the piano or the cello, for which I was being secretly groomed by my mother. But my stepfather, who had just returned from Vilna, replied that to be a good violinist is very hard and if the playing isn't good the violin is just an awful nuisance.

In 1910 or 1911, early in the summer, the whole family left Lubcza for our first visit to my grandmother Falz-Fein's estate, Preobrazhenka, in the south of Russia near the Crimean isthmus.

49

We were driven to the station. There we boarded the Odessa Express. From Odessa we were to proceed by steamer—a real seagoing craft, not a flip-flap river "yacht" like ours at Lubcza—to grandmother's harbor with its ancient Tartar name of Khorly.

My mother was of German stock. Her ancestors had immigrated to Russia in the second half of the eighteenth century and settled on the northern edge of the Taurian steppe near the town of Melitopol, a Russian derivative of the sweet-sounding Melitopolis. They fared well in Russia and by the middle of the nineteenth century had accumulated great wealth in land and sheep. The family estates stretched from the Crimean isthmus northward to Melitopol, eastward to the Sea of Azov, and westward to the Dnepr.

In addition the family had acquired land on the Crimean peninsula, houses in Simferopol, Kherson, and Odessa, an apartment house of dubious repute in Moscow, a canning factory, a steamship line, two harbors on the Black Sea, a villa on the Caucasian coast, and endless flocks of Merino sheep.

As a boy I used to find my mother's maiden name funny. Falz-Fein sounded like the fossil of a word game. The origin of the strange double name was in fact quite simple: someone called Fein married someone called Falz. But it was an "uneven status" marriage. Early in the nineteenth century a German "colonist" from Elizavetfeld near Melitopol, a wealthy landowner and famous breeder of Merino sheep, called Frederick Fein, married his only daughter to the son of a humble person called Pfalz. In the deal Pfalz lost the "p" and had to add to his own one-syllable name the weightier syllable of his bride: hence Falz-Fein.

The funny new name soon became the synonym of successful sheep-breeding and wealth. To be a Falz-Fein meant to have large flocks of sheep and plenty of money. Later on, toward the end of the nineteenth century, the name became internationally famous, at least among lovers of birds and animals. Frederick, Mother's elder brother, inherited Askania-Nova, the family's main estate, at the relatively early age of nineteen. Being an ardent lover of wildlife, he started there a little zoo of his own. He trapped and collected rare birds and mammals, bought others from the Paris, Berlin, and Hamburg zoos, and even from Buffalo Bill. He organized at his own expense expeditions to Africa, Asia, and America to populate his animal preserve on the steppes of southern Russia. By the time he was thirty he had transformed Askania-Nova into a beautiful oasis of wildlife and an important center of zoological research. He corresponded with scientists and wildlife enthusiasts in Europe and America. As a result, zoologists, botanists, ornithologists, animal-behaviorists, and other scholars connected in one way or another with animal and bird life flocked to Askania-Nova's guesthouse in the summer in ever increasing numbers and provided Uncle Frederick's zoological enterprise with an appropriate chorus of admirers.

Since my earliest days Askania-Nova had been on the lips of everybody around me. Tales of ostriches walking in winter snow, crossbreeds of European and American buffalo with Westphalian cows, wild horses from Tibet being cross-bred with the African zebra, green canaries turning white in the winter, gazelles and wild turkeys attending one's outdoor breakfast, were told and retold by everyone who had been to Askania-Nova. No wonder that to my child's imagination Askania-Nova was a lost Paradise, a Noah's Ark, and a Promised Land.

We boarded the train at Baranovichi in the afternoon, on our way to my grandmother's estate. In the midmorning of the next day we were rolling into Odessa's small railroad station. We were met there by a diminutive man, red-faced, bald-headed, with graying beaver mustaches, whose name was Mikhail Zinovich Rabinovich. He carried a large bunch of red roses and long stalks of exotic white flowers with an insidiously pungent scent. Later I was told that they were called tuberoses. Mikhail Zinovich Rabinovich, my grandmother's "Man Friday," a delightful Russian Jew of incredible gentleness and kindness, had prepared everything. A row of victorias with funny-looking white tents over them waited for us, and a flock of porters started piling the carriages with our baggage. We drove to the Gostinitsa (hotel) Londonskaya and stayed there two or three days until Grandmother's steamer, called *Lydia* in honor of my mother, was scheduled to leave Odessa on her weekly trip to Khorly.

I remember Odessa's quays with their lovely hotels, their elegant stores and flower markets, Deribassovskaya Street with its two rival cafés, and the old-fashioned music bands of the two cafés, a bit like those of St. Mark's Square in Venice. Odessa was very un-Russian, indigenously cosmopolitan—the home of thousands of Jews, Greeks, Armenians, Italians, Germans, Romanians, and Ukrainians who together with Russians formed a gay and curiously homogeneous population.

51

Grandmother's steamer, a 1,550-tonner that carried freight and a few passengers, sailed late in the evening. By the time I would have had to face the sea and its effects upon my stomach, I was sound asleep on my cabin bunk below deck. When I awoke, just after dawn, and climbed upstairs to the captain's bridge, I looked around and gasped at what I saw:

The sun ball floated low above the horizon. The S.S. *Lydia* was moving very, very cautiously through what seemed like a vast mirror. The sky was pale pink and so was the mirror. All of it melted into one silent whole, separated only by the pencil-like horizon. There was nothing to disturb the silence, not a bird, not an insect. The vast lagoon lay still and peaceful, and the ripples our little steamer was making in the lagoon's channel added the only touch of life and motion to a scene of calm beauty. On the right horizon was the coast of Crimea, in front were the Taurian steppe and Grandmother's harbor.

I stood enraptured, letting myself be taken in and, as it were, permeated by the liquid beauty around me. I felt like an inseparable part of it, to the point of melting away.

Khorly was a disappointment, drab, ugly, and flat. The harbor consisted of two wharves flanked by a half-dozen storehouses, all alike, made of wooden planks and brick joints. The dusty air was permeated with a smell of sheep's wool and untanned hides. The adjacent townlet consisted of a few straight streets with low, lonely-looking houses, whitewashed and sun-baked, surrounded by sparse greenery. At some distance facing the harbor was my grandmother's guesthouse, and in front of it was a square that looked as if someone had tried but failed to turn it into a French garden.

The harbormaster and Mr. Rabinovich, who had come along with us from Odessa, did the honors and welcomed us to Khorly. Then we boarded the *dormeuses*, landaus, and victorias Grandmother had sent to meet us, and drove off at high speed toward her residence, Preobrazhenka, some fifteen miles away.

Summer drives across the broad, unpaved roads of the Taurian steppe at the time of my childhood were formidable ordeals. I remember them vividly and with a sort of awe. Each carriage of our family caravan was usually drawn by a team of four horses, harnessed not in a suite of pairs but side by side like a Roman quadriga. The sixteen hooves of quick-trotting, powerful horses and the four wheels of each carriage produced a huge cloud of dun-colored dust, a bit like the trail of a rocket, but of a dense consistency.

In order to protect those driven from the clouds of dust, a paraphernalia of gadgets transformed each one into a strange-looking cocoon. There was an oilcloth duster that went down to one's feet and had sleeves that exceeded the hands by at least five inches. Above the duster, a shawl covered the nose, ears, and mouth, large goggles covered the eyes, and a cap or a hat was tied under the chin by an elastic ribbon. Yet despite these precautions, dust penetrated everywhere, filling ears, nostrils, and mouth, and reaching below the duster, deep into the armpits and the more secret folds and crevasses of the human anatomy.

Of this first drive through the steppe I remember mainly two things: the utter, desolate flatness of the landscape and its burnt-out, brownish surface. By the time we arrived at Preobrazhenka, the horses, the coachmen, the carriages, and all of us had acquired the same color as the landscape. We looked like those mimetically gifted moths that adapt themselves to match not only the tree bark but the moss that grows upon it.

After a half-hour of driving, our coachman turned around on his seat and pointed his whip at a dark spot on the horizon. "There it is," he said, "that's Preobrazhenka."

Gradually there appeared an oasis of gardens and houses, in the midst of which stood a white, sprawling, Miramar-like palazzo built for my grandmother by her husband. It shone bright and gay in the midday light with its endless rows of windows and indented Moorish towerlets. On the porch in front of the main entrance, rigid and solid, stood the figure of Omama, our grandmother. She was dressed in a long, white, lacy dress with a stiff collar, and a high black coiffure rose above her aquiline features. Lined up around her was the household personnel, from superintendent, housekeeper, and head butler down to a bunch of pretty girls in Ukrainian national dress. And while we were being kissed and hugged, from somewhere beyond the porch came the sounds of a band playing the tune of the Russian Imperial Anthem.

Omama, or Sophia Bogdanova Falz-Fein, *née* Knauff, was of German stock, and the story of her two marriages is a lesson in nineteenth-century mores and morals.

She was fifteen or sixteen when the three young Falz-Fein brothers, Edward, Alexander, and Gustav, came from Elizavetfeld near

Melitopol for a visit to Ekaterinoslav. They were sent there by their grandfather, Frederick Fein, for the purpose of getting themselves brides.

Judging by their portraits hanging in Preobrazhenka, the brothers were in every way different from one another. The eldest, Edward, was far from good-looking. He was stocky, dark-haired, and red-faced, with shrewd, hard eyes. His face had the kind of boorish expression of will power and endurance one finds in seventeenth-century portraits of Dutch businessmen. He looked like what he was: a descendant of pioneer settlers, a sheep-breeder, a man of the steppe. The second brother, Alexander, was taller and stouter with a jovial *bon-vivant* expression on his pudding face. The pudding was three-quarters covered by a Hohenzollern-plus-Romanov beard (Wilhelm I plus Alexander III). I imagined Oblonsky of *Anna Karenina* as looking a bit like him. The third brother, Gustav, was the opposite of the older brothers. Tall and handsome, with dreamy blue eyes and a pale, sensitive face, he looked like an intellectual, an artist, a bit like Chekhov.

The arrival of the three brothers in search of a bride, with their reputation for wealth in land and sheep, was no doubt exciting to the potential mothers-in-law of the large Teutonic colony of Eka-terinoslav. For the impoverished Knauffs it was a godsend. They knew they could supply at least one of the three brothers with a good-looking, healthy mate and reap one-third of the Falz-Feinian bridegroom harvest.

The Knauffs must have set to work swiftly and actively, for shortly after the arrival of the Falz-Fein brothers two of them, Edward and Gustav, were known to be courting the Knauff daughter. But while Edward's courtship was purely formal—probably he was simply obeying his parents' orders—Gustav's was growing more and more ardent. Gustav apparently fell deeply in love with the pretty, fifteen-year-old brunette, and she in turn found the hand-some, romantic-looking young man most attractive. At some point Edward withdrew from the courtship race and left the field open for his younger brother. Gustav proposed and the Knauffs joyfully accepted his proposal. But Gustav had not reckoned with his grand-father's will. When he returned to Elizavetfeld to announce his in-tention of marrying Sophie Knauff, the old man flatly refused to give his consent. Seniority had to be respected. Edward and Alex-ander must find brides before Gustav, the youngest, could be allowed to marry. So Frederick went up to Ekaterinoslav to look into the situation personally, to size up the Knauffs and their seemingly eager daughter.

He must have found the Knauff girl worth bargaining for, since after a short stay in Ekaterinoslav he turned the situation around. It became known that Fräulein Sophie Knauff was engaged not to Gustav but to Edward Falz-Fein, and that the parents of both the bride and the groom had given their blessings to the marriage.

Gustav withdrew to Vienna. There he sulked, distractedly studied the piano at the conservatory, and became interested in Freemasonry. I think he rose rapidly in the Masons' "degrees" and became master of a lodge while his brother ran his estates and sent him his share of the money. Sophie did not disappoint the hopes of old Fein. She was a fast and able breeder. In less than twelve years she produced a litter of six sons and one daughter (my mother). Then she visited Gustav in Vienna and traveled extensively with him in Europe. As years went by, she became more and more attached to Gustav. Edward, shut up in his domain on the Taurian steppes, grew morose and hypochondriac. He did not sleep at night, and my mother, when she was a girl of seven, would be awakened by him and would have to go to his room and sit on the edge of his bed and scratch his back.

It was rumored in family circles that two of Omama's youngest sons were fruits of adultery. Indeed, one of them, Uncle Nicolas, looked surprisingly like Gustav. He had the same dreamy blue eyes as Gustav and the same pale, elongated face.

This ambiguous situation lasted nearly ten years. Edward's life was strenuous. He got up at dawn, rode his horse far onto the steppe, watched his Merino flocks being shorn or bathed in pits of carbolic acid, an invention of his ancestor Jacob Fein (carbolic acid diluted in water was at that time the only remedy against mange), or he looked after his harvest and orchards. He came home at dusk to a cheerless household where he had instituted a reign of fierce economy. The house was ill-lit, bare, and cold, and the meals were frugal. As soon as he came home, all around him became silent. His children feared him—he was a despot to them. Gradually his health gave way. Or was it his will to live? But he died soon enough for the two lovers to get married and be blissfully happy together for a decade.

As it turned out, the impoverished Knauff girl succeeded in marrying two of the Falz-Fein bridegrooms and as a result held in her hands two-thirds of the Falz-Fein fortune. Old grandfather Fein could rest in peace. He had made an excellent deal. The larger part of his fortune was secure. It was in the hands of tough Omama and her seven children.

When we arrived in Preobrazhenka, Omama must have been in her middle seventies, yet her stiff, well-corseted bearing and high, smooth coiffure—it looked as if each strand of hair had been treated with black shoe polish—did not betray her age. She seemed ageless. Her endurance was as phenomenal as her bearing. She could outstand anyone in church and outsit anyone at the endless ceremonious meals that took place twice a day at her house. Her only trouble was that her hands shook, and the spoon or the fork seldom reached her mouth with what was intended to be in or upon it. Occasionally during these long meals, especially the holiday ones, her head would dip forward, her eyes would close, and for an instant she would fall asleep.

Grandmother Falz-Fein, like all the Falz-Feins, was a Lutheran, yet she surrounded herself and her household with all of the trappings of iconophilic Greek-Orthodoxy. In her boudoir she had assembled a cornerful of icons, a so-called "beautiful corner." Several oil lamps in blue and red cups hung in front of the icons, casting pretty rays of light up onto the dark faces of saints and virgins. Here Omama would spend several hours each day and night murmuring Slavonic prayers, kneeling and bowing her head down to the floor like any Russian peasant woman.

Each east corner of Preobrazhenka's many rooms was provided with an icon hung high up near the ceiling. *Molebens* were celebrated in Preobrazhenka on every possible occasion—saints' days, birthdays, or Imperial holidays. Opposite the main entrance of Preobrazhenka's castle she had installed a Greek Orthodox chapel. In that private chapel we had to attend excruciatingly long Vesper services on Saturdays and endless Slavonic Mass on Sundays.

A special form of pietistic agony took place every year in late May or early June. It was connected with rainfall and harvest. Early in the morning all of us including whatever guests or relatives were staying at Preobrazhenka, would be driven to a prearranged place far away in the midst of the steppe. There, at a crossroad, the priest, the deacon, the choir, various superintendents, employees, and farmhands, both male and female, would have gathered before our arrival and a sizable crowd would be waiting for us. A first *Moleben*, with special prayers for rain and harvest, was celebrated on the spot in front of a portable altar. Then a procession would start, during which the choir sang the same litanies over and over again while the priest waved his aspersion broom, sprinkling the field with holy water. After a mile-long walk down dusty paths in midday heat, the procession would stop and the priest would start his *Moleben* anew. The ritual would be repeated three or four times until we had covered many miles and our faces, hair, shirts, shoes, and socks would have turned chocolate brown. We were all of us totally exhausted.

Omama had instituted at Preobrazhenka a courtly way of life that was immutable and ceremonial. To us Nabokov children, coming from the free atmosphere of Lubcza, it seemed constrained and constricting. Although everything here was much more luxurious, the routine of daily life catered to grown-ups, not to children. Children and at times there were many of us: relatives and visiting friends—felt like a separate and a bit superfluous element.

The Preobrazhenka day was quite different from an average day at Lubcza. Its sequence was different, the timing more punctual, the meals more lavish, as were the pleasures and distractions. Our day began with breakfast at 8:30 in the smaller of the two dining rooms, called the dining room for *hors d'oeuvres*. There we drank our cocoa and ate our bread and butter with thick layers of honey. Then we climbed upstairs to my mother's apartment on the second floor. Mother with Kólo, Aunt Caroline, and the baby sister lived in spacious rooms near one of the castle's Moorish towers, and Mother's boudoir had a large balcony where she and Koló used to have their breakfast.

During that first visit my mother often sat in a pink dressing gown on the balcony, holding in her lap my baby sister, while Aunt Caroline and Koló were still in their respective rooms, getting dressed. After rambunctious kissing and hugging of everyone by everyone, Onya, Mitya, and I rushed downstairs, through the library, the adjacent *fumoir*, the spacious *salon* with its slippery parquet, to the front porch. There a contraption called a *lineika*—a Russian crossbreed between an English brake and an American covered wagon—was waiting for us. We crowded into it and drove a few miles across the steppe to the plum and peach orchard that lay on the shore of

57

Preobrazhenka's nearest *liman*, or shallow bay.

This *liman* was bordered by mounds of grayish, damp seaweed. Its water was shallow, perpetually tepid in the summer, and nearly as salty as the Dead Sea. But being very still, it was a chosen breeding place for jellyfish and for a small but nasty variety of catfish whose poisonous dart was rumored to be deadly. The last and perhaps most distinguished quality of our *liman* was the layer of black silt that covered its floor and smelled like a blend of rotting eggs and canine farts.

We were told by the elders that ours was the best and the healthiest sea-bathing spot in Russia. Our *liman*'s silt was supposed to contain iodine and also something else, something quite special that a Polish lady called Madame Curie had just discovered in Paris. We were told that the sun, the salt, and the silt (never mind the smells, the burns, and the stickiness) taken together, first in small doses and then gradually increasing, would work miracles on our bone structure, our circulatory and digestive systems, our appetite, and the general condition of our bodies. Consequently we had to rub ourselves with the silt, lie in the sun until the mud formed a gray crust, and then take another dip to wash it off, all of which took about two hours.

After this therapeutic contact with the sea we dressed and drove back to Preobrazhenka at top speed. Our reward for these odoriferous excursions was the peaches and plums we would pick in the orchard and eat on the drive back to Grandmother's castle. There followed the grand event of the day, and to me its greatest ordeal: the endlessly long dinner.

Soaped and cleansed, brother Mitya and I changed into immaculate sailor suits and descended to the ballroom. There we waited, mingling awkwardly with the assembled grown-ups, waiting for Omama to appear from her chambers and for the band to strike the *Egerski* March.

When she finally appeared and had received the *baise-main* from everyone present, the grown-ups moved solemnly to the library. We children and our ever present protectors stayed in the ballroom. We wandered aimlessly around on its gleaming parquet, peering occasionally into the winter garden, where Grandmother's band, in Navy uniform, looking like a shoal of trained seals, played waltzes, marches, and polkas, blowing their woodwinds and brasses amid a setting of semi-tropical greenery. I used to enjoy watching the emaciated, red-faced sousaphone player, his instrument curled around him like a huge prehistoric monster. The instrument seemed to belong to the same species as the dragons of St. George or St. Michael, about to sneeze flames at the saints' lances. Toward the end of the dance miscellany the head butler, Alexei, would appear and announce that dinner was served. The *Egerski* March would resound again and the grown-ups would start their solemn move toward the dining rooms. We would follow a bit sheepishly and take our seats at the end of a table that stretched all the way down the thirty- or forty-foot dining room. There we would wait until the grown-ups had eaten their *hors d'oeuvres* ("not good for children") in the smaller luncheon room next door. Finally they would reappear in the main dining room and would be seated. The dinner would begin to operatic medleys from *Il Trovatore, La Traviata, Carmen,* or *La Sonnambula.*

Dinner at Preobrazhenka was, as it is now in Russia, the central meal of the day. And, as is still the case in Moscow hotels, it lasted from one and a half to two hours. It was a strange and slightly unbelievable affair. When I think of those daily dinners in Preobrazhenka and try to recall the detailed processional of their gluttony and *gourméterie,* I cannot believe that they ever existed. They seem figments of imagination. Yet not only did they exist, but for at least six years of my childhood I endured them.

Not only were those meals ingeniously copious, including five or six courses (not counting the bonbons and savories served after dessert), but they were overabundant in fats and proteins. I still hear Omama's voice scolding her cook because the *borshch* did not have enough "pretty eyes" of fat floating on its surface. And soup was rarely served without an accompanying gruel called *kasha,* of which pre-Revolutionary Russia was so inventive and of which only one species survives abroad—the buckwheat one. A spoonful of sour cream was usually thrust into the soup, and with a variety of *kasha* came several kinds of little pastries stuffed with meat, cabbage, rice, or fish.

Soup was followed by fish, then roast meat, then fowl, then a *jardinière* of vegetables. Toward the end of the gamut came sweets: pudding with fresh or whipped cream, or else a variety of *plombières, bombes glacées,* and *parfaits.*

During these dinners the band continued playing in a somewhat subdued fashion so as to permit table talk. At dinner, our end of the

59

table was supposed to be mum. We were not allowed to disturb the table talk of the grown-up end. If we talked, we had to whisper. And the governesses whispered back at us angrily: "Where are your hands? Put them on the table! . . . Take your elbows off the table!" or more snappily: "Behave yourself! . . . Eat properly! . . . Don't kick! . . . Be quiet!"

After the meal was over and we had passed in a file in front of Grandmother to say *"Merci beaucoup,"* we would rush to our quarters on the second floor for an hour-long siesta which everyone observed. At about four p.m. we would have an hour's time free for games, walks, gathering fruit, flowers, and berries. At five p.m. tea was served on the terrace in the French garden. It was again a ceremonial affair with an overabundance of breads, cakes, cottage cheese, fruits, and berries. Then Omama would propose either an excursion or a digestive promenade through the park. The park was well laid out, equally well kept, and constantly watered by flocks of barefoot girls in peasant dress. The big lanes and even the smaller paths were covered with bright yellow sand that was raked daily and looked as impeccable as the Imperial gardens in Kyoto. The main *allée* of the park led to a pond, in the midst of which, on a promontory that looked like an island, was a grotto. In the evening on Sundays and holidays the grotto would be illuminated to give a performance of its own. Preobrazhenka had been provided with electricity in 1895, and since then the grotto had produced its series of *tableaux vivants:* sunrise, thunderstorm (while someone shook a sheet of metal), and a starlit night with a lemonish crescent floating among stars.

Beyond the park were fruit orchards, vineyards, several greenhouses, a plantation of young trees, dozens of flowerbeds for cutting, and a vegetable garden that after our small one at Lubcza seemed enormous to me. There were also a fairly deserted tennis court and a croquet lawn. On the whole, the park was ample and its very existence was a miracle, for next to it lay the endless flat space of drought-ridden brown steppe and beyond that the *liman* with its silt, sun, and stench.

Punctually at seven p.m. a bell rang. It was the call for children's supper, which, like breakfast, was served in the *hors d'oeuvres* room. Supper was, by Mother's order, light and swift, and although supervised by our tutor and one of the governesses, it was a much gayer and happier affair than midday dinner. We could speak and laugh freely and cease for a while to be victims of the grown-ups and their elaborate ceremonial.

They ate much later. But before they sat down to their supper we would be passed around from cheek to cheek, lap to lap, and hand to hand, to say our good-nights. Once we were in bed, teeth brushed and our prayers finished, the light would be put out and only an oil lamp in a ruby-red glass would quietly flicker in the eastern corner of the room in front of the icon of my saint, providing the necessary warmth conducive to sleep. Despite the zooming of mosquitoes, the chiming of the clock, the barking of sheep dogs, I would drop at once into deep, heavy sleep, exhausted by the sea, the silt, the meals, the smells, and by the pomp and circumstance of grandmother's white castle on the steppes of southern Russia.

Omama's boudoir at Preobrazhenka was a large, stuffy room cluttered with furniture, bibelots, and heavy damask curtains. In one corner stood a lectern with an upholstered prayer stool in front of it. Icons of various shapes and sizes covered the two walls of this corner up to the ceiling. On the lectern lay a large black German Bible. Red and blue oil lamps flickered in front of the icons.

Omama sat in an armchair near a closed window. It was a hot summer day in 1913. She wore her summer apparel: a long, starched, snow-white dress with a whaleboned collar. Her high coiffure was jay black, her owlish profile pale and stern. Stuck in the armchair, she looked like a Jugendstil curio: an aged goddess hewn out of Carrara marble, with an ebony top.

She did not move when I came in, nor did she greet me. Her face was stony.

I felt edgy. Never before had I been in Omama's private chambers. Inaccessible to children, they were open only to Mother, to the hunchback housekeeper, and to her private chambermaids.

After a long, awkward silence she turned her head wearily toward me, gazed at me, and said in a low, tired voice: "Come closer . . . I want to speak to you. But first kneel down, bow your forehead to the floor, cross yourself, and kiss the Holy Bible," and she nodded toward the lectern.

I did what she said. When I got up, she blessed me and let me kiss her plump hand.

"Now pull up a stool, sit down, and listen carefully. But don't forget, you'll be speaking in front of these icons. When I ask you a question, you must tell the truth. If you don't, God will punish you."

I muttered, "Yes," and sat down.

"You see," she started, still in the same tired voice, "you are growing up fast. Soon you will be a big boy. I've been watching you—oh, yes, I have," and she looked straight into my eyes. "I notice everything, you know. People think I'm gaga because I fall asleep at meals and because my hands shake. But I watch. I notice things." She lifted her eyes to the icons and her index finger toward the ceiling. "I know everything that goes on in this house. And I have people who watch for me and report," and she stopped as if to catch breath. After a pause, she started speaking in a calm, cordial tone.

"Tell me, Nikooshka," and she patted my cheek, "do you know already . . ." She hesitated. "*Noo*, how shall I tell you? Did someone tell you . . . or perhaps you noticed yourself . . . ?" and she hesitated again. "Well . . . did anybody speak to you about it?"

"About what?" I asked.

"About children," she said. "I mean . . . how they are born." She looked at me as if trying to read my thoughts. "But before you answer, think carefully and tell everything. Tell the truth . . . all you know about it."

"I don't quite understand . . . what you want me to tell." I started to mumble. "Sometimes . . . I saw strange things . . . I watched dogs and horses. How they climb on top of each other . . . And then Uncle Frederick took me once to see how elephants do it at the zoo in Petersburg. He told me that this is the way they make little ones."

"Never mind what Uncle Frederick said. Never mind dogs and horses and elephants," interrupted Omama. "I mean *children, babies* like your sister Lidochka or yourself a few years ago. Did anyone tell you how *you* were born?"

I wavered. "No, not really . . . nobody told me . . . except once, at Lubcza . . ."

"Except what?" she snapped.

"Well . . . you see, Mitya talked to me about it last summer. He tried to explain to me . . . that babies come out of our insides . . . and then . . . we looked for babies . . . inside our holes."

"What do you mean, you looked for babies inside your holes? Where? What holes? Where did you look?"

"We . . . just looked . . . around our bodies," I stuttered. "We looked for . . . holes."

"Well . . . come on," said Omama, smiling, "tell me, where did you look? Don't be afraid, I won't punish you."

"But, Omama, must I? Because, you know . . . we didn't find anything."

"Stop fidgeting on your stool and tell me where, in what holes, did you look for babies?"

"It happened this way," I said. "One morning at Lubcza, brother Mitya came to my bed. He was naked. He pulled off my blanket, lifted my nightie, sat on the edge of my bed, and started worming his finger into my navel. 'Ai,' I screamed, 'you're hurting me!' but he made, 'Sst!' and whispered, 'Keep quiet,' and he started again pushing his finger into my navel. 'You know,' he said, 'you have a hole in there!' I told him to stop hurting me. I knew nothing about a hole in my navel and did not believe that there was one.

" 'Yes, there is a hole in your navel. We all have holes in there,' said Mitya, 'and we must learn how to pry them open . . . because this is the way babies are born. They come out of a hole in the navel. They stay in our bellies until they are ready to come out. But we must help them get through the navel.'

"I looked down at my navel with interest, but was not at all convinced that there was a hole in it and a baby beyond that hole.

" 'Why don't we try to find the holes in our navels?' proposed Mitya. 'Maybe we'll find a way to pry them open and see if there are babies inside.'

" 'If there is a hole in your or my navel, it must be small,' I argued. 'How can a baby crawl out of it?'

" 'Don't be silly,' said Mitya. 'Our holes stretch, they're like rubber. Besides, when babies come out, they're like dolls made out of jelly. Once they're out, they blow up overnight, like balloons.'

"I had never seen doll-sized babies, nor could I imagine how such a baby would turn overnight into something as big, for example, as my sister Lidochka when she was a week old. But Mitya insisted. 'Let us try,' he said. 'It won't hurt. Maybe we'll find a way to open our holes.'

"So we started to dig, push, and worm our index fingers into our respective navels. But nothing happened. The holes wouldn't open. After a while we stopped. Mitya bent down and looked closely inside my navel.

" 'Your navel's dirty,' he said. 'There's something black in it. Perhaps this is why the hole won't open. Let me try to get the dirt out.' He found a penknife and started scratching my navel until it bled. He said that this was normal. He had seen dogs and girls bleed from their holes. It might be a sign that my hole would open. But I told him to stop it and leave me alone. He went back to his bed and . . . this is all . . ."

Omama listened intently to my story. At the end of it she smiled. "Heavens! What a silly story! I knew that Mitya was a brute . . . but he could have hurt you!"

She got up, bowed to the icons, crossed herself, mumbled something like a prayer, and plunged back into her armchair.

"Now listen carefully," she said. "*I* will tell you the truth: There are no holes in your navel, and no baby is hidden in either your or Mitya's belly. Remember this and stop worrying about your navel. Especially do not scratch it with a penknife! What a queer idea! You could hurt yourself badly! Promise never to do it again!"

I promised.

She hesitated for a moment and then said, as if speaking of something completely different, "Now listen. I will tell you what you should not do with your little 'thing,' " and she pointed to my crotch, "all by yourself or with others . . . especially not with girls . . . or with anybody! And I mean *never, never!*"

I bowed my head.

"Does your little thing, your *pipiska*, get hard sometimes?"

I blushed and said, "Yes."

"And what happens then? I mean, when it gets that way?" She lifted my head and looked into my eyes. "But don't forget, tell the truth! Don't hide anything!"

"I don't know, Omama," I muttered. "Sometimes in the daytime, but also at night and in the morning."

"And what do you do then?" she asked. "What do you do with your *pipiska* when it gets hard?"

"I . . . I . . . rub it," I stuttered. "I play with it."

"*Mein Gott!*" she exclaimed. "You shouldn't! Don't ever rub it! It can make you sick! When your *pipiska* does get hard, what does it do to you? Does it excite you? Does it?"

"Sometimes, yes . . . it does," I admitted. "But, Omama, what can I do? I can't help it. It does it by itself . . . and then I get excited."

"I know, I know," she said and patted my cheek. "But I will tell you what you should do. When your *pipiska* gets hard, run to the nearest faucet and stick your *pipiska* into cold water. Keep the water running until your thing shrinks. Your *pipiska* is there to make *pipi* and nothing else. You should not use it when it is hard! Will you do what I say?"

I said that I would try.

"Don't try," she commanded, "do as I say and . . . and promise me now, here, in front of the icons!"

I looked down to the floor, nodded, and said, "I will."

"The worst thing you can do," she continued, "when you are excited and your *pipiska* is . . . hard . . . is to put it into somebody else's body." She hesitated. "Into a girl's hole, for example. Girls have holes there where you have your *pipiska*. They make *pipi* from their holes. But when you stick your own *pipiska* into a girl's hole," and she clasped her hands, "then something awful happens . . . something awful!"

I looked at her, frightened.

"Promise me that you will never, never, *never* stick your *pipiska* into a girl's hole. Promise!"

I mumbled, "Yes."

"Do you know what happens to a girl when you do it?"

No, I did not know, I replied.

"I will tell you what happens." She looked at me triumphantly. "If you stick your *pipiska* into a girl's hole and rub it . . . then a milk-like liquid will come out of it, a sort of milky *kisel* [a starchy Russian sweet]. If that *kisel* gets deep enough into the girl . . . she'll have a baby," and she shook her finger at me.

"But! But! But!" she exclaimed. "It will not be a normal baby, it will be a sick baby, a *monster* . . . because God will punish you and the girl. The girl will get fat and ugly and no one will look at her. As for you!" She stood up and put her hands on my shoulders. "You will get an awful disease," and her voice grew harsh. "You will decay! Your *pipiska* will be covered with boils. Pus will flow out of it. It will get brown and fall off. You won't be able to use it any more to do *pipi*. You will have an awful disease that is called syphilis. People die from it. And they die only because they do not obey God's will!"

She took me by the hand and said solemnly, "Now come here, kneel with me in front of the icons."

We both knelt, she on her prayer stool, I on the floor.

65

"Now recite the Lord's Prayer," she ordered.

I started nervously. "*Otche Nash izhe yesi na nebesekh . . .*" (Our Father that art in heaven . . .)

"No! Recite it slowly. Start again."

While I recited the Lord's Prayer, Omama's face was buried in her hands, and after I had finished reciting she prayed for a long while. Then she turned to me and said: "Now repeat what I say."

I started repeating every word she said. I swore never to do those "evil things" she had talked to me about. I swore that if I was tempted to do them I would pray to God and ask him to remove the temptation from me. I also swore that whenever I felt "it" rising and getting hard I would rush to the nearest cold-water faucet to get the thing back to its normal soft size.

When the swearing was over, Omama blessed me again. I kissed her hand and she the top of my head. She sighed and said in her native German, "Now you can go . . . but you must never forget! You must always remember *Deinen Schwur!*" and she walked through the door to her bedroom.

I felt that someone was waiting for her there. I put my ear to the crack in the door.

I heard her chuckle or cough. And then in a hard, matter-of-fact voice she said to someone in Russian: "Well, I have frightened him all right. Now your Nikooshka is safe and scared. It will take him a long time to get over it. I'm sure he won't start trying to do it for quite some time."

I assumed that the person she spoke to was my mother, although it may have been Aunt Caroline or the hunchback housekeeper, Maria Filipovna.

Omama Falz-Fein was an early victim of the Red Terror. 1918 and 1919 were troubled years on the steppes of southern Russia. Places passed frequently from the Red to the White armies.

Omama had withdrawn from palatial Preobrazhenka to her little house at the harbor of *Khorly*. It seemed to be a less ostentatious and safer haven. But she refused to join us in Yalta and would not listen to suggestions of leaving Russia.

In March 1919, a day before the Whites liberated *Khorly*, two agents of the Cheka came riding up to her residence. The next morning a detachment of the White Army found her riddled with bullets. She was eighty-seven years old.

* * *

The only pompous thing about Askania-Nova was its hybrid Latin name. In every other way it was the opposite of Preobraz-henka. There was no ceremonial, no etiquette at meals, no "pot-pourri-ing" band, nor were there any "church ordeals." Meals were punctual, snappy, never more than three courses. But there was often strange, exotic food to eat: a roast of buffalo, a rack of kangaroo or gazelle, or a huge pink carp. Sometimes, in spring, there was a dish of scrambled egg made of one ostrich egg.

Unlike the table talk at Preobrazhenka, the conversation around the table involved everyone, from the youngest up. In other words, we children took part in it. Meals were gay and exciting. The talk usually centered on Askania-Nova and its latest news. Had someone noticed something new in one of the aviaries or in the garden?

"How are your young nightingales coming along?" Uncle Frederick would ask a Pan-like, wiry old creature at the end of the table, called Herr Konraetz. Herr Konraetz, an Austrian and a former tutor of my uncle, had developed a technique for breeding nightingales in captivity and teaching them how to sing.

"Two of them died last night," would mumble toothless Herr Konraetz.

"You must have given them vodka instead of water," joked Uncle Frederick.

Konraetz's face would get red: "*Aber bitte, Herr Friedrich!*" he retorted. "What do you think I am, an idiot?"

Someone at the table reported news from the waterfront. He or she had seen a brood of Icelandic geese flying in circles above the pond. Did that mean that they were training the young ones to fly and soon would be away?

"Maybe—who knows? Sometimes they fly away, sometimes they winter here," answered Uncle Frederick.

Someone had noticed a pair of flamingoes building a conical structure on a secluded island.

"That's strange. It is much too late in the year. So far not a single flamingo has hatched here at Askania-Nova."

At times Uncle Frederick would announce the birth of a rare cross-breed, or that a brood of Caucasian eagles had been spotted.

"How did the Caucasian eagles come here?" I'd ask.

"Well, that's what Askania-Nova does—it attracts." Uncle Frederick smiled benevolently.

But there was a precondition to being happy in Askania-Nova and feeling "at home." One had to show active interest in what was being accomplished and participate in its animal life. If a visitor did not show such an interest and seemed indifferent, he would be neglected and soon would be given to understand that he was undesirable, and hence would leave.

Fortunately, indifferent visitors were rare. Most people who came to Askania-Nova had heard about it beforehand and came for a definite purpose. Around the dinner table there were always a few scholars, nature lovers, directors of zoos, or explorers.

Askania-Nova possessed a magic of its own, and with the adroit help of Uncle Frederick it turned most people into nature lovers. Even a dumb *chinovnik* (a civil servant) on an inspection tour would be affected by it and ask Uncle Frederick's permission to come again. Most visitors, like Askania-Nova's migratory waterfowl (the lakes and ponds were vast and hospitable), came back seasonally. A few of them had come for a brief visit and stayed for life. They found in Askania-Nova their life's interest. Three such visitors outlasted Uncle Frederick and all of us by decades: a famous Tibetan explorer of the turn of the century, General Kozlov, with his wife, and a charming lady, Iulia Ivanovna Igumnova, sister of a famous piano pedagogue at the Moscow Conservatory and one of the many "last secretaries" of Tolstoy.

At the very first contact with Askania-Nova, I fell in love with it. It excited me, amazed me, made me happy. It was a welcome relief after stuffy Preobrazhenka. It even surpassed in charm and beauty my beloved Lubcza. Here at Askania-Nova nature enveloped me with its extraordinary abundance and variety. I felt like a diver into exotic waters discovering strange shapes and scapes of the sea bed. All around me was a huge Noah's Ark floating peacefully on the Taurian steppes. And I was a part of that Ark, an initiate to its mysteries. My mind, my senses, my emotions were on the alert, watching, observing, loving.

Uncle Frederick was a tall, corpulent man with a round Bismarckian head. His eyes under heavy eyebrows were brown and had a stern, hard look. He was prematurely bald and wore a short beaver mustache. He drank no alcohol, not even wine, did not smoke, rose at five in the morning, took a daily afternoon nap, and went early to bed. When at Askania-Nova, he always wore the same clothes: a jacket (like Stalin's or Mao's) and high boots; gray in winter, white in summer. He always looked neat and well groomed. His house was immaculately clean, its glossy, whitewashed rooms filled with Russian country-style Empire mahogany furniture.

His mornings started with a meeting with his aides, superintendents, surveyors, keepers, breeders, and gardeners. He would be briefed by them as to what had happened overnight. Then he would tell them what to do during the day and how to do it. First came the agricultural discussions, then the zoological ones. In the latter, Rieberger, Klim Sianko, and at times I. I. Igumnova or Professor Ivanov took an active part.

The rest of the day, except for meals and his afternoon nap, he was continuously on the go, inspecting, advising, or showing visiting notables his beloved Askania-Nova.

He liked to joke and laugh and play practical jokes on people but he had no patience with small talk or stupid people, or, rather, with people who showed no interest in Askania-Nova. He got rid of them rather expeditiously.

He was thrifty but not miserly. His tastes were simple and unluxurious. Preobrazhenka, with its ostentatious opulence and courtly ceremonial was alien to him. He went there very rarely. Only when my mother, whose judgment he trusted, would persuade him that it was time for a visit to his mother would he drive the thirty-odd miles that separated Askania-Nova from Preobrazhenka, staying briefly.

He had little interest in art, literature, or philosophy, nor had he any religious inclinations. He always made cracks about his mother's addiction to Greek-Orthodoxy and her exaggerated iconophilia. (There were no icons at Askania-Nova.) His younger brother Nicolas leaned toward mysticism, so when Uncle Nicolas came Uncle Frederick teased him mercilessly and made cracks about religion and his Tolstoyan mysticism. Uncle Nicolas would obligingly lose his temper. To Uncle Frederick religion, philosophizing, and literature were "unnecessary ballast," good for lazy men and indolent women. What he liked to talk about was discoveries in zoology, in botany, and in other applied sciences. But he also talked about history and politics when those he talked to were intelligent people ready to argue with him.

His views were a curious mixture of modernism and conservatism. "Russia is no England," he would say. "Just look around and see how unprepared we are for Parliament and freedom. We need time to develop, but under a strong, capable government."

69

Yet at home at Askania-Nova he applied the most advanced modern techniques of his time both in farming his land and in his zoo. He paid the employees and workmen much better salaries than his neighbors, built schools and hospitals on the estate, and pensioned aged people (a thing unheard of in pre-Revolutionary Russia). All in all, Uncle Frederick was a rare example of a pragmatic realist, a builder, a modern man. On the other hand, while many of his neighbors among the Russian land-owning gentry were often on the brink of bankruptcy, his fortune steadily increased, despite the large sums of money he spent on his zoological and scientific hobbies.

One of the things I liked best about Askania-Nova was its aviaries. They were close to the house, in the midst of the shady park—spacious quadrangles surrounded on three sides by chicken wire and on the fourth by a wall with several open doors. Behind those walls was a house, heated during winter. Inside each aviary were quaint Japanese-style gardens with miniaturized shrubbery, treelets, rocks, artificial waterfalls and brooks. All of it looked perfectly natural and, despite the presence of thousands of birds it was clean and neat.

I liked to sit on a bench in front of these aviaries. The concert inside started at dawn and lasted until dusk. It was a boisterous, virile, and gay concert that enraptured me. It sounded like a 1,001-part counterpoint, perpetually "aleatoric" and indescribably intricate. There was a beauty in it that seemed to me more intense than any organized sound invented by humans.

My frequent companion at these concerts was Herr Konraetz. He told me which bird was singing what "part" and how to recognize their songs with my eyes closed. He always carried a little pillbox containing woodworms. He would pick up a worm and hold it close to the chicken wire. Instantly a bird—finch, warbler, cardinal, or Chinese nightingale—would fly toward the hand and take his prey.

"When you come in spring," he would say, "I will show you how to make nightingales sing."

And the first spring we spent at Askania-Nova, Herr Konraetz took me before dawn into the thickets of the park. We sat silently holding our breath. Herr Konraetz started rubbing a rough sheet of paper with a brush. Suddenly a nightingale started throbbing. Soon there were two and then three answering one another and throbbing together. As we went home, old Konraetz explained which of the nightingale *Meistersinger* was a *"famoser Walther"* and which was an *"abscheulicher Beckmesser."*

"What are those animals called?"

"Which?"

"Those cream-colored ones with a hump on their back and horns like corkscrews."

"They are called *Elenbock* in German—the largest African antelope."

"And those there? The funny-looking gray ones like horses with a ram's head and a goatee?"

"They're also antelopes—called gnu."

"Why do they jump all the time and kick with their hind legs?"

"Because they're wild and difficult to tame."

"And why is that big bird running away from the others?"

"Because it's an emu, an Australian ostrich. It's afraid of African antelopes—especially wild ones like the gnu."

Rieberger, the overseer of Askania-Nova's animal preserve, a *Kolonist*, looks down at me, picks me up, and plunks me on his shoulders.

"Look! They're all coming toward us and some of them are galloping. Why?"

"Because it's feeding time," says Rieberger. "See those carts there? They're bringing in forage. It will be spread all over the place. Else they'll start fighting."

"But why do they fight?"

Rieberger smiles. "Because animals are accustomed to fight for their food. It's in their blood."

We have been standing on a platform, a kind of promontory on top of a fence made of wooden planks. The fence, which seems to stretch endlessly to left and right, encompasses some forty acres. Its far side can barely be seen: a faint pencil line across the surface of the steppe.

Two staircases lead to the platform: one from the outside, the other from the animal enclave. Uncle Frederick walks slowly down the stairs to the animals. A gazelle walks up to him and he gives her a cigarette. She spits out the cardboard tip and walks off chewing tobacco. He remounts the platform and, pointing to the *Elenbock,*

7 *1*

the gnus, and the other fifty-odd animal species gathered in front of us, he says with pride: *"Pochti vse nashi!"* (Nearly all ours!)

"What do you mean?" I ask.

"Most of those animals down there," he explains, "were born and bred at Askania-Nova."

"But where did they come from? Where did you get their parents?"

"From animal dealers, some from zoos. We organized expeditions to get the rare ones. It cost a small fortune getting all those animals and birds. And it took a lot of patience and many years to breed these here. But now they're all ours, born and brought up here. To-morrow you'll see large herds of *Elenbock*, buffaloes, and other animals grazing on the open steppe—like cows or sheep."

In the spring of 1917 Uncle Frederick fled to Moscow. In October, when the Bolsheviks came to power, he was put in jail. Jail in those early days of the Revolution was relatively humane. The terror started later, in 1918–19. I understand that while in jail he gave lectures to his jailmates on zoology and subjects related to wildlife. The jails were full of scholars and intellectuals. I was told that even Commissar Lunatcharsky attended his lectures in jail. I do not remember upon whose intervention he was freed and allowed to emigrate to Germany.

I saw him in 1920, at a sanatorium in Berlin. He was a broken man. The news from Askania-Nova was disheartening. Civil war and hunger raged all over Russia. Askania-Nova was pillaged, animals and birds were killed, the gardens went untended. He wrote letters to scholarly colleagues in Moscow asking for help. But nothing was done before the end of the civil war. In 1922, when a commission from the Academy of Sciences finally visited Askania-Nova and the Soviet government declared it a national wildlife center, Uncle Frederick had died.

When I got the news of his death I suddenly remembered a conversation between Mademoiselle Verrière, Rieberger, and other people on the staff: "What will happen to all of this? Look at what Frederick has built up here! Will it all now fall to pieces and be destroyed?" There was real despair in their voices.

But despite two great wars and the upheavals of the Revolution, Askania-Nova still exists. Ironically, it is now called "Professor

Ivanov's State Preserve" after one of Uncle Frederick's colleagues and friends, the late Professor Mikhail Fedorovich Ivanov. Ivanov's monument stands in front of the master's house. On it the legend reads: "To the creator of the State Wildlife Preserve."

Yet everyone in Russia knows the name of the real "creator" of Askania-Nova. When I went to Moscow in 1967 and told someone in the Ministry of Culture that I was a nephew of Frederick Falz-Fein, I was instantly urged to visit "Professor Ivanov's State Preserve." But my loving memories of the old Askania-Nova were too powerful: I declined.

In the autumn of 1911, in mid-September, our little paddle-steamer took us downstream from Lubcza to the railroad junction at the Neman bridge. We boarded the train in the afternoon and arrived next morning in St. Petersburg.

I remember Mademoiselle Verrière at Askania-Nova exclaiming: *"Ah, quelle chance!* How lucky you are to go to St. Petersburg!" and paraphrasing Custine, she added, *"C'est la ville des plus belles façades du monde."* But that drizzly morning the famous façades looked glum and inhospitable, and the drive in the landeau seemed endless.

"What is it going to be like," I thought, "living here, among all these gloomy houses, in this sad place?" And suddenly I wanted to be back home, to feel warm again, to be at Lubcza or Askania-Nova.

The carriage turned to the left at a bridge and stopped almost immediately at the third house from the corner of the Nevski Prospect. On top of its gates I read a luminous sign in Russian lettering: "Fontanka 25, Snkt PTRBG."

A liveried porter with a conical beard came rushing from under a portico and led us into the front hall.

Suddenly everything was well again. The hall was warm, lit by a large chandelier and brass sconces with milky white globes. Under our feet was a soft rug and the walls glimmered with brown and gilt Cordovan leather. Servants came down toward us smiling and started unloading the luggage. We walked up to the second floor upon a broad, carpeted staircase whose brass railing shone and whose bannister was covered with soft, deep-red velvet.

Upstairs the entrance door to the flat was wide open. Mother stood on its threshold in a pink peignoir and Koló in a camel-hair dressing gown. All of us started kissing, embracing, and hugging.

From inside, somewhere from the left, came the comforting smell of *café-au-lait*.

"Now, children," said Mother, holding me by the hand and leading all of us into the flat, "here it is, here is your new home."

In a few days the ritual of the Fontanka flat was fully established. As was true of most things that Mother organized, the household machine was well oiled. Meals were simple and punctual and the day had a well-defined schedule. Everyone except Mitya and me had his own room. The two of us shared a large one. A classroom and our tutor's room were next to ours, so that the supervision was effective and continuous.

A few days after our arrival brother Mitya entered the preparatory class of the Alexandrovski Litsei, while I started going to the School of the Reformed Church, one of the three German Protestant schools that had the reputation of high scholastic standards. Sister Onya had already been at St. Catherine's boarding school for girls for a year.

Despite the comforts of our new home, despite Mother's care and solicitude, it was a very different life that I had to face as of September 1911. Instead of gardens, country homes, and meadows, there were treeless squares, canals, bridges, and buildings—small ones, drab ones, large and grand ones, luxurious palaces, and official government buildings. Many of them were part of Russian history, others had no history whatsoever. All of them were full of people and those people had unfamiliar faces. They were not Mademoiselle Verrière, or Rieberger, or coachman Anton. The crowd in the street was anonymous, strangely unsmiling, and shadowy.

This applied above all to everyone in the school. Before coming to St. Petersburg I had always been taught by tutors and governesses. Now I had to sit in a class with about thirty strange boys and try to understand what the teacher was saying at a desk that looked like a pulpit. Then, like all my classmates, I would have to copy into my notebook figures or words that he had written on a blackboard. It all seemed mechanical and unconcerned with me. My fellow students, as I soon discovered, were a tough lot. They were mostly Germans and Balts, with a crop of rich Jewish boys, but very few Russians. They liked to fight and play rough games.

I did literally nothing in school. I was so disoriented by the sudden burst into collective life that I did not even try to understand what was being taught or expected of me. Nobody told me how I was to behave, how to deal with the subject matter that was being taught, or simply how to listen, how to follow a dictation or to learn by heart those beastly multiplication tables or irregular French verbs.

Toward the end of the school year it became clear that not only was I a social misfit in the school, but that I was appallingly bad in my studies. My mother was informed that if I was to stay I would have to start the same class over again. My mathematics were rotten and so was my spelling in all languages. I only managed limpingly to get a passing mark in history.

Rather than have me repeat the year, I was given a year of intense training at home, and in the spring of 1914 I passed the entrance examination to the preparatory class of the same Imperatorski Alexandrovski Litsei, where my brother had been studying for two years. During the year of study at home, except for relatives and family friends, I did not see many new faces and had no friends of my own.

But there was one consolation. By 1914 the tedious piano lessons had borne fruit: I had become proficient enough to enjoy playing for my own pleasure. By the time we moved to St. Petersburg I had developed the habit of spending most of my free time improvising or sight-reading at the splendid new Becker piano my mother had bought to adorn the ballroom of our flat. Soon I had a sizable repertoire of various kinds of music, mostly pieces I had gleaned from my mother's, my sister's, and my brother's music racks. I had, however, begun to develop my first set of independent critical judgments about the music I was deciphering, and I began to write down those particles of my own improvisations that stuck in my memory.

My first original composition, a "berceuse for piano" with bits of Caucasian Orientalia, was written for my mother's birthday in 1912. I recall the long hours of constant erasing needed to put down that brief piece on paper. My manuscript was received with enthusiasm, and my new piano teacher, a very kind and very timid Jewish lady, was entrusted with teaching me the rudiments of music theory and harmony.

My earliest musical enthusiasms conformed with the musical taste of my environment. In fact, it was probably quite similar to the taste of most other Russian children of my time in whose households the art of music was being practiced.

First I developed a tender affection for the Nordic-spring rumblings of Edvard Grieg—the prickly heat of music, one of the most inoffensive children's diseases. I used to spend hours playing the polite "Anitra's Dance" and the sorrowful "Death of Ase" from the *Peer Gynt* Suite. The Grieg rash came and went quickly. Next came the measles of Frédéric Chopin, or rather of Chopin's preludes, a few nocturnes, and one or two easy mazurkas. This second illness lasted much longer. For several years the living room of our apartment resounded with Chopin's Nocturne in C Sharp Minor or the E Major Prelude.

After Chopin came a serious and protracted case of esoteric mumps: the music of Alexander Scriabin. It began mildly with the discovery of the Chopinesque preludes and the first three piano sonatas. Gradually it grew in intensity and began to revel in the more "transcendental" sonatas of his later period until I became addicted to such esoterica as the *Poème du Feux* and *Poème de l'Extase*. Scriabin's music kept me in total subservience for at least three years, but then it left me abruptly.

Curiously enough, all through these years I felt indifferent to the older Russian composers, such as Tchaikovsky, or the bearded panoply of Russian nationalists, Rimsky-Korsakov, Borodin, and Moussorgsky, nor was I moved by any of the classics—that is, by Bach, Mozart, Haydn, or Beethoven. Their music seemed boring and stale because of what I felt to be sadly dated harmonies and dull, trivial melodies. Only after I started participating in our homespun quartet—my sister, my brother, my sister's violin teacher, a young Diaghilev cousin, and myself as stand-in for the last—did I begin to react to some of the early Beethoven quartets.

I suppose that I should be ashamed of such a tortuous development of musical taste. Yet I believe that it is more natural for children and adolescents to like the music of Grieg, Scriabin, Chopin, and Wagner (and nowadays Stravinsky, Webern, and Schoenberg) than to like the music of Mozart and Bach. A child loves primarily the outward symbols of art; he cannot comprehend and is totally unaware of its inward qualities. He likes the harmonic language of his time. Older music seems too simple, and hence is boring to him. This is why most of the so-called "children's pieces" do not amuse children. They are too simple for them. In reality these pieces usually represent a sugar-coated image of what the grown-ups dream is a child's musical taste. A child rarely senses the depth and beauty hidden behind the conventional musical language of past centuries. The outward simplicity of Mozart and the contrapuntal complications of Bach are equally impenetrable to a child.

Stravinsky entered my life very early, but by sheer accident.

On a balmy summer Sunday in 1912 or 1913 I was led by my tutor into a neo-Gothic glass-topped pavilion, part railroad station, part *Kurhaus*, at Pavlovsk, one of St. Petersburg's greenest suburbs. The pavilion served as a concert hall for the summer concert season of the Imperial Court Orchestra. The concerts were given each Sunday throughout the summer and were a deservedly famous attraction for music-loving Petersburgers.

My mother, like many other Petersburg mothers, patronized them zealously. They provided her offspring with a propitious combination of a countryside outing, for which Pavlovsk's shady parks and spacious meadows, were ideally suited, and a cultural event in the evening. As for us, the offspring, the excursion to Pavlovsk with its midday picnic was obviously pleasurable and the evening concert, at its worst, endurable.

The evenings were north-lit until midnight; the gardens smelled of bird cherry, lilac, and syringa (which Russians insist on calling jasmine), and the breeze from the Finnish Gulf was cool and bracing.

The Pavlovsk concert programs, as I remember them, were a mixed fare of light and serious music. Nineteenth-century repertoire pieces, from Bach to Offenbach and from Johann Strauss to Richard Strauss, commingled with native classics of a well-established variety. Occasionally there would be an excursion into "tame" modernism, but never anything eccentric, shocking, or controversial.

The symphonic journey usually started in a standard way: first would come a familiar overture, then an equally familiar symphony or a concerto played by a soloist. Then the intermission. The grown-up males went outdoors for a smoke, while the children with their female chaperones queued up according to sex in front of exiguous lavatories.

After intermission the journey generally went wrong, or, rather, got unbearably tedious. Although the musical numbers were usually gayer and lighter, the hall grew progressively oxygen-less. Many children and quite a few elders started dozing or falling asleep; others grew edgy and whimpery. Toward the concert's end the music in the hall accompanied the music from the stage in the form of rhythmic yelps and sobs.

It was at such a concert at Pavlovsk that I was shocked out of my wits by a brief, weird, and bumpy piece of music, the like of which I had never heard before. The instruments whizzed, shrieked, trilled, shot up and down their registers, sparkled, and clattered, and before I could realize what was happening, the piece came to an abrupt end with a tremendous thud on the bass drum.

I grabbed the program and in the pavilion's dim light deciphered: "Fireworks" by Igor Stravinsky.

Little remains in memory of that first encounter, and nothing of the "Fireworks" except their shock. We walked silently to the Pavlovsk railroad station under a pale pink sky and shuttled back to St. Petersburg in an overcrowded train.

"Why are you late? *Il est presque cinq heures!*" says a voice from inside, while Onya, Mitya, and I and our gubernatorial escort unscramble our feet from galoshes and hang up our coats in a tiny anteroom.

The room from which the voice comes is penumbral, the ceiling low, and the walls darkened by a panoply of frames. After sunlit snow it is hard to see anything.

"Now show yourselves," says the same voice in a milder purr.

Gradually I begin to make out objects. A sofa in front of me, several armchairs and chairs around an oval table, a steaming silver samovar, a few small, cluttered tables, and a chaise-longue.

While Onya and Mitya bow and kiss the hand of the chaise-longue's occupant, I scrutinize her.

She—for it is a she, despite the masculine voice—is immersed in lace and ribbons, a sort of morning peignoir. She reclines, propped up by a mound of embroidered pillows. Around her neck is a mauve dog collar with a golden pendant. Her coiffure is high and looks like a puffed-up meringue cake. Another mauve ribbon, tied in a bow, crowns the top of the cake.

Her face is chalk white with a few black dots on it. Later on I learned that she sticks on those *mouches* every morning. Her features are strikingly angular—a straight nose with a protruding tip, a small mouth, and a well-shaped, sharp chin; deep-set eyes hiding under heavy penciled lines drawn in broad arcs in place of eyebrows; and large, doggy ears, the lobes weighted down by pear-shaped earrings.

78

She turns my face toward the light and stares at me with her clever, pale blue eyes.

"Hm . . . hm . . . rosy . . . blond . . . ," she mutters, "and those Tartar eyes . . . slanting upward like your mother's . . . or maybe like Dimitri Nikolaevich's [my paternal grandfather] . . . he had those narrow Tartar eyes!"

And then louder to someone in back of me: "Khristina, come closer, look at them, they have finally arrived."

And to the three of us: "This is Khristina, she lives with me in this hovel."

Khristina's moonface shines with a warm peasant smile. She puts down the tea tray, comes over and kisses each of us three times on both cheeks: "How pretty they are, truly delicious, and all of them so much like Dimitri Dimitrich [my father]."

"Now, children, sit down at the table and have tea," says Babushka. "I'll stay here on the couch and look at you. Khristina, give me a cup."

This was our first visit to Grandmother or Babushka Nabokov's house and the first time I remember seeing her. I may have seen her before, but if so I don't remember it.

I was about nine. The train to Gatchina was late, so we arrived past four o'clock. The sun was low but still very bright. The thaw had turned the snow on the road into a slush, and a mild spring breeze caressed my face as I walked with the others toward Babushka's *dacha*.

"At last!" I thought. "Now I am going to see Babushka Nabokova, of whom I have heard so many tales. I hope she'll be different from the grandiose Omama of Preobrazhenka. Because this Babushka is a real baroness, not a German *kolonisten* matron, and she is a grand lady. She has been married to a famous man, my grandfather, a minister of the good Tsar Alexander II. Perhaps from now on we will enter a new world, the world of my 'absentee father,' and we will become a bit more Nabokov—that is, less German and more Russian."

Babushka's villa lay in a narrow lane not far from the Imperial palace of Gatchina. It was a small clapboard house painted brown. Babushka had been given that "government issue" villa as the widow of a retired minister, but she lived in it only during the cold season. When the weather got warmer and the roads were passable, she went to Batovo, the Korffs' family estate, which lay near the station Siverskaya on the southern shore of the Finnish Gulf.

Although Babushka Nabokova was born Mademoiselle de Korff, she was thoroughly Russian. Only her tall figure and limpid blue eyes betrayed a Nordic ancestry. Babushka's ancestors, the Korffs, were neighbors and friends of Alexander Pushkin; Mikhailovskoe, Pushkin's family estate, was close to the Korff estate. The name of Korff is therefore woven into Pushkin's biography.

From 1911 onward the yearly schedule of our family's movements took on a steady routine. We spent the autumn, winter, and spring seasons in St. Petersburg and migrated each summer homeward to Lubcza. Only once—in 1913—did we split the summer between Lubcza and the Taurian south. And there, besides visiting Preobrazhenka and Askania-Nova, we went on an extended tour of other Falz-Fein estates. Another time we spent a brief Easter vacation at Omama's castle. I remember well that visit and the enchanting beauty of a drive through a blood-red sea of wild tulips.

Then came the ominous summer of 1914 and our migratory routine broke down.

We were at Lubcza when it happened.

One day in August the square between the hayloft, the cowshed, and the machine shop of Lubcza's farm was suddenly filled with peasant carts and horses attached to them. Officers in brilliant uniforms were walking briskly among the carts, inspecting the horses' teeth, hoofs, bellies. In front of the administrator's house, the *Kontora*, there was a long queue of glum young peasants. Older peasants were gathered near the *Kontora*'s porch. One of them was reading aloud a printed proclamation that was pasted on the door. He enunciated carefully the syllables of foreign words—*Mo-bi-li-za-tsi-a, Re-kvi-zi-tsi-a, Re-mont*—as if enjoying their strangeness and their mystery. The rest of the courtyard was totally silent except for the occasional barking of a dog, a child's whimper, the beating of horses' hoofs.

At home in the castle everyone was agog with excitement. Mother was packing for Koló. He had received urgent telegrams and was leaving for St. Petersburg. The *Novoe Vremya* bore huge, ominous headlines: ASSASSINATION, ULTIMATUM, DECLARATION OF WAR. Our hunchback housekeeper Maria Filipovna, Aunt Caroline, and other female members of the household transformed our playroom into a workroom for sewing hospital shirts and preparing *korpia*, or lint, a tradition dating from the Crimean War.

At dinner Koló announced that most of our coachmen, stable-boys, and farmhands were being drafted! Lubcza was a strategic point of national defense and we would have to leave as soon as possible.

The next day he and Mother left for St. Petersburg. A week later the rest of us, led by Aunt Caroline, took the train to the south, but not the usual comfortable way, by sleeper to Odessa. This time trains were crowded. No one paid attention to what was first, second, or third class. Eight or ten people squeezed into each compartment. Baggage cluttered the corridors and WCs. We had to change trains several times with long stops in between and take the oncoming one by assault. Most of the station restaurants had run out of food; even the traditional *kipyatok* (boiling water to make tea with), was hard to get. The platforms were crowded, untended, covered with sunseed peelings.

At railroad junctions, especially at important ones, while waiting for our train we saw long military transports made up of freight cars. All of them were moving westward. In the open doors uniformed recruits stood or sat dangling their legs. Some of them sang, others looked impassive; only a few smiled or joked.

We reached Preobrazhenka after three or four days of travel. All of us were grimy and exhausted.

Pyotr Sigismundovich was to join us later at Askania-Nova, but he never came. He volunteered to join the Army and was given a lieutenant's commission. We started getting letters and postcards from him in his neat, angular handwriting. He was in a garrison town, waiting to be sent to the front.

We stayed late into the autumn at Askania-Nova, and returned to St. Petersburg, now rebaptized as Petrograd, in October. Once back in town, a new routine emerged rapidly. The war was now something far away, something we had to live with as a normal state of affairs. Our homespun quartet had meanwhile expanded to a chamber-music ensemble. We started to play on Sundays with both Diaghilev brothers, our violin, viola, and cello teachers, and other instrumentalist acquaintances of our age. I practiced the cello and the piano and spent a lot of time "improvising" or reading books.

When 1915 came along and our armies started their steady retreat, Lubcza fell to the Germans. But somehow that did not touch me then. Petrograd was lively and exciting now that I was twelve years and could enjoy life there.

BAGAZH · *Nicolas Nabokov*

In those first years of the war everyone and everything around us became feverishly patriotic. For patriotic reasons Aunt Caroline tried to change her German name, Muller, to its Russian equivalent, Melnikova. Mother and sister Onya joined the Red Cross and served occasionally as day or night nurses in an improvised Army hospital at somebody's private home. Koló was made head of the Red Cross for the South of Russia and started shuttling back and forth from Petrograd to Odessa and Simferopol.

I pasted the walls of my room full of portraits of famous Russians: generals, statesmen, musicians, poets, and writers, and even two tsars: Peter I and Alexander II. Above my bed hung a beautiful *tableau vivant* printed on yellowish linoleum. It represented Field Marshal Kutuzov surrounded by famous generals of the 1812 Napoleonic War: Barclay de Tolly, Bennigsen, Bagration, and a dozen others at the war council in a peasant house of a village called Fili after the Battle of Borodino. Underneath it hung a small engraving, a caricature of the period: Bonaparte in a sleigh fleeing from his straggling army in the winter of 1812.

I learned by heart and could whistle the tunes of the national anthems of the principal Allied nations. I even knew the second British one: "Rule, Britannia." I liked its quick and gay verses, ending with the assertion that "Britons never, never, never will be slaves." I also knew the odd-sounding Japanese anthem, composed, I believe, or perhaps only orchestrated by Alexander Glazunov.

"The Star Spangled Banner" joined my hymnodic medley much later, in 1917, when America entered the war. And then it turned out that it was literally unknown in Russia. At the Imperial opera house, the Mariinski, the orchestra performed instead, "Yankee Doodle." (Before the start of each performance the national anthems of *all* Allied nations had to be performed. First came the Russian one, then the "Marseillaise," then "God Save the King" *and* "Rule, Britannia," then the Belgian "Brabançonne," then the Italian, Serbian, and Japanese anthems and, as of 1917, the American one.)

Most stores in Petrograd carried signs saying: "It is requested not to speak German." One such sign, but *in German* ("BITTE KEIN DEUTSCH"), hung in the Germanic Department of Petrograd's Public Library.

We continued our weekly outings to symphony concerts, to the Mariinski opera house and the Alexandrinski theater. I began to learn how to read orchestra scores and acquired at Bessel's music shop the scores of Tchaikovsky's Fifth and Sixth Symphonies and Rimsky's *Scheherazade*.

Mother kept having her *jours fixes* and once or twice a year gave a grand dinner party for thirty or forty (the remains of which we enjoyed the next day). On these days the front rooms of our flat continued to smell of Guerlain's Herbes-marines, and there were heaps of sable coats in the anteroom.

This seemingly stable and well-protected life went on through the winter seasons of 1914 and 1915 in Petrograd and the summer ones at Askania-Nova and Preobrazhenka. Only the motorcars were requisitioned and we traveled again in *dormeuses*, landaus, and victorias. A lot of young men we knew were away, or in uniform. Omama's music band ceased to exist, and in Petrograd the newspapers had more and thicker censors' or empty unprinted columns. Otherwise life seemed to go on as if the war were being fought somewhere in Africa and not at the gates of Riga, Kiev, and Minsk.

Pyotr Sigismundovich came to visit us in Petrograd. He looked handsome in his trim uniform and high, polished boots. He stayed for a few days, went with us to the theater and the circus, and left again for his garrison town.

One summer he came to see us at Askania-Nova. Mitya and I traveled to his mother's home in Evpatoria on the Crimean coast. Pyotr Sigismundovich's mother, a slight, gentle woman, was consumptive. She had been married to a Pole, was widowed, and lived on her husband's pension and what Pyotr Sigismundovich could provide for her. Her house was tiny, close to Evpatoria's flat, lonely beaches. Pyotr Sigismundovich was her only child and one felt that between them the umbilical cord had never been severed.

We played on the beach and baked potatoes in seaweed in the evenings. She liked me and I was attracted to her. Just before we left, she took me aside.

"Did he tell you," she asked "that he is going to be transferred to the front?"

"No, I did not know," I said.

"I'm so worried . . . it is awful." She hesitated. Then she said: "I don't think he will come out of it."

But early next autumn, on a sunny September day, Pyotr Sigismundovich came to see us in Petrograd with a shiny St. George's cross dangling on a black-and-yellow ribbon. I was proud to walk

83

in the streets of Petrograd with a hero.

He came again a few weeks after "The Bloodless Revolution," but this time without epaulettes, cockade, and the St. George's Cross —officers were hunted by mobs of "revolutionists." He looked worried and concerned as he spoke of revolts at the front. His mother was dying in Evpatoria. "The future of Russia is black," he said. I never saw him again, nor did anyone of us ever get a letter or postcard from him any more. Rumor had it that during a soldiers' revolt he was killed by a bullet in his forehead.

At home our tutors and governesses changed more frequently than before. A few went back to their countries (via Sweden), others replaced departing teachers at schools and universities, or got drafted.

It was during that last autumn before the February Revolution that I acquired a tutor who was supposed to coach me in Latin and mathematics. He wore the uniform of a sergeant of the Petrograd *oborona* (a corps to supplement the capital's garrison). He turned out to be a member of the Bolshevik wing of the Social Democratic Agitprop. From him I heard outlandish names, and he showed me photographs of Marx, Engels, Plekhanov, Martov, and his special hero, Ulyanov-Lenin.

Instead of "coaching" me, he spent his time reading to me party pamphlets whose meaning seemed obscure. He also brought other photographs—he called them "documentary evidence." One of them showed a peasant in a white Russian blouse and a priest's beard among a group of ladies in extravagant hats sitting around a tea-table. In another photograph the same man sat with the four Grand Duchesses and the Empress.

I recognized the man. I had seen him twice before. Once in the autumn of 1914 I went with my mother to the studio of a sculptor who was making a portrait bust of her. The sculptor lived on the top floor of an apartment house on Gorokhovaya Street. As we walked up the stairs, a door on one of the floors opened and a woman started out crabwise. Behind her in the door's frame appeared the tall figure of a man in a white peasant blouse. He had a black beard and long hair. He looked intently at my mother and followed her with his gaze as we climbed to the top floor. I asked my mother who this *Batyushka* was. She pulled my hand and muttered: "Come on . . . don't look . . . don't stare at people."

84

The Lubcza Castle with its thirteenth-century tower.

Grandmother's castle, Preobrazhenka, ca. 1900.

Father and mother during their voyage de noces.

B.F. GOTLIEB   ODESSA
· RECOMPENSE AUX EXPOSITIONS ·

Mother in court dress.

Grandmother Falz-Fein.

*Grandmother Nabokov
with my father.*

Mother with NN in her arms, Sister Onya, and Brother Mitya in Nice.

NN with Brother Mitya, 1913

Preobrazhenka, 1913 or 1914. Seated (left to right): *Aunt Caroline Muller, Mme. Révat, Grandmother Falz-Fein, Sister Lida, Stepfather Nicolaï Fëdorovich von Peucker, and Sister Onya.* Standing: *unidentified girl, Captain Petrash, unidentified girl, a governess, Brother Mitya, NN, General Révat, and our tutor.*

*Our quartet with our viola
teacher at Askania-Nova, 1916.*

picnic at Grandmother Falz-Fein's.

Uncle Frederick standing next to Emperor Nicolas II at Askania-Nova, 1914.

Stravinsky, Diaghilev, and Serge Lifar,
photographed by NN in Monte Carlo, 1928.

Léonide Massine, photograp
by NN while rehearsing Od
in Monte Carlo, May, 1928.

Diaghilev on his deathbed, Venice, 1929.

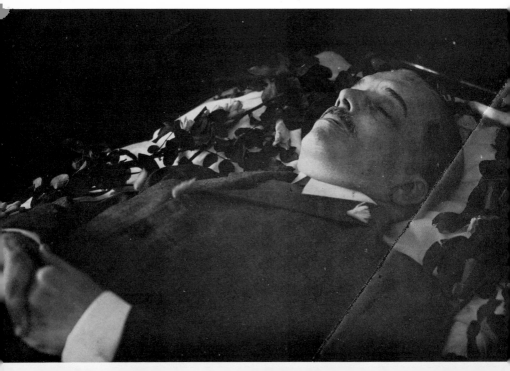

La Sérénade, *at a concert in Strasbourg, 1931*. Left to right: *Vittorio Rieti, Antoinette Grunelius, Madeleine Milhaud, Henri Sauguet, Darius Milhaud, Professor Pautrier (the host), the Marquise de Casa Fuerte, NN, Alexandre Grunelius, an unidentified lady, Jacques Fevrier, and Mr. and Mrs. Wolf (the music patrons of Strasbourg).*

La Sérénade (*reduced version*). Left to right: *Vittorio Rieti, Henri Sauguet, Darius Milhaud, the Marquise de Casa Fuerte, NN, an unidentified lady, and Jacques Fevrier.*

Henri Cartier-Bresson in New York, 1936.

Stalin, NN, and an unidentified American colonel at the Berlin airport, 1945.

Father with NN at his officer's billet in Berlin, 1946.

Stravinsky, Balanchine, and NN in Hollywood, 1947.

Igor and Vera Stravinsky with Balanchine (left) *and NN in Hollywood, 1950.*

Stravinsky at his studio door
in Hollywood, 1950.

Stravinsky smelling a rose in his Hollywood garden, 1950.

Igor and Vera Stravinsky in Hollywood, 1950.

Stravinsky reading a press statement (prepared by NN) at the 1952 Paris Festival.

NN, ca. 1965.

Photograph by Gjon Mili.

NN, Balanchine, and Suzanne Farrell at a rehearsal of Don Quixote, *1965*.

NN submitting his
second Berlin Festival
program to Willy
Brandt in Berlin, *1965*.

Photograph by
Harry Croner.

Photograph by Harry Cron

Lucas Foss, NN, and Mstislav Rostropovich in Berlin, 1966.

NN and Balanchine in Alsace,
1966.

NN, while composing Love's Labor's Lost, *Aspen, 1971.*

NN and Stravinsky in Zurich, 1969.

Richard Dufallo, Isang Yun, Elliott Carter, and NN in Aspen, 1973.

NN and Cousin Vladimir Nabokov at the Montreux Palace Hotel, May 1, 1974.

A year later I had a closer view of the same man. I was at a children's party where most of the children were older than I. I was left stranded between empty chairs and a buffet in a corner of the dining room. The older children were dancing in the adjoining ballroom.

Suddenly a door next to my hiding place opened and the man I had seen at the Gorokhovaya Street apartment house appeared, followed by the hostess and several other smiling ladies. He was dressed in a white blouse, but had on top of it a long black frock like a coachman's *poddyovka.*

He must have noticed me in my corner, for, as he passed, he turned around and his eyes shot at me angrily. His face was pale against the blackness of his beard. There was something unsettling about him.

This time I did not have to ask who the man was. By then everyone in Russia knew Rasputin's features.

On December 29, 1916, I was taken to the opera at the Narodny Dom, a large new auditorium on the right bank of the Neva. We lived on the Neva's left bank, and left the house early to catch a tram. The evening was dark and damp, and an icy wind was blowing from the Finnish Gulf. Trams were scarce and it took my chaperon and me over an hour to get to the opera.

But despite the cold and the wind and the crowded tram, I was excited and happy. I was going to hear *La Traviata* (whose music I knew well) for the first time in my life. The famous Maria Kuznetsova, one of Russia's best and prettiest sopranos, sang the part of Violetta. The rest of the cast was good and the conductor was, I believe, Albert Coates.

I loved every bit of that evening's performance. At the end of the opera the applause was thunderous and Kuznetsova received a long, standing ovation.

It was an anticlimax to have to go out into the cold and wait for the tram. My chaperon snatched an evening paper from a vendor at the tram stop. The vendor was shouting something I could not understand. I glanced at the paper's front page. At the top was a headline in huge black print, bigger than the paper's name: "RASPUTIN IS MISSING." The rest of the front page was a smudge of censor's tar.

The tram was damp and crowded. Many people carried under their arms the same copy of the *Evening Times.* But no one spoke, nor did anyone look at each other.

When Fritz, the porter, opened the front door of our house, he started at once: "Did you hear what happened?"

"Yes, yes—here it is," said my chaperon and he showed Fritz the paper. "Let's not talk about it. I have to take him to bed."

I lay in bed with open eyes. I could not sleep. It was all too exciting. First *La Traviata*, then the sinister headline. "Who did it? Who abducted him? Where is he? Is he alive?"

Very much later, in the dead of night, I suddenly woke up. There was a shuffling noise in the corridor as if someone was trying to walk very silently. I slid out of bed and opened the door to the corridor. There was a light at the far end of it. I seemed to hear voices whispering and then someone closed the front door. I waited. Again the shuffling noise, this time coming toward me. It was Koló in a dressing gown and slippers, returning to his bedroom with a candlestick in his hand.

Next morning before dawn I was on my way to school. I noticed that both doors to Koló's study were closed and that my school pass, which had to be signed every day by one of my parents, was lying in the front parlor near the telephone. This was unusual. Normally the pass lay on Koló's desk in his study.

I had a cup of cocoa, put on my coat, took my briefcase, but the temptation to look in Koló's study was much too great. I opened the door noiselessly. The study was dark, the curtains drawn. Yet in the dark I could distinguish that there were sheets on the study's large leather sofa and that some sort of form lay wrapped in those sheets.

I closed the door and rushed down the staircase. "Could it be," I thought, "could it be he? Rasputin? But why? Why in our house?"

A few days later the truth about Rasputin's disappearance started to leak out. The body was found in the Neva and the protagonists of the clumsy murder were identified. Yussupov and Grand Duke Dimitri became overnight the saviors of Russia and national heros. The other two *compères*, the Deputy Purishkevich and an army doctor, were scarcely mentioned.

Rasputin's murder has entered historical mythology as a kind of curtain-raiser to the February Revolution of 1917. On the surface this is, of course, true, but only on the very tenuous "chronological" surface. In reality the murder had much less to do with the Revolution than with the war that caused it. Rasputin was doubtless a horrible creature. But he was also one of the very few "Russians of influence" who had been consistently against the war. His peasant's instinct knew that the war was absurd, that it was alien to the Russian peasantry, and that the people surrounding the foolish Tsar were nonentities incapable of leading Russia through to victory with the country and the Army totally unprepared.

From the very beginning of the war, and even before it began, Rasputin was warning the Tsar against it in his coarse peasant language. "Don't fight with Wilhelm," he used to say, "you can only lose." And once the war had started, he repeatedly argued with Alexandra and Nicolas about it. "Stop that butchery, make peace, throw out all these Boyars," as he called the Tsar's courtiers and ministers, "and your son will become a peasants' Tsar."

And who knows how much the foreign services of antagonist countries had to do both with Rasputin's life *and* with his murder. Rumor has it that the first phone call made from Yussupov's palace the night of Rasputin's disappearance was to an Allied embassy.

Two years later, during the last languorous and beautiful spring in Yalta (with its "lilac-colored sea," as Chekhov saw it), the Deputy from Bessarabia who took part in the murder and was the *de facto* assassin came to visit us in our flat.

He had known my mother in her youth and had, I believe, courted her in Kharkov or Odessa. He talked in detail about Rasputin's murder, and had just written a booklet called *How I Killed Rasputin*. He admitted that after the quartet of assassins disposed of Rasputin's body they lost their heads and did not know what to do with themselves for fear of the police. He did not go back that night to the hospital train he was in charge of. Instead he sought refuge at a "private home."

Koló had died. I had never asked him, or rather had never dared to talk to him about that night in December 1916. Why was he shuffling through the corridor in the dead of the night? Why were the doors to his study closed the next morning, and why was my school pass lying near the telephone in the anteroom and not in his study?

February 1917 . . . dusk . . . snow . . . large flakes sliding down the windowpanes. No light—the current has stopped at noon.

Two candles on the desk in the study, two in the dining room. The rooms are cold, someone has forgotten to attend to the stoves.

The doorbell rings. No one goes to answer. When it rings again, I go to open the door. Behind it stands a tall, uniformed shape. It is hard to see the face. But a voice says: "*Zdrastvooytye*, Nika," and I recognize Colonel N.

"Is Lydia Eduardovna home?" he asks.

"Yes, I think so."

His coat is white with snow; I help him out of it.

"I finally managed," he says. "I had to walk all the way from the other side of the river. No trams . . . and patrols everywhere."

I take him to the study and call Mother. She comes with a candlestick in hand. Others come in after her. But Koló is out.

"Well," says Mother, "has it started?"

"I think, yes," says the colonel. "But who knows? Rumors . . . rumors all around us," and his huge shadow moves across the wall.

There were only two classes that morning. The priest did not come, nor did the history teacher. During English class our tutor came in and whispered something in the teacher's ear. The Englishman's face turned crimson. He stopped the class and told us to go home.

"There will be no trams after noon," he said.

A crowd beleaguered the tram stop. The tram came late and was packed when it screeched to a stop. The crowd assaulted it and squeezed me inside. There the human brew steamed, swayed, and jerked, but everyone was silent, glum. A little old man next to me, a servant at my school, whispered in my ear: "You'd better take off that uniform, young man—it is no good now."

I got home before lunch. I asked Alexei, the butler, what was going on.

He shrugged his shoulders. "They say all kinds of things—disorders, rumors," and he went off with the dishes.

"Rumors, rumors," says the colonel, "the Putilovtsy workers are on strike. There is unrest at the Semyonovski Regiment barracks . . . also in the garrison." His voice is hoarse, halting. He seems frightened and excited.

"But what do *you* think will happen?" stutters Aunt Caroline.

"*Tout ce désorde* in the streets, these queues . . . who will put an end to that?"

"I read Khabalov's proclamation," intervenes my mother. "It is preposterous! How can that help?"

"Yes, yes, you are so right, Lydia Eduardovna!" The colonel's voice gets louder. "It cannot help. Even if they bring thousands of tons of flour to Petrograd. Nobody trusts them any more. It cannot go on like this . . . Don't you think so?"

"There haven't been any papers," says someone else in the room. "No one knows where the Germans are."

"And before that? Before that?" says the colonel. "What did we know from those papers? Nothing! Empty sheets blacked out by censorship. All the rest . . . rumors . . ."

The door opens and Koló walks in. He goes to his desk and sits down. He looks exhausted.

"I have just heard," says Koló, "at the Red Cross . . . there was a telegram . . . the Germans have taken Riga . . . our army is in retreat . . . the losses are enormous . . ."

"You see, Nikolai Fedorovich," exclaims the colonel, "I told you a month ago, here in this very room, that it would happen! How can it be otherwsie when our fate is in the hands of—"

"I know, I know," interrupts Koló impatiently. "Yes, you predicted it and still I hope I was wrong."

"Well!" says the colonel in an aggressive, flamboyant tone. "We sat still much too long saying to ourselves, 'What should be done?' and we never did it. Now 'it' will come. *It* is here."

The colonel is staying at our flat for the night. He will sleep on the sofa in Koló's study.

When everyone has taken a candle and gone to his room, I slide back through the dark corridor to the study. The colonel jumps up.

"Platon Ilyich," I say, "is that down there the Revolution?" and I point to the window.

"Yes . . . I think so," he replies in a drowsy voice and yawns loudly, "but of course I don't know. You'd better go to bed . . ."

A week later it was all over. The Imperial eagles' double heads had fallen to Petrograd's pavements. Those of stucco got smashed, the wooden ones helped stoke the fires of documents and office debris in front of ransacked police stations and ministerial palaces.

To Mademoiselle's dismay, her native "Marseillaise" overnight became Russia's national anthem.

"What has all this to do with the 'Marseillaise'?" whined Mademoiselle, looking out of the window and pointing at the carnival-like procession moving slowly up Nevski's slush with bannered slogans.

The Tsar and his brother Michael had abdicated. Referred to now as Nikolai Romanov, he was interned with wife and children at Tsarskoe Selo. Nobody seemed to know what to do with him.

A provisional government had been formed, and it met continuously at the Taurian Palace, the seat of the Duma. A parallel organization had emerged under the name of Soviet of Workers', Soldiers' and Peasants' Deputies. But everyone was jubilant. I put on a large red armband with a ribbon and joined the excited crowds clogging Nevski and adjacent streets.

The victims of "The Great Bloodless Revolution," as those days of late February 1917 were then called, were buried at the Marsovo Pole, the beloved exercise square of mad Emperor Paul I.

We spent the post-Revolutionary years partly at Askania-Nova, partly at Preobrazhenka, and mostly at Yalta. First we came under the wing of the German occupation army, then under the "Reds," and then under the insecure wing of the Whites.

In Yalta I started serious studies in harmony and composition with a strange-looking, aging colossus of a man, Vladimir Ivanovich Rebikov. He was a pupil of Tchaikovsky and was known in Russia as the composer of a children's opera called *The Christmas Tree*. Rebikov was a true "original." He had huge, fleshy lips and a large purple-plum nose. He was immensely shortsighted and wore telescope lenses in an old-fashioned metal *pince-nez* that hung around his neck on a broad black cord. The top of his head was as bald as a billiard ball, but on its sides grew long strands of salt and pepper hair. At each side of his concert grand he kept a square of cardboard—on the left a black square, on the right a white one. When a hair would fall from his head, he would fumble shortsightedly with his fingers upon the keyboard until he found it. If it was dark, he would put it on the white cardboard square; if it was white, on the black one. Then he would turn to me and say sententiously: "I've been collecting my hair for over ten years. When I grow old, I will make myself a wig out of my own hair."

He was terribly sensitive about etiquette, and if his official visit to our house—and he made one every month—was not returned by my stepfather immediately, or at least within a week, he would shout at me and refuse to give me a lesson.

He wore galoshes throughout the year, a broad *lavallière* tie with traces of many meals upon it, and an exceedingly broad Panama hat whose color had reached the *café-au-lait* stage. "It's the same kind of hat Napoleon wore on St. Helena," he would say proudly.

Our composition classes consisted largely of his showing me pieces of his own music in which he had outfoxed Debussy by using unorthodox harmonic progressions several years before Debussy had used them. "*C'était moi, l'avant-garde!*" he would exclaim in his *tenorino* voice.

He was a bachelor and lived in a dingy cold-water flat near Yalta's harbor. He refused to let the maid clean his workroom, especially the piano, for fear she would wipe the hair off the cardboard squares.

"Besides," he would whisper in my ear in French, pointing at the old chambermaid with a huge wall-eye, "*c'est une espionne*, she works for the German General Staff and for Trotsky and his *Cheka*."

When I would bring him a piece of my own music, he would shout my piece down. "It is not only bad, it is infamous! It's as stale as a cold potato! Do you understand me! Throw it out immediately and start anew!"

And later on during the lesson he would admonish me in a milder, somewhat wailing tone: "Why do you try to become a composer. Don't you see *my* misery! Why don't you become a conductor? You are tall and handsome and all the beautiful women will be at your feet. You can *baiser* them to your heart's content. You can have a real harem! And if you prefer boys, you can buy Arab boys at the market at Damascus very cheaply and have them especially prepared for you and even castrated if you wish!"

From the autumn of 1918 onward, after the Germans left and Yalta was occupied by the Bolsheviks, things became rough. Rebikov used to wander along the quay and scan the seascape with an old-fashioned portable telescope. "I am informed by reliable sources," he would whisper, "that President Wilson is sending a cruiser to fetch me."

I was told many years later, long after my family and I left Russia, that all through 1920 one could see the large, anachronistic bulk

91

of Rebikov in his Panama hat and galoshes walking up and down
the quay of Yalta, still scanning the horizon with his telescope.
President Wilson's promise was apparently not very reliable.

In 1921, in the dead of Russia's coldest and hungriest winter,
Rebikov, dressed up as usual, was found in his Yalta flat, frozen on
his bed.

Askania-Nova. August 1918.

Mother's eyes are swollen. Red with tears. She stares in front of
her. She has been staring this way since yesterday, when they had
told her.

She won't speak, she won't sleep, won't eat or drink. She just
stares and weeps.

No, she does not weep, she howls, she wails like a peasant woman.
She buries her face in her hands and wails.

When I come close to her, she pats my hair, but does not look
at me. She continues to stare and her lips tremble. . . .

It was a sultry August afternoon. We sat on the airy veranda
of the old master's house at Askania-Nova. Koló was away in Simferopol. It was after teatime, but the sun was still blazing hot.

There were gypsies milling around at the opposite side of the
courtyard. One of them, a very dark young girl, came over toward
mother. "*Davai pogadayu?*" she asked, showing the palm of her
hand. But Mother did not notice. She was looking the other way.

"Mistress . . . Mistress," nagged the gypsy, coming closer, "let
me tell your fortune. I'll say the truth . . . only the truth . . .
show me your hand."

Mother turned around, smiled, and asked: "From where are you
people? When did you come?"

"*My tut taborom . . . s Dona* [We're here with our camp from
the Don.] *Barynya!* Mistress! Show me your palm."

"All right," said Mother, stretching out her right hand. "But
you're so young. Can you really read palms?"

Aunt Caroline intervened: "Please! Lidochka, don't do it. *Ar-
rête!*"

"But why?" asked Mother. "Why don't you want this girl to tell
my fortune?"

"Because! Because *cela ne se fait pas*," grumbled Aunt Caroline.
She went toward the gypsy girl dangling a twenty-*ruble* bill.

"If you let them do it, Madame," chimed Mademoiselle Verrière, "they will never go away! They're a nuisance. They'll stay here all night. *Et puis ils volent.*"

"That's exactly what I mean!" exclaimed Aunt Caroline. She turned to the girl and the other gypsies in the courtyard and shouted: "Now will you people please go away! Go back to your *tabor.* This is a private home."

But the young gypsy did not move. She did not even look at Aunt Caroline. Instead she put her palm to her cheek, shook her head, and stared at Mother. Then, very, very softly, as if she were talking to Mother alone, she said:

"*Oi-oi, Barynya! Oi-oi,* my poor one! *Plakat Budesh.* You will cry! Soon! Bitterly, bitterly . . ."

"You see what I say!" exclaimed Aunt Caroline, her face flushed with irritation. "They are crows, ravens! They bring bad luck!" And again to the gypsies, but louder, angrier: "Will all of you people *please* go away! For heaven's sake."

While Aunt Caroline was shouting, I heard the far ring of the telephone in the pantry. A servant came out to the veranda and whispered something in Mademoiselle Verrière's ear. She slipped into the house, but came back a minute later and started making signs at Aunt Caroline. Both disappeared and closed the front door behind them.

"Where have they gone?" asked Mother. She turned to my sister and told her to find out who had called.

I followed Onya into the house. The butler stood in the hallway looking distraught.

"What's happened?" I asked. "What is it? Tell me." But he put his fingertips to his lips. "Don't speak too loud, Master," he whispered, "*Barynya* might overhear. There's bad news! They called from the post office. A telegram from Simferopol. Nikolai Fedorovich . . . your stepfather . . . he died in Simferopol . . . an attack."

Yalta. March 23, 1919.

On the crowded boat from Yalta to Sevastopol, Mother and I find a young lieutenant, Seryozha T., a friend of the family. He is to join his outfit at Sevastopol. He says there is little hope . . . the Allies won't help . . . there has been mutiny on the French cruiser . . . the White Army is retreating. . . . He comes from the Caucasus. "It's a worse mess there than in Yalta," he says.

Nothing to eat on the boat. In our haste we have forgotten about

93

food. Seryozha T. finds an Armenian who sells stale *pirozhki*. The sea is rough. The boat will rock. I hope I won't be seasick.

At noon we move. Mother and I wave goodbye to the rest of the family on the pier. Mother shouts: "I will call tomorrow! Prepare everything!" but her voice is drowned by the boat's siren.

Sevastopol. March 26, 1919.

Hotel Rossia is packed. Speculators, bourgeois families, film actors and actresses . . . the lobby is abuzz . . . not a free seat . . . heaps of luggage everywhere. Uncle Sergei Nabokov is here. He arrived by road a few days ago. He's waiting for his family to join him. "I have one room here," he says, "and another one in town. But I do not know what Vladimir [Uncle Sergei's brother] will do when he arrives with his family. He says the French do not give visas at all. But there are two boats leaving Sevastopol in a few days with Greek refugees for Constantinople and Greece. One of them, the bigger one, is called *Trapezund*. We must get space on it, with or without visas. Otherwise we're stuck."

The town is seething with rumors, all alarming. The Reds, they say, have broken the last line of White resistance. They are about to cross the isthmus. None of the Allies will help.

Sevastopol. March 27, 1919.

Mother and I go to the Quartier Général Français. We make our way through a glum-looking crowd. The sentries check passes. Mother got one through the hotel *portier*. We are told that Commandant X. is away in Odessa. He is due back *"peut-être demain."*

The streets are lined with ambulances. Seryozha T. says that all hospitals, hotels, and private homes are crowded. "Nobody knows what to do, or where to go. There is no one in command. Complete anarchy. The town hall is closed."

The day is gray. A continuous, cold drizzle. We hide in the lobby or in the restaurant. It is open, but there is no food. Mother and I share a room. The room is small, damp, and airless. I have nothing with me. Not even a nightshirt. Only my toothbrush.

Sevastopol. March 28, 1919.

Commandant X. came to see Mother this morning, straight from a French corvette that appeared in the harbor at nine. He says he can't do much. He has strict orders not to embark foreigners. He can only repatriate French citizens. *"Je regrette, chère Baronne,"* he apologizes, *"ce n'est vraiment pas possible!"* Mother tells him about the Greek boat *Trapezund.* Perhaps he could get us passes? He says he will inquire.

Mother telephones Aunt Caroline. It takes hours to get through to Yalta. She tells Aunt Caroline, "Pack up and come as soon as possible with Onya, Mitya, and Lida and the maid Manya. Don't wait for a boat. Come by bus." Another day goes by. Many new arrivals in the lobby—where will they sleep?

Sevastopol. March 29, 1919.

Mother meets an acquaintance in the lobby of the hotel. He is a rich Karaite named Solomon Samoilovich Krym (like Crimea in Russian). He has connections. He calls up Yalta and arranges for a car to drive our family from Yalta to Sevastopol tomorrow.

"Lydia Eduardovna," he says with a soothing smile, "do not worry! You will see, everything will turn out the way you want it. And if you need something, just tell me—I'll get it for you."

He is kind and sweet. He looks very Oriental. A black wedge-like beard and a bald head, like an ancient Assyrian. Koló and I visited him two years ago among his huge orchards at Karassubazar, in the heart of the Crimea.

S. S. Krym regales us with a luxury dinner in a *cabinet privé* of the hotel's restaurant. Gloved and liveried waiters. Immaculate silver. Caviar and sturgeon.

"From where did you get all this?" I asked.

He laughs. "It is my secret. I buy it from the Bolsheviks. Now that you know, will you eat it?"

Sevastopol. March 31, 1919.

Seryozha T. has received orders to join his outfit in Rostov. He is leaving by boat on the 2nd of April.

"Did you hear the cannonade last night?" he asks.

No, I did not. He tells me that the Reds have advanced to the edge of Simferopol, but were thrown back.

"Of course all this is rumors—who knows what happened? Except that there was a cannonade."

My sisters Onya and Lida, brother Mitya, and the maid Manya

95

arrive in the late afternoon, tired and grimy. Aunt Caroline decided to stay behind. Mother is upset. She tries to call her, but can't get through. "All communications with Yalta are cut," says the *portier*.

Mitya has brought me a pillowcase full of stuff. But not my new cello! The stuff is helter-skelter. Three shoes for the right foot, none for the left. But now I can change my shirt and underwear. I take a cold bath in Uncle Sergei's bathroom—We have none.

The lights go out at nine. But the French fleet in the harbor is aglow. I can see it out of the window. Everything else is dark: the hills, the sea. Only the men-of-war are illuminated.

Sevastopol. March 30, 1919.

Commandant X. calls. He will obtain passes for all of us, for the Greek refugee boat *Trapezund*. "*Aussi pour monsieur Serge Nabokov et sa famille.*" But we are not supposed to say a word about it to anyone.

Seryozha T. is bitter. His boat is delayed. "It's a bloody mess here," he grumbles. "Everyone thinks only of how to save his skin. To hell with Russia! Serves them right if the Bolsheviks get them and hang them by the balls."

Mother comes back triumphant. She got the passes for us, also for Uncle Sergei and his family. And she has found a case of canned foods. "I found it at the harbor depot," she says. "It is the last case they had from Grandmother's factory in Odessa."

The lights go out earlier tonight. We undress in the dark. There are no candles.

Sevastopol. March 31, 1919.

At two in the afternoon we board a tug. Besides us there are Uncle Sergei and his family and about twenty other persons with French passes. We reach the *Trapezund* in the outer harbor and climb a crowded staircase to the upper deck. We are aghast! Our haven turns out to be a charred, burned-out shell. It was supposed to be repaired in Yassy in Romania, but was abandoned by the fleeing Germans. "It can't possibly make more than eight knots at the most," says the captain. The captain is a former vice-admiral of the Baltic Fleet, unctuous and unpleasant. With him are his dromedary-looking wife and two skinny daughters.

We find two cabins with charred bunks. The bunks are damp,

but there is no water around, except a faucet near one of the smoke-stacks. The cabins are for the women. We boys find space in the hold. Toilets and latrines are burned out. Uncle Sergei, Mitya, and two sailors build WCs toward the prow of the *Trapezund* with lumber they found in one of the holds. The boat is empty except for our two families and those who came with us on the tug. In the evening Onya, Mitya, and I with our cousins Muma, Katya, Seryozha, and Kolya sit in a circle at the stern and sing songs.

On the Trapezund. April 1, 1919.

I wake up at dawn. There is a huge noise around me—clatter of chains, squabble of voices, shouts, chatter. I go up to the deck. Crowds of people are swarming all over. Weeping children. Women of all ages. Men carrying food. They speak a language I don't understand. They seem angry, exasperated.

I ask a sailor: "Are these the Greeks?"

"What else!" he answers glumly.

We spend most of the morning defending Mother's and Aunt Dolly's cabins. The Greeks are furious. None of them speaks Russian. They shout insults in Greek and try to push us out. Finally, by noon, they give up and settle down. They've occupied the whole boat—all the holds, the decks, even the captain's bridge.

By dusk the boat is dark. Only a few weak bulbs. None in the cabins.

The rain stopped yesterday. There's a warm breeze from the sea. Spring is in the air. I can't sleep. All is silent now; only an occasional whimper, a bit of a woman's song, strange and sad. I look at the sea into the dusk beyond the harbor and back at dark Sevastopol. Scarcely a light visible.

Suddenly, I hear Mother's voice calling: "Nika . . . Nikaaa . . ."

I walk over to where the voice came from. I find Mother in the penumbral dark of her cabin. She is exhausted, anxious. "I don't know what to do," she says. "The captain won't sail with us on board. He says it's illegal. The Greeks complained. The boat has been chartered for them by the Red Cross. He won't even look at the French passes. Uncle Sergei has gone to talk to him."

She starts crying. Poor Mother. Unnerved, helpless. I press close to her. I kiss her hands. She strokes my head and smiles through tears.

We wait for a while. Uncle Sergei returns, smiling. "All arranged," he says. Mother and he will pay a sum of money in foreign currency. "Our vice-admiral is more vice than admiral," laughs Uncle Sergei. Mother is now calm, sad but proud. She has done what she believed was her duty: she has saved us.

I go back to the stern. Above me, stars. In front, the sea . . . endless.

II

Between Wars

ALTHOUGH FROM 1912 onward I saw Babushka Nabokova regularly, I was too young to form an opinion about her. I felt that she was something special, a creature out of the ordinary, if only in appearance. But I did not, I could not, make out what it all amounted to.

There was a lapse of five years when none of us saw Babushka Nabokova. In 1917 we fled from St. Petersburg to the south, and she stayed in Gatchina.

My true discovery of Babushka—the *Generalsha*, as Khristina called her—took place in the early years of my exile, in the 1920s, when we all lived in Berlin. She had escaped from Gatchina with the retreating White Army and joined Uncle Vladimir and his family in Berlin. They lived close to my mother's flat in one of those spacious, bourgeois apartment houses built at the turn of the century when Berlin was hospitably cosmopolitan.

By that time I had discovered the attractiveness of Uncle Vladimir and of his family. To me they represented the summit of the Nabokov clan. In a way, they also discovered me. When we first met in Yalta, in the autumn of 1917, I felt that there was among them (and among the Nabokovs in general) a certain unease, a reticence as regarded me. Whether it was because of the gossip that surrounded Mother's divorce or for other reasons, I do not know, but I felt distinctly that there was a barrier between the Nabokovs and me, and that I must make an extra effort to be accepted by them and win their favor. Fortunately, circumstances helped. We fled together from Sevastopol to Greece and were thrust upon each other in Phaleron near Athens for several months. By the time all of us reached Berlin in 1920, I had been adopted by Uncle Vladimir and Aunt Lyolya as a member of their family and all uneasiness had disappeared.

It was an extraordinary household. Aunt Lyolya and her husband brought with them to their Berlin flat the full flavor of a wealthy, enlightened St. Petersburg home. Uncle Vladimir had been active as a liberal member of the first Russian parliament, the Duma of 1905. Then, several years after that parliament had failed, he became one of the editors of Russia's liberal newspaper *Rech*, and one of the leaders of the liberal party, the Constitutional Democrats. After the Revolution of 1917 he was a member of the first post-Revolutionary provisional government. When I met him in Yalta, he was a famous man and represented that generation of the Westernized Russian intelligentsia that had hoped to move Russia swiftly toward a parliamentary form of democracy.

Both he and Aunt Lyolya had brilliant minds, quick wits, rounded educations, and strong political and cultural convictions. To me, personally, Uncle Vladimir had an added attraction. He was one of the rare Nabokovs who truly loved music. On Sunday mornings we would take the Berlin subway to the general rehearsals of the Berlin Philharmonic Orchestra. They were open to the public at that time. We stood in the back of the hall (seats were much too expensive and standing room cost the equivalent of fifty cents) under a light so as to be able to follow the music in pocket scores that Uncle Vladimir brought to the rehearsals.

It was at those Sunday-morning concerts (and the discussions with Uncle Vladimir that followed) that I received the first truly useful and lasting part of my musical education. We heard admirable conductors conduct an admirable orchestra, and I learned in this pragmatic way the basic symphonic repertoire of the time. The outstanding figure among the conductors of those years was the aging Arthur Nikisch, but there were also many younger men around. During those years Berlin was the world's biggest showplace for conductors, instrumentalists, singers, and, to a lesser extent, composers. Besides Nikisch and Furtwängler, there were Bruno Walter at the Charlottenburg Opera House, Erich Kleiber at the Staatsoper, and Otto Klemperer at the Kroll Opera and Sing Akademie (to name but the five most famous). Plane travel did not exist and conductors in the twenties stayed put. Like Oriental pashas, they ruled over their un-unionized orchestras as over a harem. Only very occasionally did they go on conducting tours.

Berlin was also stuffed with excellent choirs, chamber-music groups, and solo performers. The Chilean pianist Claudio Arrau soon became a close friend of mine. In fact he was the first artist to play my music in public.

At those Sunday-morning concerts Uncle Vladimir liked best "the classics"—in particular, Beethoven. He did not care for Tchaikovsky, whom I, like most Russians, adored. We used to argue about Tchaikovsky and he would usually close the argument by saying: "I grant you that he is a brilliant orchestrator. But I cannot accept his sentimental melodies. They sound like gypsy stuff! It is all *très mauvais goût.*"

At one of the Sunday-morning concerts we heard Tchaikovsky's Fifth Symphony conducted by Nikisch, who knew how to avoid the Scylla and Charybdis of Tchaikovsky's bombast and sentimentality and how to model those suave melodic lines so dangerously close to *Kitsch*. He brought out their genuine lyricism. The strings of the Berlin Philharmonic changed their character and tone after the Mozart overture that preceded Tchaikovsky's Fifth. Instead of being thin and sharp, the tone became round, full of what Pushkin used to call *nega* ("bliss") and a kind of Slavo-Jewish voluptuousness. And yet there was no imprecision of intonation hiding behind the strings' vibrato. Normally I do not trust the "round" tone of orchestral strings. Often it conceals imprecise intonation and what the Germans call *unsauberer Notengang* ("unclear-sounding passing tones"). But when the Berlin Philharmonic played under Nikisch's direction, the roundness became an indispensable aesthetic device that it rendered truthfully the style of Tchaikovsky's music.

Nikisch conducted, as was customary in his time, from the score. His gestures were "imperatorial," but his beat was precise and commanded obedience. There was absolutely no "showmanship" in his conducting, yet it was by no means devoid of temperament and grace. His bearded appearance and the funereal frock coat he wore gave him a kind of old-fashioned, solemn dignity. He looked a bit like those photographs of French senators of the *Troisième République*, or like a Russian Academician of that same period.

To our contemporary taste, Nikisch's *tempi* were probably much too slow. But *tempi* in music conform to psychological habits of receptivity. When those habits change, the *tempi* get slower or faster. Fifty years ago the tempo of urban life was somewhere between the *Andante* and the *Allegro moderato* of the metronome. Now it is far beyond the *Allegro*. This fact alone may perhaps explain the general trend toward faster *tempi* nowadays. As life goes faster, so does the music.

I remember what a relief it was in the mid-thirties to hear Toscanini perform Beethoven's gay scherzos and finales *al italiano* (with all those exaggerated, witty, off-beat accents) after the traditionally much slower "doldrum" nineteenth-century Germanic *tempi*.

But there are, of course, national traditions that rule the metronome. Until lately—that is, before conductors became suave "cosmopolitans"—German Beethoven was slower than Italian or Anglo-Saxon Beethoven, and J. S. Bach in Alsace, probably under the leadership of his famous doctor-biographer, was as a Volkswagen to a Porsche. Besides, there still lingers in the Mitropa world the misunderstanding about the word *Andante*. Translated into German, it means *gehend* ("walking"). But the fat Germans walk slower than the wiry Italians, and *Andante* for an Italian means "at a fast walking pace," whereas for the Germans it is a *langsamer Spaziergang* (a slow walk).

It is very much as with food. Germans like steak well done, Americans eat it while the steer is still grazing, and today's Russian steak tastes like pot roast and swims in a tub of grease.

Every Sunday as Uncle Vladimir and I shuttled homeward after a concert rehearsal, he gave me a *post-mortem* résumé of what he had liked or disliked in that day's concert. On the day we heard the Berlin Philharmonic's splendid performance of Tchaikovsky's Fifth Symphony, Uncle Vladimir admitted to having been completely persuaded by its musical qualities and by its great "lyric" beauty. But he made a point of emphasizing the word "lyric" as opposed to "romantic." Later on we defined very carefully the distinction between the terms "lyricism" and "romanticism" in music. It has remained for me a criterion of critical judgment in music, but only for a special category or type of music and especially as to its performance. It applies fully to Tchaikovsky's symphonic music and is useful as a guide both for its "understanding" and its "misunderstanding."

When Tchaikovsky is treated as a *romantic* composer—that is, when his symphonic music gets the romantic treatment, with all the exaggeration and overstatement that this implies—the weaknesses of his music come to the surface, the melodies become oily and sentimental, and the dramatic passages grandiloquent and shallow. But when Tchaikovsky is treated as a *lyrical* composer and his music is played with reserve, precision (which does not exclude warmth), and an understatement of its emotional content, then he becomes one of the most poetic and accomplished symphonic masters of the late nineteenth century. I believe that Tchaikovsky does not need emphasis. Everything is "inscribed" in his scores. He is not a romantic *sans-culotte*, but a bourgeois dandy, and, I would add (referring to a famous Russo-American conductor whose performances of Tchaikovsky's symphonic music were notorious for their schmaltziness), one mishandles the content of his music by playing it with exaggeration and excessive vibrato. To hear a good "lyrical" performance of Tchaikovsky's symphonies, one should go to Leningrad, whose Philharmonic Orchestra under its "imperatorial" conductor Mravinsky has kept the lyric tradition alive.

I experienced in an empirical way this distinction when I wrote (in 1930) my first ("Lyrical") Symphony. I chose as a motto a verse of Pushkin:

> *Dusha stesnyaetsya liricheskim volnenyem*
> *Stenaet i zvuchit i ishchet, kak vo snye*
> *Izlitsya nakonets svobodnym vdokhnovenyem.*

In English:

> The soul is seized by lyric tremor,
> it moans and sounds. As
> in a dream, it seeks a way for
> the free flow of inspiration.

Later on, and much more succinctly, I experienced it again when in 1945 I was writing my cantata, *The Return of Pushkin*. I had to keep under control my own musical invention in order to "contain" and not "exceed" the emotional flow of Pushkin's verse.

There is and there always will be a dichotomy between romanticism and lyricism in music. It has to do with interpretation, but also with perception. Logically, the dichotomy is of course erroneous. The two terms are not opposites. But if one detaches the term "romanticism" from its historical and semantic connotations and regards it as a form of musical "behavior," the dichotomy begins to be valid and can become a useful approximation for the understanding of musical styles. And since aesthetic terminology in music is, at best, made up of parables and metaphors (and, at worst, of a "journalistic" intoxication with adjectives), why should one refrain from employing useful but logically "approximate" dichotomies? If they are helpful and lead to a better understanding of a musical phenomenon, and if language cannot provide us with semantic equivalents, they should by all means be used.

Language, however inadequate, remains our only means of reaching the periphery of understanding, even though the understanding may remain incomplete or approximate. (All this has, of course, nothing to do with "communication," for which we have now at our disposal a set of new techniques). It is of no use to pretend, as did Schumann, that the only way one *can* for example "understand" (and he used the word *verstehen* and not *Erkenntnis*) the Ninth Symphony of Beethoven is to write another Ninth Symphony about it. This leads nowhere. It sounds like a joke by Erik Satie and is tautologically useless. The only way to deal with a piece of music is to listen to it well and then "bombard" it with the best words one can find.

The Nabokov flat in Berlin was, during those years, a center of *émigré* cultural life. There was a constant flow of visitors: writers, scholars, artists, politicians, and journalists.

Some of them were recent arrivals. One had to see them through the labyrinth of the Police Headquarters and help them· obtain a temporary residence permit. It was not easy to get that long-winded document. The Germans, though at that time less rude than the French, were also less corruptible. In the Paris *Préfecture* there was a big fat man (God bless his memory!) whom one could approach carrying an envelope jingling with coins which had the same effect as Pavlov's bell: it aroused his appetite. He dropped the envelope adroitly into a half-open drawer and saw to it that the *carte d'identité* was issued. In Berlin such tricks were impossible.

There were visitors who stopped on their way to Paris or to Prague, or even to London or New York. There were also quite a few on their way back to Russia. They had only temporary visas, and with pangs in their hearts they had to travel back to our dangerous motherland.

A few years later there was a wave of intentional returnees. They had decided to go back for different, often highly moral reasons. They would argue with Uncle Vladimir about the need for all *émigrés* to return to Russia.

But Uncle Vladimir was a prudent man. He would listen compassionately and then say that it was a decision each one must make according to his own conscience. Personally, he could never cooperate with the Bolshevik regime.

With several colleagues of his party Uncle Vladimir started a Russian-language daily called *Rul* ("The Rudder") and a publishing house called Slovo ("The Word"). Both were eminently successful as long as the center of the Russian emigration was in Berlin. Slovo published remarkable historical documents in a series of books under the title *The History of the Russian Revolution.* Among them were the appalling diaries of Nicolas II and the tender correspondence between him and Alexandra, as well as excellent editions of Russian classics.

When *Rul* was in its second year, Aunt Lyolya and Cousin Sergei suggested to Uncle Vladimir that I try my hand at musical criticism. Uncle Vladimir agreed and told me to write a review of the concert of a young Russian pianist. Several days later I came to *Rul*'s office with my first review. I felt uneasy—I thought that my piece was rubbery. But Uncle Vladimir called me up and said that the editorial staff liked it and that the review would be printed.

Soon I became one of *Rul*'s regular concert reviewers and acquired the music critic's indispensable adjectival jargon. I was very proud that my pair of press tickets enabled me to invite someone to a concert. But for some time my reviewing was limited to concerts to which the older staff members did not want to go. These were mostly Russian musical events of dubious quality. Press tickets for the better ones were reserved for the senior staff members. But sometimes these gentlemen got colds or were out of town, and I was then able to go to better concerts. I do not remember who it was— it may have been my cousin Sergei—who suggested I write, on *Rul*'s stationery, personal letters to the "grand" musical organizations of Berlin and ask for tickets. For a while it worked, until one of the "grand" German organizations wrote to the senior staff member that press tickets for *Rul* had been asked for by me. I nearly got fired. But Uncle Vladimir and Aunt Lyolya intervened. So, instead of being fired, I was raised in the hierarchy of *Rul*'s critical staff. From then on Uncle Vladimir and I had comfortable seats at the

Philharmonic concerts on Monday evenings, and we went together to some of the best recitals and chamber-music concerts I have heard in my life.

Aunt Lyolya, Uncle Vladimir, my cousins, and the stimulating ambience of their home was for me a new Russian haven and the intellectual catalyst I badly needed. After one and a half years of ascetic exile—studies in isolation, in Stuttgart, where I had been studying music at the conservatory—I felt suddenly as though I were back in Russia. No wonder I preferred to spend my evenings at their house rather than stay home with all those exes—ex-generals, ex-colonels, ex-landowners, ex-counts and barons, and all sorts of other relatives, most of them of German stock, who invaded Mother's flat on the Landhausstrasse.

I had my personal friends, of course, both Russian and German, but the Nabokov flat was, so to speak, my newly acquired "Russian" home.

Uncle Vladimir was strikingly handsome. He looked like his mother, but his facial features were much less angular. In addition he had something lordly about him, something imposing and yet very attractive. He was often thought of as "snobbish," and someone (could it have been Trotsky?) in a bilious comment about the first days of the Revolution of 1917 called him a *nakrakhmaleny angloman*—a starched Anglomaniac. Uncle Vladimir had·in his bearing, his manner of speech, and his whole appearance something distinctly aristocratic, and, like many liberal Russian gentlemen of his time, he was worldly, ironic, a bit haughty, and cosmopolitan. But when he was *en famille,* he became gay, amusing, and a source of exciting ideas and information.

Aunt Lyolya was quite different. She was nervous and shy, very intelligent, but much more complex and brittle than her husband. It was not easy to win her friendship. But once she liked someone, as happened with me, she became a friend forever.

The table talk at the Nabokovs' was always gay and lively. We spoke about politics, cultural events, literature, and the arts. When cousins Vladimir and Sergei were around (both studied in England, Vladimir at Cambridge and Sergei at Oxford), the talk turned into a marathon of questions and answers, accompanied by a certain amount of teasing. The teasing game consisted of asking a victim, usually Babushka or me or cousin Olga, questions we couldn't answer. (Who was the world champion in chess before Lasker? What did Napoleon say when he crowned himself? What caterpillars feed on privet leaves? What did Pushkin write to Gogol after reading what book?) Or else cousin Vladimir would invent a writer or a poet, a king or a general, and ask questions about his nonexistent life. The victims would get upset (especially cousin Olga) and call the teaser names. But these games always stopped short of cruelty.

Soon Elena, the younger girl cousin, and I grew fond of each other. Aunt Lyolya was happy about it and considered us as being engaged. But both of us were too young to get married, and my mother was by no means favorably inclined to my youthful infatuation. Circumstances separated us, alas, much too soon, and nothing came of it (though cousin Vladimir often reminds me of my unfulfilled engagement to my charming cousin).

The Moscow Art Theater, or at least part of it, was in Berlin at that time. Stanislavsky had fled with one part of the company (with costumes and sets) to Serbia in the wake of the civil war. The other part, under Nemirovich-Danchenko, stayed in Moscow. The Stanislavsky company performed in Berlin to full houses, and all of us went to see their Chekhov, Tolstoy, Dostoevsky, and Gorky productions.

Stanislavsky and Olga Leonardovna Knipper-Chekhova (Chekhov's widow) were close friends of Uncle Vladimir and Aunt Lyolya. Other actors and actresses of the Moscow Art Theatre also visited the Nabokovs quite often, and once, I remember, Aunt Lyolya gave a party for the whole company. Stanislavsky was already aging and getting corpulent, but he still played the role of Vershinin in *The Three Sisters* opposite Olga Knipper. They both performed masterfully, but in a style that even then seemed stale to me. Stanislavsky was a big man, well groomed and impressive. He had a suave, velvet voice and intelligent, languid eyes. Once he came to tea at the Nabokovs' with Reinhardt's most famous actor, Moissi, a slight, pale, and extremely sensitive-looking man. I had to act as interpreter. They argued about the interpretation of Tolstoy's hero in *The Living Corpse*. Stanislavsky was politely but firmly critical of Moissi's pervasive hysteria in that part. Moissi was visibly disappointed by the lack of compliments from the man he so greatly admired. It was by no means a satisfactory encounter, though both protagonists remained excruciatingly polite to each other.

Stanislavsky was then caught in a dilemma. His Russian-language theater, despite its fame, had no real place abroad. The Russian emigration was very large, and two-thirds of it belonged to the audience that had supported Stanislavsky in Russia, but that was not enough. Stanislavsky knew that he would have to make his way back to Moscow. He discussed the matter often with Uncle Vladimir, but the latter as usual remained noncommital. Finally Stanislavsky and most of his flock returned to Russia. Only a handful stayed abroad and became zealots of the "Stanislavsky method" in Europe and America.

Olga Leonardovna Knipper-Chekhova would talk about theater, and especially about her late husband. To her the quality of Russian plays, and especially Chekhov's, lay in their truthfulness to life.

"You know," she said, "a foreign visitor once asked Tolstoy what the difference was between Russian and foreign literature, and Tolstoy replied without hesitation: 'We, here, are always concerned with truth, while your writers are not always concerned with it.'

"This is what makes Chekhov's theater so good," she continued, "he never exaggerates, never underlines anything, and he always is concerned with life as it is, with truth." And then she started to speak about acting: "The main thing is the mood. If the mood is truthful, then all is well!" and she smiled at me short-sightedly.

Of my two older cousins, Vladimir and Sergei, in those Berlin years I was closer to Sergei. Sergei loved music and Vladimir did not. Rarely have I seen two brothers as different as Volodya and Seryozha. The older one, the writer and poet, was lean, dark, handsome, a sportsman, with a face resembling his mother's. Seryozha, although as lean in his angular way, and handsome, looked more like Babushka. He was not a sportsman. White-blond with a reddish tint to his face, he had an incurable stutter. But he was gay, a bit indolent, and highly sensitive (and therefore an easy butt for teasing sports.) Sergei worshipped Wagner, whom at that time I did not care for. Most composers of my generation were in revolt against Wagner and the Wagner cult. Fortunately Sergei and I agreed on Verdi, and went together to listen to his operas admirably sung in wretched German translations at the three Berlin opera houses. Sergei also knew a great deal about literature and history, and conversations with him were always interesting and profitable to me.

Volodya always did everything with *une superbe sans égal*, and I was a bit scared of his awesome store of information. If I made a clumsy statement, or gave an inadequate answer to a precise question, or misquoted somebody's verse, he would scoff at me and tease me mercilessly. But this did not keep me from becoming fond of cousin Vladimir soon after we first met in Yalta in the autumn of 1917. We remained friends, and not only because of the *cousinage*, throughout our migratory life.

In the autumn of 1917 three Nabokov families had converged on Yalta. We came in November from Askania-Nova, via Preobrazhenka, horse-drawn as in 1910. Uncle Sergei's and Uncle Vladimir's families had come a few months before us. The *Sergeievichi* part of the clan had settled in Yalta itself, while the *Vladimirovichi* occupied a commodious villa a few miles to the west of Yalta near the palatial mansions of the Imperial family.

At that time the southern tip of the Crimea was untouched by the anarchy that prevailed in northern and central Russia. Consequently thousands of *ci-devant* families, those whom the Bolsheviks nicknamed "the yet unslaughtered" or rather "to be slaughtered bourgeois," invaded Yalta, transforming it for a while into a miniature St. Petersburg on the shore of the Black Sea.

At first cousin Vladimir appeared to me to be haughty, conceited, and snobbish. He did not mingle with us—with my sister, my brother, and me—as did my other cousins, the Sergeievichi. Only toward the spring of 1918 did we start seeing each other more frequently.

Like his father, cousin Vladimir was immensely industrious, already talked about in family circles as the clan's poet. (He had published, I believe in 1916 or 1917, the first book of his verse.)

I remember setting a poem of his to music in Yalta, in the autumn or the winter of 1918. It was a tableau vivant of "The Last Supper" (Leonardo's, I suppose), written in a lilting anapest meter with elegantly carved dactylic rhymes.

Cousin Vladimir always led a carefully circumscribed life. Though by no means a recluse, he was uninterested in our homey games, our music-making, our amusements. He had his own hobbies—butterfly-collecting, chess, tennis. Very soon those hobbies turned into disciplines and he excelled in all of them.

We fled from Sevastopol to Greece the same day, but on different boats. Then, in the early Berlin Diaspora days, I became a member of his family's "Russian home." In those years he wrote in Russian and wrote a great deal. Soon he was acknowledged as the leading writer of the young generation of *émigrés*. Every new work of Vladimir Sirin—a pen name he adopted to distinguish himself, I suppose, from his namesake father—was a literary event in *émigré* circles. Instinctively I felt that Vladimir Sirin was the last great writer of a particular Russian civilization that started several decades before Pushkin and was gradually but thoroughly despoiled by Russia's twentieth-century tyrants.

Yet during those 1920s Vladimir Sirin was virtually unknown beyond the Russian *émigré* community.

In those lean years, making a living was a perennial problem for any Russian *émigré*. Harshest it was, of course, for *émigré* poets and writers. Their crafts depended on a language community. And though the *émigré* community was enterprising and remarkably literate, it was inevitably and irretrievably dwindling. *Emigré* newspapers, journals, and publishing houses led a precarious existence. They could not afford to pay proper fees even to their most celebrated contributors. Vladimir had a hard time making ends meet.

From 1925 onward, the center of the Russian Diaspora was gravitating from Berlin to Paris. But Vladimir stayed entrenched in Berlin. When I asked him why, he told me that he wanted to "protect" the purity of his Russian language. He did not speak any German, but knew French *à fond*. Moving to Paris would have exposed him to language temptations and contagions. In Germany he could remain a mum observer, and, as it turned out, he was a brilliant one.

To make a living, he invented chess problems for newspapers, gave tennis and swimming lessons, and occasionally played as an extra in the thriving German cinema.

He stayed in Berlin with his wife, Vera, and an infant son, Mitya, far into the dangerous years of the Nazis. They lived in a small, sparsely furnished flat in West Berlin in nearly total but splendid isolation. Vera worked at the French Embassy (which, to a degree, was a protection from the Nazis). Vladimir continued to give his sports lessons and wrote his longest and best Russian novels.

Yet, despite a pervasive financial *gène*, the family went every year on a remote lepidopteral vacation. Nor did they ever complain or lose their innate cheerfulness. They appeared gay and delightfully amusing when I visited them in Berlin, or when they visited me in my little house in Alsace.

Cousin Vladimir lived in want and in "noble poverty" throughout the greater part of the first threescore years of his life. I remember him and Vera always in cramped, furnished flats, even as late as his first years in America, in New York and on provincial college campuses.

It is only when the Russo-Biblical bird Sirin moulted into the American writer Vladimir Nabokov and, in fact, only after *Lolita* that affluence and world fame came to him.

Our warm familial friendship continued unchanged. Every time I visit cousins Vladimir and Vera at their Montreux Palace retreat, *je gourmande*, their sharp, brittle, a bit abrasive, and at times boisterously hilarious wit, their all-pervasive sense of humor, his mannerisms and his "strong opinions," his biases, his loves and hates, and his bottomless, punctiliously precise memory . . . and all of it bathed in grand, lordly, but amiably unostentatious hospitality.

Maria Ferdinandovna Nabokova, or Babushka, had quarters in the Nabokov flat in Berlin at the far end of a long corridor, close to the kitchen. Her room was large, but was cluttered with furniture and had a greenish tiled stove in one corner. Babushka usually reclined on a couch, while Khristina, who had been "given" to her as a play-mate serf at the age of six, sat nearby on an upright chair. Babushka appeared the same as in Gatchina. The same lacy morning negligee, the same mauve dog-collar carrying a pendant and the meringue of hair on her head encircled by a mauve ribbon. On her chalk-white face were the usual *mouches*, and her eyebrows were heavily penciled.

One of the windows was open, there was always a smell of coffee, and both ladies were engaged in embroidery and in administering pinpricks to each other.

"You forget to flush the toilet," Khristina would say acidly, looking down at her embroidery.

"And on what evidence, may I ask," retorted Babushka in her crackling basso, "do you think that it was me? And why must you talk about it in front of him?" and she would point at me. "How vulgar!"

Khristina would leave the room and, having flushed the toilet, would return, wiping her red eyes and muttering: "Lord! Lord!"

"That's all they do," sighed Aunt Lyolya. "They sit all day near their open window until one of them starts sneezing, they drink coffee, quarrel, and do those useless *petit-point* embroideries."

Babushka got up from her *chaise-longue* only to go to meals. Then one would notice how much she had shriveled since her

Gatchina days. After meals she returned promptly to her room. There was no adequate *chaise-longue* for her in the living room. Aunt Lyolya used the only one available and would not surrender it to Babushka.

Sometimes she came to lunch at Mother's flat (she liked all those "exes" I fled from) to visit an aged couple, an ex-senator and his wife.

Otherwise her life was confined to the back room of the Nabokov apartment, where she complained to anyone who came to see her about everything: the food, the rudeness of Khristina and her grandchildren, the lack of comfort, the visitors of Uncle Vladimir, *"tout cette bande de Dieu sait qui et quoi,"* but above all about Aunt Lyolya's being a poor *maîtresse de maison*. True enough, Aunt Lyolya's household talents were not conspicuous. In Russia she had been wealthy and had had cooks, butlers, and many servants, but in her Berlin exile she had to rely on devoted friends and a family factotum, Evgenia Konstantinovna, and a German *Putzfrau*. As a result, beds remained unmade, ashtrays unemptied, books unreturned to their shelves, and the food, although abundant, was unrefined.

Babushka would remember with nostalgia the Lucullan menus of the time when she was the wife of an Imperial minister and one of St. Petersburg's most elegant hostesses. *"Alors là,"* she would say, "one ate really well, not all this German *Sauerkraut* and *Klopsen.*"

I liked to visit Babushka in her room. I knew that eventually she would stop complaining and start telling me stories about herself, about the past, and above all about the Nabokov family.

Babushka Nabokova was married off at the age of fifteen to a civil servant. Her husband was her mother's lover. As sometimes happened in the prudish nineteenth century, it was convenient for lovers to have an official link. It gave them easy and free access to each other and made things look *convenable*. The trio traveled abroad together and, from Babushka's accounts, the lovers were very happy, protected by Babushka's legalizing presence. "I was their chaperone," she said, "but, believe me, I did not like my role at all."

Dimitri Nikolaevich Nabokov, the lover and husband of this *ménage à trois*, was much older than Babushka. But apparently he performed his duties with the two baronesses, mother and daughter, very well. Within six years he fathered four children with Babushka, though she did not like sharing his bed. "He had cold frog's feet," she said.

She never grew to love her mother's lover, and this is why the fatherhood of her five other children was never quite certain. Three of them were attributed to various persons in high places, one was doubtful and the last was apparently the result of a tender affection for one of her children's tutors. She talked about all of this in innuendos, never mentioning names or dates.

"*Après tout*," she would say, "didn't Peter the Great's mother have many lovers, and wasn't Peter's father a certain Streshnev and not Tsar Alexei?"

Babushka, like so many eccentrics of the nineteenth century, talked freely about everything. When I once asked her what was hidden in the golden medallion she wore on her neck, she opened it, showed it to me, and said wickedly: "It is hair . . . but not from your grandfather and not from anybody's head. You see how curled it is?"

Another story, typical of Babushka, concerned two of her sons. The older one was a homosexual. When his younger brother reached the age of consent, the older brother started being a bit too interested in him. "And so," said Babushka, "quite properly I called the older brother to my room and told him: 'Stop looking at your brother with dirty eyes.' *A quoi bon sont les domestiques?*" (What are the servants for?) And Babushka chuckled.

Babushka had traveled a great deal, first *à trois* with her mother and husband, then alone, leaving her husband to take care of state affairs. Being very attractive and elegant, she belonged for a while to the "fast set" of Paris. Together with other celebrated *beautés* of her time she performed all sorts of pranks. For example, they undressed in the anteroom of a box in the new Palais Garnier (as the Paris Opera was then called) and sat stark naked through the first act of an opera. An usher finally turned them over to an officer of the Garde Républicaine, who was, as Babushka said, "*très ému et consterné*." "But you know," she exclaimed, "it was wonderful to sit there in the box and to see all the binoculars turned on you and not upon the stage."

Babushka had been on friendly terms with Emperor Alexander II (Grandfather Nabokov's patron) and had hated his son Alexander III (who dismissed my grandfather after Alexander II's murder). She always had Alexander II's photograph in a silver frame on a table next to her *chaise-longue* and called him "dear Sasha."

Her escape from Gatchina was typical of her. The commander of the White Army that was fleeing from Gatchina sent an adjutant to pick up Babushka. She would not leave. "I will not move unless Khristina comes with me, and this *chaise-longue* upon which my mother died, and a trunk full of old Valenciennes and Spanish lace." The officer tried to argue. The army had no transport, there was no time left, the Reds were about to invade Gatchina. "Well, young man," she said haughtily, "then I'll stay here . . . and . . . come what may. Adieu." She was finally packed off with Khristina, couch, and trunk in a freight car filled with wounded officers. It was the last train to leave Gatchina westward.

"And you know," she said, "we spent several days in that beastly car without sleep and barely a handful of bread to eat. But I was so happy! I gave up my couch to a beautiful young officer who was wounded in his head. Khristina and I nursed him day and night. We spent the rest of the time sitting on this lace trunk. Unfortunately he died before we reached safety. What a pity! He was so handsome and so young."

After she had settled at Uncle Vladimir's, she started writing letters to everyone she had ever known, complaining about Berlin and everything around her. "A miserable hole, *aucun respect pour moi*, Uncle Vladimir works too much while nobody else does anything, get me out of here," and so on. But most of this was epistolary rhetoric. She knew that she would not be better cared for anywhere else. Yet when she came to see my mother, she begged her to arrange things so that she could come and live with us.

But her life was to have one more splendid chapter. An old ex-Russian senator of Baltic extraction had moved to Dresden. He and his wife had just celebrated their golden wedding anniversary. He was in his late eighties and Babushka in her early eighties. The senator fell madly in love with Babushka when, after the death of Uncle Vladimir, she moved to Dresden. He visited her daily, brought her roses, and spent long hours with her in cozy chit-chat.

The senator's wife, also not in her prime, felt abandoned. She wrote furious letters to my mother calling Babushka a Messalina and a strumpet. Babushka apparently enjoyed the situation greatly and was happy to be courted by such a grand old man (the senator was seven feet tall, had a round, gleaming ball for a head, a red face, and a strawberry nose). But fortunately, or unfortunately, it all came to an untimely end. One day, with roses in hand, the senator was attacked by a taxicab and died. The two ladies, draped in black veils, made their peace over the senator's coffin. After the senator's death Babushka moved to Romania, where Queen Marie installed her and Khristina in a flat at her palace on the Black Sea. No sooner had she been installed there than she started bombarding my mother with letters: "Lidochka, for heaven's sake, get me out of this gypsy hole! It is so boring here! Romania is not a country, not a nation, it's a profession!" Babushka would have lived for another decade, had she not fallen downstairs and done something irreparable to her insides.

Uncle Vladimir came to a tragic end. He was assassinated on March 21, 1922, in the chamber-music hall of the Berlin Philharmonic, next to the hall where we had heard so much music together. Two Russian right-wing extremists wanted to kill a different person, Pavel Miliukov, the leader of the Russian Constitutional Democratic Party, at a party meeting being held in that hall. Uncle Vladimir was the only man in the hall who, after the first shots had been fired, thrust himself upon one of the assassins. The rest of the people in the hall fell flat on the floor, and a few tried to make their way to the side doors. Uncle Vladimir fell on the floor with the gunman, trying to wrest away his gun. The second man walked up from the back of the hall and fired several shots into Uncle Vladimir's back. He died a few minutes later.

Cousins Volodya and Seryozha were in England. Someone called me at midnight and told me what had happened. The next morning I had the awesome task of identifying Uncle Vladimir's body at the Berlin morgue.

Aunt Lyolya was totally shattered, but did not show a trace of it at the funeral. Uncle Vladimir was buried at the Russian cemetery in Tegel, several yards from the place where Glinka lay buried for quite some time.

Soon thereafter cousin Volodya got married, Babushka moved first to Dresden and then to Romania, Seryozha to Paris, and Aunt Lyolya, with Elena and the other two cousins, to Prague. I never saw her again. My vital center, my Russian home in Berlin, ceased to exist.

My circle of acquaintances in Germany soon grew, and through a stroke of luck I met some of the more interesting personages of the Weimar Republic. In The Hague, in the autumn of 1919, Natalie Peterson, one of my father's sisters, was approached by a German diplomat who wanted to take Russian lessons from her. Germans at that time were tabu in the pro-Entente diplomatic milieu of The Hague to which Aunt Nata belonged. Her husband, Uncle Putia Peterson, was an Imperial leftover, a Russian consul general in Holland, still officially holding to his past.

It was considered improper to meet Germans and receive them in one's home. Consequently, Uncle Putia and two of his sons, who were just about to go to Oxford or Cambridge, were infuriated when they learned that Aunt Nata had agreed to give *"ce Boche"* Russian lessons and had invited him to tea. "You can't do that!" they shouted. "What will the Van-der-Xs say?"

"If you don't want to meet the man," replied Aunt Nata, "you can leave. Nika will help me entertain him."

I too had mixed feelings about it. But curiosity prevailed, and a few days later I was sitting in Aunt Nata's living room waiting for the ominous creature to appear.

The surprise was baffling. The person who came into the room was young, good-looking, a man of medium height and somewhat stocky. He was dressed in elegant clothes, obviously of English cut. His manner was urbane, amiable, a bit timid, his voice soft and pleasant, and his pale blue eyes looked kind and gentle. There seemed nothing Teutonic about him. He spoke fluent French and English, devoid of any German accent, and with much greater ease than either Aunt Nata or myself.

I do not remember what Aunt Nata and the young diplomat talked about. I was too much absorbed with watching him. I had expected to be confronted by a brutish beast; instead I saw a friendly, civilized person who could well have passed for an English peer or an Oxford don.

This German diplomat turned out to be deeply interested in Russia's cultural heritage, and that, of course, attracted me to him at once. Very soon we became friends. In fact, except for Aunt Nata, he was the only friend I found in The Hague. When I left The Hague for Germany, he gave me four letters of introduction to German friends. Two of them were addressed to persons living in Stuttgart, where I was going to study music; the others to friends in Berlin, Count Albrecht von Bernsdorff and Felix von Bethmann-Hollweg, the son of the ex-Chancellor. It was through the chain reaction to these four letters that I came to know some of the cultural milieu of the Weimar Republic. The one to Albrecht von Berns-dorff led me to Count Harry Kessler.

Berlin in those early twenties was, as I said earlier, the capital of the Russian emigration. It was the first and the most lively station of its Diaspora, a Russian Antioch.

The bulk of Russia's intelligentsia and large segments of the bourgeoisie and aristocracy that had escaped the Bolshevik terror had made their way to Berlin and established themselves there. They lived in cheap boarding houses, pensions, hotels, furnished rooms, and flats, or, in rare cases, sumptuous villas in the Tiergarten and Grunewald. But the Russian refugees in Berlin were by no means a humble, frightened lot that fretted and trembled in a hostile environment. They seemed to have taken over Berlin and transformed it into a Russian camp.

There were Russian newspapers, Russian theaters, Russian schools and churches, Russian cabarets and libraries, Russian literary clubs and publishing houses, Russian foreign-exchange speculators, Russian bookstores, Russian art galleries, grocery stores, confiseries and antique or bargain stores that sold false and real Fabergé jewelry and a lot of genuine and fake icons.

The center part of West Berlin, from the Wittenberg Platz past the Gedächtnis Kirche and down the Kurfürstendamm, seemed to have surrendered to the Russian takeover. Every other person in the street, in cafés and stores, spoke Russian or a heavy, consonant-laden German. All around, on the walls and on the advertising pillars, one saw announcements, sometimes in Russian, not only of Russian opera performances and concerts given by Russian artists, but also of Russian political meetings, officers' clubs, welfare committees. Dowager ballerinas opened ballet schools, writers held forums and public readings of prose and poetry. Above all, there was (as there always is when Russians meet) a flow of benefit functions: concerts, dinners, and balls, to which natives and other foreigners were lured by the promise of "authentic" Russian entertainment, and which helped replenish the ever dwindling funds of Russian welfare committees and concomitantly increase the meager incomes of those who worked for them.

Yet the Russian *borshch* that splashed all over Berlin did not penetrate deeply into the life of the Berliners. It remained a kind of detached superstructure. Astonished and perplexed by this eastern in-

119

vasion, the Berliners went about the complicated business of their own lives, disoriented by the loss of the war, their economic and political crises, and the galloping inflation that had started immediately after the war, and by 1921 had reached incredible proportions.

I settled in Berlin in the early spring of 1921, after one and a half years at the Academy of Music in Stuttgart. My mother had sold a part of her forest land in Poland and had moved into a large Berlin apartment in Wilmersdorf, a furnished flat whose living and dining rooms were filled with light-oak Jugendstil, and black Moroccan furniture inlaid with mother-of-pearl, and other contraptions of the same period.

As soon as I arrived in Berlin, I carried my two letters to their respective addresses. Both responded at once. We met and, as in The Hague, I was startled to discover Germans who did not conform to my biased picture of them. Both Albrecht von Bernsdorff and Felix von Bethmann-Hollweg were intelligent, well bred, charming, urbane, and thoroughly cosmopolitan. We became friends at once.

Sometime in 1921 Albrecht von Bernsdorff called me up and asked me to come to lunch at the Automobile Club. "I'm arranging for you to meet Harry Kessler," he said. "There will be no one else at lunch—only you, Kessler, and I—so please come."

Graf Kessler's name was already surrounded by a legendary halo. He was known not only as a discriminating lover of the arts, a Maecenas, and a friend of Hofmannsthal, Richard Strauss, and Max Reinhardt, but also as a liberal political figure with a post in the Foreign Office. He had played a brief but important role in the first years of the Weimar Republic. I knew that Kessler was a true and generous friend of artists. Being well off, he was able to assist a number of famous artists financially, and had helped to promote their careers.

I remember how awkward I felt entering the grand, oak-paneled dining room of the club, its tables laden with silver and crystal, shiny brass chandeliers hanging low from the ceiling, and a swarm of swallowtailed waiters flitting to the entrance door to greet the incoming guests with an obsequious *"Jawohl, Herr Graf," "Aber selbstverständlich, Herr Generaldirektor," "Guten tag, Herr Baron."* My clothes were baggy, my shoes worn, my appearance much too juvenile for the club's sedate surroundings. Besides, I had lost the habit of plush places.

I looked around disconcerted and at first could not find Albrecht von Bernsdorff. But a waiter led me across the big room to a table near the window, where Bernsdorff was waving at me. I was nervous, late, and ill at ease. Kessler greeted me coldly, or at least it seemed to me that he did, and continued talking to Bernsdorff as if I were not present. I watched him as he spoke. He looked more German-Junkerish than I had expected, but, at the same time, smaller and frailer than in the photographs I had seen in the papers. His hair was brown-blond and was as carefully glazed as the shine in his light blue eyes. His hands were small, with dainty fingers and well-manicured nails. His clothes were dark, tweedy, and dapper. He spoke in a soft monotone, as upper-class Germans often do, and as he spoke his face did not move at all, only his eyes blinked at rhythmic intervals, very fast, like camera shutters. He clipped his sentences, and while speaking looked intently at Albrecht von Bernsdorff.

Fortunately the swallowtails arrived with menus and we started ordering. Only then did Kessler turn to me and look at me intently, as if sizing me up. He started showering me with questions.

Did I know Diaghilev? No . . . at the time I did not. But I explained that he was a half-brother of a half-uncle of my half-sister, and that we had played chamber music in St. Petersburg with Diaghilev's half-nephews. Well, all those halves did not seem to interest or impress Kessler at all.

Did I like Maillol? Who's he? I asked.

Did I prefer Rilke to Valéry? I did not know who Valéry was. What was Meyerhold like? And Trotsky? And what did I think of Pavlova and Nijinsky? I did not know Meyerhold (I met him later in Paris). I had never seen Trotsky. As for Pavlova and Nijinsky, the latter was only a name to me (albeit a famous one) printed under the photograph of a ludicrous creature in rose-petaled tights. And Pavlova? Yes, I had seen her dance, but only once, here in Berlin at a benefit performance. She seemed much too bony and haggard; besides, she was dancing to that oozily sentimental piece of Saint-Saëns's—her famous "Dying Swan"—and I did not like it.

Kessler listened to me with a condescending smile. He did not argue or discuss anything. Soon he stopped talking to me at all. He turned to Bernsdorff and for the rest of the meal spoke to him about German politics.

Suddenly, in the middle of dessert, he looked at his watch, and exclaimed: *"Mon Dieu!* I'm late. I was supposed to see Flechtheim at three o'clock and it's already three fifteen." And to Bernsdorff: "Uhde is in town, he arrived from Paris yesterday, and I have to talk to Flechtheim about Uhde's article for the *Querschnitt.*"

He turned to me, shook my hand hurriedly, and said: "Well, *au revoir*, young man . . . keep well . . . and good luck at the *conservatoire*," and he was off.

"Flechtheim, Uhde, *Querschnitt*," went through my head like an echo—three more names I did not know anything about.

Quite obviously Kessler must have found me a bore. I did not know any of the names one should know, nor did I seem interested in learning anything about them. I was not *au courant*, not concerned with what was the talk of the town's art patrons and art lovers. Fancy, a Russian not knowing Diaghilev and Nijinsky, not having met Meyerhold, and admitting that he did not like the great Anna Pavlova!

But I, for my part, was disappointed by Harry Kessler. All of his questions seemed "planted" in order to disconcert me. And the condescending way in which he listened to my monosyllabic replies was, to say the least, unkind. I was, after all, only nineteen, and could not possibly have known all that he thought I should know. Besides, I had just surfaced from a protracted immersion in various cultural hinterlands and had been busy surviving some rather serious ordeals.

"Why didn't he ask me a personal question?" I thought. "Why wasn't he interested in knowing where I came from, or who I was, or what I was doing, or what were my hopes and ambitions?"

Bernsdorff tried to comfort me. "Never mind," he said, "don't pay any attention to the way he behaved today—he's often like that with strangers. But he only *acts* like a snob; he isn't really one. He is quite different. He can be charming. And he's full of concern for the people he admires. Don't worry, you'll have other occasions to meet him."

The next occasion to meet Count Harry Kessler came sooner than I had anticipated.

There was from about 1920 to 1925 a curious Russian club in Berlin. It was called Dom Iskusstva, the House of the Arts, and was located in the western part of town, at the Nollendorfplatz. From the outside the Dom Iskusstva looked like any Berlin house: peeling, gunpowder-gray stucco covering a misshapen Jugendstil building. On two of its floors was a *Kaffee Restaurant*. It was large, ill lit, with a pervasive smell of German cigarettes and cigars mixed with sauerkraut, fried onions, and stale coffee. Half a dozen glum waiters in long skirt-like aprons waited on a clientele largely, if not exclusively, Russian.

Each Friday evening a throng of Russians, mostly poets and writers, invaded the Dom Iskusstva to listen to prose or poetry readings, or forum discussions, or lectures given by major and minor Russian intellectuals.

The Dom Iskusstva and its "Fridays" were run by a delightful, roly-poly, and exuberantly friendly ex-Symbolist poet called Nikolai Mikhailovich Minski. Anyone who had the slightest claim to being part of the Russian intelligentsia (except, of course, extreme right-wingers) visited those Friday-evening gatherings and in one way or another took part in them. At that time the umbilical cord between the Soviet Union and the *émigré Diaspora* was not yet entirely severed. A considerable number of Soviet citizens could still travel abroad, so consequently there was always a trickle of Soviet intellectuals in Berlin, on their way either westward or eastward. Most of them liked to stop in Berlin and enjoy the various entertainments offered by the Russian borshch circuit and the native Berliners.

Normally, Soviet citizens did not mingle with *émigré* Russians. But there were a few places where they did, and the Dom Iskusstva was one of them. So there was always a sizable complement of Russian intellectuals from the Soviet Union at Minski's Fridays. And being often famous people, they were usually the stars of the evening. In those years all intellectuals, the *émigrés* and those from the "heartland," still shared common roots.

In retrospect, it seems difficult to imagine that once upon a time, in the drab surroundings of a German *Kaffeehaus* in post–World War I Berlin, barely three or four years after the seizure of power by the Bolsheviks, so many diverse, famous, and at times antagonistic personalities could have met peacefully and fruitfully and have enjoyed their time together. Such a confluence could never have been produced within the borders of the Russian motherland before or after the Revolution, and less than five years later it would have been impossible abroad. Only a particular combination of seemingly unrelated circumstances—the simultaneous bankruptcy of Russia

123

and Germany, the new economic policy in Russia and the inflation in Germany, and, of course, the massive emigration of Russian intellectuals to Berlin—could make it possible.

In 1923 the German mark was revaluated and stabilized. Suddenly Germany became, at least outwardly, calm and sedate, but also as expensive as France and the other countries of postwar Europe. Russian *émigrés* started moving out of Berlin—to Paris, to Prague, a few to England or the United States. In Berlin, Russian establishments began closing. Berlin rapidly lost its Russian flavor. It was reverting to the natives.

Then, in Russia, Lenin lay dying. The rumblings of the power struggle became audible. For Soviet citizens, even the illustrious ones, travel abroad became more cumbersome. In a few years it would be reduced to "official delegations," or to a trickle of people upon whose allegiance the Soviet government could count. The Stalinist era was in the making, and the Golden Age of the Russian Diaspora was on the wane.

One Friday evening when I arrived at the club and climbed the stairway, the place was packed. People stood shoulder to shoulder in the doorway. I looked above their heads and saw that someone was reciting something on the podium. Minski was sitting in the front row, but he did not notice me waving at him. I said, *"Pardon,"* and pushed myself through the crowd.

Minski noticed me, jumped up, and tiptoed toward the entrance. "Ah, you're so late," he whispered. "I saved a seat right next to them. See there?" and he pointed at an empty chair in the front row. "They're both a bit tipsy," he buzzed into my ear. "They had a brawl. She has a black eye. But please, make as if you don't notice anything."

I recognized at once the ash-blond head of Esenin. He was talking to someone in the second row. He looked astonishingly young and pretty—the freckled face of a Russian peasant kid.

Next to him, her fur coat spread on two chairs, sat the Diva, Isadora Duncan. I had heard that she had aged, but I was stunned by what I saw. She looked like a Roman matron after revels. Her baggy face was glistening and red. One eye was covered with a black patch. Mascara and lipstick were swimming inordinately on her lips and her brow. She wore a rumpled-looking Greekish tunic with a deep decolleté and an equally rumpled mauve shawl that covered her hair and neck.

In contrast to Isadora, Esenin was well groomed: gray-checked tweeds, a neat stiff collar with a crimson tie, and light-colored spats.

"*Et voici, Madame, si vous permettez,*" started Minski in his quaint French, introducing me to Miss Duncan, "this is the young composer Mr. Nicolas Nabokov, who speaks fluent English."

"Oh!" mumbled the Diva, and smiled.

"Why don't you sit between them?" suggested Minski. He took Isadora's fur coat off the chair to make room for me.

Esenin turned around, looked at me with bloodshot eyes, and said: "Who are you? What do you want?" His tone was gruff and hostile.

Fortunately Minski was still standing next to me. "Oh, dear Sergei Konstantinovich," he said with a suave smile, "this is the young composer I talked to you about.

But Esenin interrupted him. "Okay, okay," he said, "don't worry, I won't hit him," and he smiled in a childish way.

The evening was long. One after another, poets—young, middle-aged, and older ones—climbed up to the podium and recited or sing-songed their stuff. The place was getting stuffy and hot.

"Is it always this way here?" whispered Isadora Duncan. "Can't we leave? It's boring and the air is filthy! Don't you agree?"

Esenin had gotten up in the middle of one of the elegiac numbers, muttered an obscenity, and made his way to the bar. A minute later Minski appeared on the podium. He asked for silence and announced with a face full of smiles: "Ladies and gentlemen, I have an important announcement to make." He looked down at Miss Duncan. "We have . . . yes, we have the pleasure and the honor to have among us tonight the famous and beautiful Miss Isadora Duncan and her faithful companion, our great national poet, Sergei Esenin."

He was interrupted by thunderous applause. He raised his hands and added: "Sergei Esenin has very kindly offered to read tonight a few of his new poems."

Another burst of applause followed the announcement. But Miss Duncan did not react and Esenin remained at the bar. His chair was empty.

Minski, looking contrite, started to climb down from the podium. Suddenly there was a bang, and sounds of angry cursing came from the direction of the bar.

"There he goes again!" exclaimed Miss Duncan. She turned to me and started speaking very quickly. "Listen, young man," she said, "would you take me down and find a taxi for me? I want to go to the hotel. I've had enough of it! Please come!"

She got up and started walking toward the exit. The eyes of the public followed her, aghast.

Minski came running after Isadora Duncan: "*Non, non, Madame,*" he exclaimed, "*ne partez pas, ne partez pas.*" He stopped her and asked me to tell her in English that everything was all right. It was a silly accident. A waiter with a tray of beer had bumped into Esenin, that's all. "*C'est tout, c'est fini!*"

But Isadora's face flushed. "*C'est fini,* my eye!" she shouted. "Goddammit, let me pass, you silly little man. I'm going home." And to me, "Come on, mister. Help me get out of here!"

Suddenly I saw Esenin making his way toward Isadora and me. He looked disheveled, his suit and shirt and face were wet. He grabbed Isadora's hands. "Let go of me!" she shouted. He retorted with a string of obscenities in Russian.

I rushed downstairs, out of Minski's club. For some reason the lights on the stairs were out, but gropingly I found my way to the front door. I had opened it and was still holding the handle when I heard a voice pronounce my last name and a hand came down on my shoulders.

"Sorry," said Esenin, "I did not mean to insult you, Nabokov. Won't you come with us—that is, with me and my mare—to a night club? Just for a bit? Please?" he asked in a gentle voice.

I said that I had promised to be home early.

"Oh, come on," said Esenin, "let's go together to a pederast night club. I'm told it's close to here. Men get undressed there and bugger each other on the stage. I want to see it. Come with me and the Dunkansha."

I wanted to say no, but he stopped me. He took me by the arm, smiled like a child, and said, "You have a good face. I like you. Please come with us. The bitch is making herself up. Then we'll go. Okay?"

The cabaret or night club to which Esenin wanted to go was supposed to be right around the corner, in the Bülowstrasse. He could not remember the name of it, he only knew the second word, *Diele.* It turned out that the Bülowstrasse had many *Dielen.*

We trudged, Isadora, Esenin, and I, from one dingy joint to another until after a half a dozen *Dielen* we found the one Esenin was looking for.

The place, darkish and noisy, was divided into three sections. In the front part, near the entrance, were tables as in any Berlin café, with clusters of people around them. In the middle, a bar ran the length of one section, with a dance floor in front of it, also crowded with people. From beyond the dance floor came sounds of "sloe blues." The place reeked of Egyptian cigarettes, sweat, cheap cosmetics, and Coty's Lorigan.

"It stinks like a brothel," grumbled Miss Duncan.

I pushed my way to the bar, found a sour-looking waiter, and explained to him who we were and that we needed a table.

"*Jawohl, jawohl,*" he mumbled, "I'll tell the manager. *Augenblick.*"

I went back to the entrance and watched the waiter chase several people from a table. The manager, in a cutaway with a carnation in his buttonhole, came up to Isadora Duncan and led us to the vacated table.

"*Zamechatelno! Vanderfull!*" exclaimed Esenin. "I never saw so many *Tyotki* [queens] in one place! . . . Look! Look! Look! They're raising the curtain in the back. We are just in time for the spectacle."

We sat down at the table squeezed between dancing couples and clustered tables.

"It is better to be sitting," roared Esenin, "it is safer for us."

"Will you stop, Sergei! Stop being obscene!" interrupted Miss Duncan.

But Esenin did not pay any attention. "Do you think they'll undress completely?" he asked.

"Meyerhold told me that he saw them bugger each other on the stage."

"*Wollen Madame etwas trinken?*" asked the manager.

Esenin ordered champagne and vodka. "A bottle of each," he said to the manager, and, showing his wallet, added: "*Mir hab valiuta.* [We have foreign currency.]"

Gradually my eyes were getting accustomed to the *Diele's* twilight. I began to notice that around the tables, at the bar, and pressed cheek to cheek on the dance floor were slinky, effete male creatures rouged and powdered. Heavily mascaraed and rouged transvestites in short skirts and white aprons, with pink ribbons in their wigs, were moving about with trays, waiting on tables.

"*Was wird Kommen auf Scene?*" Esenin asked one.

The transvestite laughed and answered in a squeaky baritone,

"*Wirst schon sehen, liebling.* [Don't worry, you'll see, lover.]"

Suddenly, to my acute embarrassment, I noticed that at a table next to ours was sitting Harry Kessler with two other persons.

I did not know what to do. I moved my chair closer to Isadora's and turned my back on Kessler, hoping that in the dim light of the *Diele* he would not recognize me. But I was interested in who he was with at this kind of joint. I turned around and looked. One of the persons was, or at least seemed to be, a girl. She was strangely dressed. She wore a large, glistening top hat and a dress suit with a *jabot.* Her face was chalk white and one eye was squeezing a monocle. The other person was like most creatures in the place, made-up, powdered, blond, and effete.

The girl looked at me, at Isadora and Esenin, and smiled. "Dammit," I thought, "she recognized *La Diva.*"

Fortunately at that moment the transvestite waitress brought champagne and vodka, and then the lights in the place went out. At the back of the *Diele* a tiny stage with alpine scenery lit up. Esenin and I got up to see what was going on.

There were two girls in Bavarian *Dirndl* dress on the stage, rather obvious transvestites, and a kind of gnome in *Lederhosen.* All three wore feathered Bavarian hats. The band started playing a noisy *Schuhplattler.*

I sat down again, but Esenin remained standing, grinning, and looking at the stage. Every now and then he would pick up one of the bottles, champagne or vodka, drink from it, and shout: "Bravo! Hurrah!"

"Sit down, you fool," exclaimed Isadora and grabbed him by the sleeve.

"Stop it, mare!" retorted Esenin; he laughed and poured champagne on her head, making a lewd remark.

I could not see what was going on on the stage. Isadora and I were screened from it by the crowd that packed the dance floor.

Suddenly Esenin neighed like a horse and grabbed me by the arm. "*Smotri, smotri!* [look, look]," he shouted.

I got up and saw that the two *Dirndl* girls had turned male and that the three of them stood naked on the stage, facing the public and bowing. From out of their crotches, covered by large fig leaves, protruded long, blown-up rubber sausages, the kind one buys at fairs. The sausages wore tiny Bavarian hats covering their tips. The public cheered.

128

Esenin sat down and started explaining in obscene Russian what had gone on during the number.

Isadora looked glum and flushed in her face. "Is there a lady's room here?" she asked. "I must throw up."

"Come on, old bitch," shouted Esenin, "vomit right here," and he pointed to the floor.

I caught a transvestite by her apron and told her to take Isadora to the *Damen Toilette.*

Esenin cursed. He was visibly drunk, getting noisy and unruly.

Suddenly I noticed the girl with the top hat bend over to Kessler and whisper something into his ear. Kessler turned and looked at Esenin and me. I saw him shake his head. It seemed he did not recognize me.

But Esenin noticed him and shouted at him in vulgar German: "What d'you want, *alte tante?*"

"Sergei Konstantinovich," I said, "please stop. It is someone I know. Leave him alone."

"Oh, shit!" shouted Esenin. "Tell him to stop ogling or I'll smash his . . ."

At that moment Isadora reappeared at the door of the *Toilette* with her patched eye. She waved at me to help her get through the crowd.

I left Esenin and went after Isadora. As I was leading her back to the table, I saw Kessler pushing his way toward us. There was nothing I could do—he had recognized the Diva. She was within the realm of his iconography.

He said hello to me and asked, ceremoniously, to be introduced to "Miss Duncan."

Esenin looked furious. I thought he was about to hit Kessler. I nudged him and whispered: "Don't. He's perfectly harmless. Try to be nice."

"*Garçon!*" shouted Esenin. "*Noch Shampanskoe! Und vodka.*"

Soon everyone was greeting each other and fraternizing. Even Isadora smiled.

I was fascinated by Kessler's female companion. When she got up to move to our table, I saw that she had no trousers on—only the shirt with its *Jabot,* the topper, and the jacket. The "tails" were cut off, and below she was nude. Through the studless shirt one could see firm, girlish breasts. Her eyes were "blued" underneath, brows heavily mascaraed, and lips colored a dark vamp-like burgundy. The face at close range appeared even whiter than from afar. Despite the cosmetics, one could see that it was a very young face and a very pretty one in an ostentatiously sensuous way.

I do not know how it happened—was there a chair missing, or was it by design?—but the girl planted herself squarely upon my lap. She smiled engagingly, put her right arm around my neck, and said: "I hope you don't mind. I'm *nur ein Mädchen.* [only a girl.]"

The male gazelle next to her twittered something in my ear and moved to my other side. "My name is Max," he said, "and hers is Doderl. Don't you know her?"

I said that I did not.

Kessler, much more ceremoniously, introduced his companions to Isadora and Esenin.

No sooner were we seated than Kessler started to reminisce. He told Isadora he had first seen her dance before the war in Paris. It was a revelation to him, he said, like a "rebirth of ancient Greece." He told her how he had raved to Reinhardt and how sorry he was that he had missed her when she appeared in Berlin.

The waitress brought a bottle of champagne, poured it into glasses, and gave Esenin the bottle of vodka. Esenin began to doctor the champagne by pouring vodka into the glasses.

He exchanged seats with the male gazelle and told the girl to turn around so he could pat her —— and he said the word in funny German.

Kessler heard it and winced.

"Sergei, I'll leave if you won't stop!" shouted Isadora across the table.

"Oh, damn you!" snoted Esenin. He got up and asked the transvestite waitress, "*Wo kann pissen?*"

"*Da, mein liebchen,*" smiled the transvestite, "come, I'll show you," and she led him to the men's room.

"What's your name?" asked the girl on my lap.

I told her.

"You look cute," she whispered.

Suddenly the room started to spin around me. I was trying to pick up my glass, but could not. The girl continued to laugh and whisper in my ear.

"I'm getting drunk," I mumbled, "I better go," but instead of getting up and leaving, I remained seated with the girl's bottom on my knees.

I looked around, and felt that everything was suddenly getting very gay and awfully funny: Kessler's glistening face, the patch on Isadora's eye, the girl on my lap, Max's blond hair, the transvestite, the dancing couples, the music and even the noise . . .

The night began to melt, its visions unconnected, inchoate: Isadora's purple, irate face as she tried to hit Esenin with a vodka bottle . . . Kessler leading Isadora away . . . I remember Esenin and myself, supported by the girl and by Max, standing in the slush and writing huge Russian obscenities on a show window with lipsticks. I am being pushed into a cab and . . . and . . .

. . . and I wake up with a mammoth headache and acute nausea, stark naked on a sofa in a room I have never seen before.

I look around and hear a girl's voice. It is Doderl standing at the foot of the sofa in a light dressing gown. "God, were you drunk! Both of you," she says and laughs. She goes out and returns bringing a bottle of Apollinaris and hands me a pill. "Swallow this, you'll feel better in ten minutes," she says, "or, better still, vomit if you can."

She is dark-haired, very young, tall and well built. She has a lovely, tender face. She laughs.

"We took the other man to his hotel," she says. "Max knew where he and Isadora Duncan were staying. It was quite a struggle to get him out of the way. But we didn't know what to do with you. Max didn't know who you were and where you lived. So I brought you home. Your clothes are a mess. Would you like to try on my brother's clothes? I'll go and get some."

I thank her, swallow the pill, and drink a glass of Apollinaris. I find my dirty clothes and put them on.

She goes out of the room, but comes back a minute later. "My mother would like to meet you," she says, "but I told her maybe another time. Okay?"

I hear someone playing the viola in the next room. "That's my brother," she says, "he's a well-known viola player. He plays in the X Orchestra. Do you like the sound of a viola? I hate it."

I tell her that my brother played the viola until he was eighteen. I tell her what I do and who I am.

"Must you go?" she asks. "Because you can just as well stay here until lunch. Maybe you'll feel better. Then you could come with me and have lunch at the Adlon with Mistinguett. She has just arrived from Paris. I'm dying to meet her. Come with me, will you?"

I say that I cannot. I must go home. I'm sorry.

"Well, maybe another time," she says with regret in her voice. She takes me to the door and kisses me goodbye.

Soon after the Eseninesque saturnalia, the attitude of Harry Kessler changed. He started inviting me to the theater, to concerts, and to the opera. We met quite often at Helene von Nostitz's salon, especially when she had celebrities from abroad, or went out with a group of his friends to have dinner together and after dinner to night clubs.

It was not Albrecht von Bernsdorff but Doderl who "imposed" me upon Harry Kessler.

Doderl led a helter-skelter life. At the time we met, she was, I believe, eighteen or nineteen. Her interest in music, in literature, in the arts, and in culture in general was genuine and her love for writers, musicians, actors, and movie people was, like Kessler's, *inépuisable*. But she was much less snobbish about it, and her enjoyment of "celebrities," native or imported, was open, frank, and naïvely gregarious. Late in May 1922, Doderl phoned me to say that Kessler had invited her and her boyfriend to visit him in Weimar. But her boyfriend was sick—would I like to go instead? Rainer Maria Rilke was spending a week at the villa.

Doderl and I arrived in Weimar on one of those fragrant June afternoons when the small towns of central Germany smell of lime blossoms, cut grass, and tar. Kessler had sent his car to meet us. It was a pale blue Mercedes driven by a liveried chauffeur. We drove along cobbled streets lined with blooming linden trees; we passed the opera house, the princely palace and its gardens, and stopped at a tall wrought-iron gate. The chauffeur honked and a liveried porter opened the gate. The tires grated upon a graveled *allée* that curved gently upward toward a colonnaded portico.

"Look," said Doderl, pointing to flowerbeds of white iris, stock, and alyssum, "Harry makes a fetish of flowers—he likes only white ones."

We entered a spacious hall paved in black and white marble and saw in front of us, through a wide doorway, a salon with sofas, easy chairs, and tables bearing bouquets of white flowers. At the opposite end of the salon were five sunlit French windows. Two curved staircases led from the hall to the second floor. An elderly lady in a dark dress, an apron, and a lace headgear, and a youngish butler in a bottle-green velvet uniform, white stockings, and patent-leather shoes with silver buckles met us in the hall. They led us upstairs to our rooms, with a footman behind us carrying our luggage.

Two chambermaids were waiting for us. They curtsied, said "*Gut'n abend*," and opened our bags. The elderly housekeeper showed us our rooms and the bathroom in between. "Herr Graf," she said, "thought that the *Herrschaften* would not mind sharing a bathroom. The other bathroom is occupied by Herr Rilke."

While the maids were unpacking our luggage, we undressed in the bathroom and took a bath together in a steaming tub. We soaped and scrubbed each other and laughed.

"Wouldn't Harry and his friend Max be surprised to see us?" said Doderl. "I'm sure that men are seldom seen with nude girls in this house!"

We dressed and went downstairs.

The butler was waiting for us. "Herr Graf has been detained," he said. "But if the *Herrschaften* wish to have tea, it is served outdoors." He led us through the salon to the terrace.

"Isn't this beautiful, Nabi?" exclaimed Doderl, making a large gesture with her arms.

The terrace was surrounded on all three sides by flowerbeds of various shapes and sizes, but all of them white. White roses and white iris, white petunias, Nicotiana, and stock. The flowerbeds were bordered by white alyssum, miniature white carnations, and boxwood. All of the flowerbeds seemed to fall into a kind of abstract pattern of squares, circles, quadrangles, and ellipses set within a frame of neatly trimmed bright green. There was not a pebble, not a bit of gravel in sight. At the far end of this white-and-green expanse, opposite the terrace, was a clipped yew hedge, and behind it a much higher hornbeam hedge. The garden consisted of a vast quadrangle bordered by ancient linden and elm trees.

Here and there in the middle of flower-beds stood pieces of sculpture or large earthenware pots with white geraniums in them. The air was filled with the honeyed scent of flowers and with the buzz of bees.

"These here," said Doderl, pointing to two milky nudes, "are by Maillol, and the torso there is by Rodin. I don't know who did the others. You'll have to ask Harry when he comes."

Harry and Max arrived while we were having tea. Both were smartly dressed in light-colored tweed coats and Oxford-gray flannels.

133

"Well, how do you like my roses?" asked Kessler while Max was pouring tea. "They are just beginning to flower. You're lucky, the weather was beastly till yesterday."

And he turned to me: "And how are you, *jeune homme?* Did you bring your music with you? I told Monsieur Rilke about you."

"Oh, Harry, show Nabi the house," interrupted Doderl, "he's dying to see it."

Kessler frowned. "We've been working all day. Can't we wait till tomorrow? Tomorrow is Sunday, we'll have plenty of time."

But Max offered to show me the house after tea.

Count Harry Kessler's Weimar villa was famous in Germany. It was the first Art Nouveau house built by a young but already famous Belgian architect and interior designer called van de Velde, in 1909 or 1910. A large two-storied house in light, cannon-powder stucco, it had French windows on the ground floor, smaller German *Schloss* windows on the second floor, and a series of oval dormer windows peering out of a mansard roof. The wooden frames of all the windows, the entrance door, and the glass door leading to the terrace were not, as is usual in Germany, lacquered white, but painted a pale shade of dull gray. The roof was covered with square French tiles interspersed with slabs of slate. There were no bearded caryatids upholding the portico, nor were there any Jugendstil bas-reliefs of nude damsels around the cornices. The general appearance of the large villa was that of an elegant and comfortable German residence.

But the particularity of Kessler's Weimar villa was that it was one of the first experiments in *Gesamtwerk*—that is, a house designed entirely by one person, its Belgian builder, inside and out.

The architecture, the size and shape of the rooms, the design of the furniture, the patterns and colors of the draperies, the wallpaper, the carpeting, and the upholstery, the choice of woods, the forms of the bathtubs, sinks, and toilets, the design of the silver and china were all of them the invention of Van de Velde. Even such details as locks and keys, lamps, ash trays, the forms and lines of the cornices, were designed by him to form, as Max said, "a whole— *wie aus einem Guss.*"

First Max showed me the large salon, stopping in front of each Impressionist picture, drawing, and *bibelot*. Then we went to the smaller salon. Here the furniture was of light birchwood with rose-colored silk upholstery. One wall was taken up by a Blüthner concert grand in a birchwood casing. Above it hung a picture with a blue horse and a blue rider. "This is the picture that gave the name to the movement," said Max. "You know, of course, the 'Blue Rider' group?"

The dining-room furniture was of pale pigskin, and the walls were lemon yellow. There were more large Impressionist pictures and one or two Fauves, all of them recognizably "famous."

One-third of the ground floor was taken up by the library. Here the bookcases were birch, as was the huge, low rectangular table filled with expensive-looking art books and journals. Contrary to most private libraries, there was not a single antique book on the shelves. "Graf Kessler keeps his collection of rare old books in Berlin," said Max. "Eventually he wants to move them to Weimar, but not before he has built a pavilion for them in the garden. Here in Weimar we have only books published in Germany in this century."

One of the shorter walls of the library was filled, I was told, with art books, opposite it was a wall of translations of foreign writers, and a third wall, the longest, was packed to the ceiling with rows of books, all of them of the same format and in the same neat-looking modern binding.

"This is all that has been published so far by the Insel Verlag," said Max, pointing to the longest of the three walls. "You may know that Graf Kessler was one of the founders of the Insel Verlag. He started it long before we began printing books here in Weimar at the Cranach Presse. We run it together, as you probably know. But at the Cranach Presse we print only rare and special kinds of books, and we do it by hand. These books, for example," and he went to the table and showed me two very large saffian-bound volumes. "This is all of *Faust*," he said. "First the sources of *Faust*, then the *Urfaust*, and the two parts of Goethe's *Faust*. All of it printed on the finest Japanese paper. Now we are doing the same for *Hamlet*."

Between the three garden windows of the library stood tall, pretty cabinets of the same light wood as the rest of the room. Max pulled out a drawer and said: "These cabinets contain a cross-reference catalogue of all the books Graf Kessler owns, including those in Berlin. It was prepared for Graf Kessler by the librarian of the Prussian State Library in Berlin."

On the second floor we went first to see Kessler's and Max G.'s adjoining bedrooms with a huge bathroom between them. I was

135

startled by the sunken tub seven feet square, inlaid with Ispahan-blue tiles. It was framed by two glass-and chromium cubicles; one was an American-style shower, the other contained a john with a chamois-leather seat. The walls of the bathroom were covered with rose-colored tiles and the ceiling was pale blue. On the floor lay a rug made of zebra skins. Near the window stood a black-and-gold Japanese lacquered dresser bearing tortoiseshell brushes, hand mirrors, and many scent bottles. On one corner of the dresser was a small bunch of miniature carnations in a fluted silver vase.

Harry Kessler's bedroom was the epitome of meticulous orderliness. The room was paneled in the same light birchwood as the music salon and the library downstairs. The paneling concealed, Max G. told me, a vast quantity of closets and drawers. The bed was large and covered with a cream-colored vicuña rug. Near the bed stood a small night table bearing a silver-and-crystal lamp. There was no other furniture in the room except four chairs made of the same wood and upholstered in chamois. Bookshelves filled the space between the windows. Above those shelves hung three death masks: Schiller, Napoleon, and another I did not recognize.

"This is the death mask of Oscar Wilde," explained Max G. "It was cast for Graf Kessler from the original, which belongs to an English peer."

After the seigneurial bedroom, we went on tiptoes past the doors of the poet's apartment toward the end of the hallway.

"Mr. Rilke arrived in Weimar with a cold and has been keeping to his rooms for the past three days," said Max.

At the end of the hallway was another large room filled with books. It was also a breakfast room.

"We eat lunch and dinner here," said Max G., "when we are alone. Alas, it happens rarely," and he smiled. "The books here," he explained, "are all French and English . . . and there on the table are magazines and newspapers. Graf Kessler gets at least a dozen dailies from all over Europe and the same quantity of magazines. We have two students, young men who speak English and French, who read them and prepare weekly résumés for Graf Kessler. They draw the Graf's attention to articles of particular interest. Then, every Monday, I have the magazines taken to our fireproof archives in the cellar, and the papers are thrown away. The archives are next to the wine cellar. Would you like to visit the cellar? It is supposed to be one of the best private cellars in Germany." I thanked Max G.

and suggested that we save the cellar for tomorrow.

In my room I found my clothes freshly pressed and hung on a valet rack. Even the mother-of-pearl studs were screwed into my stiff shirt.

"Nabi, *komm hier*," called Doderl from her room. I went in. She was lying naked on the bed. "God, I'm tired!" she said in a whining voice. "I went to sleep at three in the morning and made love all night. D'you think you could go to supper alone and tell Harry that I've gone to bed and can't come? I'm sure he'll understand."

But the Graf did *not* understand. He did not like it at all. The guests he was expecting from Cologne had motor trouble and did not arrive. The poet stayed in his room. Kessler looked tired and sulky. "At least she could have told me earlier that she wouldn't have supper," he grumbled. The three of us were alone—he, Max G., and I, dressed in starched shirts and dinner jackets.

"I'm exhausted," he said, leading me into the candlelit dining room. "I hope you don't mind if after supper I leave you and go to bed."

Max G. kept talking at the table about Diaghilev and Strauss, but Harry Kessler remained silent. Obviously he did not like it when plans did not work out the way they were supposed to. After dessert he got up, waved goodbye, and said in an acid tone: "I hope that your *Mädchen-freund* will feel rested tomorrow." He disappeared upstairs to his quarters.

Later I turned the lights off, went to the window, and opened it as wide as I could. The night was bright and starless, the air cool and sweetly scented. Not a breeze, not a sound. I sat on the windowsill, looking into the sleeping garden. "Why on earth did I come here?" I thought. "This is not my world. Not at all. Except for Doderl, of course."

Then my thoughts moved across the hallway to the other end of the house. "What is he doing now?" I thought. "Is he asleep? Someone told me that he is leaving Germany for good, settling in France. Why, I wonder?"

Suddenly, from behind the trees at the far end of the garden appeared the round, rust-colored face of the moon. "*La lune rousse*," I thought. "The first full moon of the summer, the moon of Merlin and French fairy-tales."

And, as if by order, a nightingale started a loud, ecstatic trill from somewhere quite close to the moonrise. I waited for an answer, but there was none. Instead, slowly, very, very gently, a poem made its way to the forefront of memory. A poem I had learned to love a few years before. Did it creep to me from across the hallway by some unknown telepathy . . . by someone's order? It was one of his earliest . . . surely one of his best.

> *Süddeutsche Nacht so reif im vollem Monde*
> *und mild wie aller Märchen wiederkehr.*

> South German night so ripe in the full moon
> and mild as the return of all the fairy-tales . . .

I forgot my irritation. I was happy again. At peace.

He reclined, cuddled up on a sofa in the corner of the music salon opposite the Blüthner concert grand. The lunch guests had departed to visit the Cranach Presse. Only Kessler, Rainer Maria Rilke, and I remained at the villa. He had huddled up in shawls and a Scotch plaid. Only the face, a very pale, emaciated one with drooping mustaches and light-gray, watery eyes, was visible inside the woolen package. The package looked as if someone were trying to comfort a very sickly lap dog, and as if the creature would start whimpering if deprived of its woolen warmth.

Kessler introduced me, as usual in French. "*C'est Monsieur Nicolas Nabokov*," he said, "the young composer I told you about. *C'est un Russe*. He arrived yesterday from Berlin."

"*O ja, ja! Je suis enchanté*," said the pale-faced creature in a barely audible voice. "Sit here beside me," and he made room for me on the sofa.

"He speaks German," said Kessler, "he speaks it as well as he does French."

"Oh, good." The face smiled at me. "Are you from St. Petersburg or Moscow," it asked, once the cough had subsided, "or maybe from somewhere else in Russia? Russia is so very large, isn't it?" And the face smiled again.

I told Herr Rilke that I had spent some of my early childhood abroad, some in the country in Russia, then in St. Petersburg, and that I had never been in Moscow except to drive in a sleigh from one Moscow railroad station to another.

Rilke looked astonished. "Isn't it rare," he said, "for a Russian not to have visited Moscow? It is such an extraordinary city. It is Russia's saintly place. So very special. Like no other city in Europe.

Half Asian, half European." And he looked at me searchingly. "But then you are young . . . you will get to Moscow sooner or later." And he mused awhile, as if remembering Moscow.

"Count Kessler told me that you are studying at the Music Academy in Berlin. I suppose that you will be going back to Russia after your studies, won't you?"

"He is an *émigré*," interjected Kessler. "His family left Russia a few years ago . . . after the Revolution."

"Oh, I see," said Rilke. "What a pity! But I am sure you will go back. It is, I am told, changing rapidly, now that the turmoil is over and Lenin's government is firmly in the saddle. They are bound to call on you. They will need educated young Russians." He smiled benignly and asked: "Where were you during the great Revolutionary years?"

"My mother and most of my family left Russia in 1919," I said. "None of us have any intention of returning."

There was a moment of silence. Rilke seemed perplexed, as if he did not know how to go on with the conversation. "Did you know Chekhov? He must have been a delightful person?"

"No, I did not know Chekhov," I replied. "I was much too young. Besides, my family wasn't in Yalta when Chekhov lived there. Chekhov died abroad," I said, "in southern Germany."

"Oh, yes, yes, I know," said Rilke, "there is even a monument there, in the municipal garden of Badenweiler. And I was also shown the room where he died."

"My family was acquainted with Chekhov's sister, Maria Pavlovna Chekhov," I said. "I visited her flat once in Yalta with my aunt and uncle."

"Oh, you did?" asked Rilke, getting interested. "What was she like?"

I hesitated. "It is difficult for me to say. I saw her only that one time. I remember she gave us tea with mountain honey and showed us Chekhov's room. It had been left untouched. I remember Chekhov's working table. Very orderly. A large, dark inkwell with many neat pens in penholders. There was a beautiful view from his table, far down to the Yalta harbor and the sea. When we left, my uncle told me that she was worried about the events in Russia. She had little money and food was hard to get in Yalta. That is all I remember."

"Thank you for telling me, *cher monsieur*. Only . . . only I do not quite understand what . . . what Chekhov's sister was worried about? Surely no one would hurt her, do harm to Chekhov's sister! Certainly not in Russia!" And Rilke looked at me, raising his eyebrows.

I evaded the question. I said that there was civil war at the time. Nobody knew what was going to happen. There was also an epidemic of typhoid fever.

"Never mind, never mind," interrupted Rilke, "it is difficult to know what people worry about and why they worry. Especially in such apocalyptic times. Because those years were apocalyptic years in Russia." In a pensive tone he added, "And not only for Russia . . ."

There was again a moment of silence. The butler brought in a tray and started arranging a teatable near the poet's sofa.

Rilke pulled out a large white kerchief and wiped his forehead. "I can't get rid of this beastly fever . . . it makes me feel so weak." He started coughing again.

"Maybe we should stop," suggested Kessler. "Perhaps you should go back to bed."

"No, no," said the poet through the cough, "I am interested to hear him. Perhaps you know that I have been to Russia. I was quite seduced by it. I loved its people, the places and the wide, open spaces. Of course, I was there before the Revolution . . . before the war."

He fidgeted with his shawl and, having arranged it, asked me: "But if you were in St. Petersburg at the time of the Revolution, and if your family, as Count Kessler told me, was concerned with the arts and the letters, you may have met Russian writers and poets. There are, for example, two poets of whom people speak incessantly, but whose works I think have so far not been translated into either German or French. Alexander Blok and that young revolutionary poet whose name begins with M . . ."

"Mayakovsky?" I asked.

"Yes, yes," said Rilke, "Mayakovsky. Did you meet either one of them?"

I said that I was too young at the time of the Revolution to meet poets.

"Blok died last year, in Petrograd," I added.

"I know, I know. It's a pity," said Rilke, again in a barely audible voice. "It's a great loss for Russia. I am told that he was one of Russia's best poets since Pushkin."

And again, silence. Max came in and poured tea for everybody. Rilke turned his face toward me and said: "A German publisher is asking me to translate Blok's poems. But I can't make up my mind. I do not know Russian, and it is a very difficult language, isn't it? And Russian is, I believe, not very pliable for translation. It is a complex and subtle language, so far as I can judge. When one translates a poem," he continued, "some of it inevitably gets lost. There is not only the meaning and the mood but the meter, the scansion, the rhythm, the word life, and the music of the poem . . . one's ear must be keenly aware of them," and he stopped again.

"I told the publisher," he continued, "that I would need three things before I would even attempt to translate a poet as complex as Blok must be. I need a literal word-by-word translation of the poem with indications of its Russian grammatical structure, then I need a careful and phonetically precise transliteration, and lastly I would need a civilized Russian, like you, for example," and he smiled at me, "a reciter, who would recite each poem aloud over and over again until I penetrate the poem's inner music. This is how I have translated poems from the Portuguese."

Suddenly the smile disappeared from his face. It grew thoughtful. He started speaking hesitantly: "I am a bit embarrassed to ask you this question—given your upbringing and milieu, you may be hostile—but I always ask every Russian that I meet this question." He looked at me sternly.

"I am fascinated by Lenin, and I know very little about him. What is your attitude? What do you think about Lenin? Because it seems to me . . . but I may be wrong . . . that he is . . . he must be . . . a great man. . . . A great man of our time . . . Tell me, what do you think of Lenin?"

I started by saying that Lenin was very little known in Russia before 1917. Then, that same year, in the wake of the Bolshevik power takeover and the ensuing terror, none of us liberal Russians could possibly like the Bolshevik regime and its leadership: we were its victims. Besides, they came to power by a *coup de force*, completely illegally.

Rilke listened attentively. But I felt that he was disappointed, incredulous.

"You know," I continued, "I have heard Lenin speak. I saw him at close range. It was in April 1917. He spoke from the balcony of the villa of the ballerina Kshessinska—"

Rilke interrupted me. "Oh, really!" he exclaimed. "How interesting. How was he?"

I said that it was not so much what he said but how he said it that impressed me.

"What do you mean?" asked Rilke.

"Well, you see . . . it was the tone of his voice. The manner of his speech amazed me. The contrast between the harsh things he was saying and the elegant way he was saying them. I should really tell you how it happened, but I don't want to tire you."

"Not at all. Please tell the story."

"Well, in April 1917 my tutor offered to take me to hear Lenin speak. As I've said, at that time Lenin was very little known in Russia, and just a vague notion to me. But I was eager to go. The trams were on strike. We marched along the quay toward the Neva to the villa of the famous ballerina, no less famous because she had been a mistress of Russian royalty. The day was damp and drizzly and there were only a handful of people, mostly women in shawls under black umbrellas. My tutor pointed out to me Boukharin, Zinoviev, and, I believe, Lunatcharsky and Kamenev. Then, suddenly, Lenin appeared, dressed in a winter coat and a worker's cap. He had mounted a platform which made him look taller than anyone else on the balcony. Immediately he started to speak. He spoke in a shrill, high-pitched voice, rolling his r's in the manner of upper-class salon snobs and using many 'barbarisms,' words of foreign extraction gleaned from the West European vocabulary of socialist political tracts. At that time the Russian language was still relatively pure and, as you know, very lovely. The language used by Lenin enhanced the feeling of elegant foreignness that his rolled r's conveyed. In addition, Lenin pronounced these foreign terms in a European manner.

"Only brief phrases remain in my mind's ear—*annexia, kontributsia, restitutsia*—but I remember how surprised I was by the contradiction between the content of what he was saying and his tone, accent, and vocabulary. I had read somewhere that Robespierre spoke elegant, upper-class French, and that it was the manner of his speeches that used to strike terror in the hearts of his occasional 'aristo' listeners.

"I remember shuddering at Lenin's performance that day, feeling a lump of fear clogging my throat. It seemed ludicrous. Here was a worldly man saying all these unpatriotic things in such upper-class-sounding Russian. Immediate peace without contributions or annexations, immediate abolition of landed property without any remuneration of the landowners, immediate demobilization, immediate takeover of power by the worker and peasant Soviets, and complete abolition of private property.

"I came home bewildered and deeply worried. There was something ominous in this early experience of Bolshevik ideology. Barely six months later all of us whom Lenin called the bloodthirsty wretched bourgeois class knew that he meant what he said."

When I finished speaking, there was a long silence. From a crouching position Rilke had switched to a sitting one. He had taken off his shawl and suddenly looked diminutive. He stared at the floor. He had picked up an ebony cane and was doodling on the rug with its tip.

"Thank you," he said in a somber voice. "Thank you very much, Monsieur Nicolas. It is not a gay story . . . but thank you for telling it so . . . candidly." He stood up and was about to leave.

But Kessler intervened. "Wouldn't you like Nabokov to play some of his music? He is writing a piano sonata, he told me. Perhaps he could play some of it, if you are not too tired?"

"Oh, no, I'm . . . not too tired."

I went to the piano and started playing. I played the first movement of my Scriabinesque piano sonata. I played it clumsily and noisily. I was glad when I came to the end of the first part and got up.

There was an awkward silence. Rilke did not say a word. Fortunately the butler came in and started rolling out the teatable.

Rilke undid his Scotch plaid, took it off his knee, and folded it. Then he looked gravely into my eyes and said in a tired whisper: "*Ich danke Ihnen sehr. Das war ein grosses Slavenereignis.*" (Thank you very much. That was a great Slavic experience.) I still do not know what Rilke meant, or whether he liked my music.

It was in Paris in 1934 that I saw Kessler for the last time. He was then an *émigré* in France. I had lunch with him at his sister's home, spent the day with him, and in the evening I took him and Misia Sert to see my ballet *La Vie de Polichinelle* at the Paris Opera.

I remember the despondency in his voice when he spoke of Hitler, the Nazis, and the outrage they were perpetrating in Germany.

I felt that the hurt in Harry Kessler was real and deep, and that there was a hopelessness in his sorrow.

We went together to Vespers at St. Julien le Pauvre. It was a warm spring day. The Romanian rite is the same as the Russian, lovely and peaceful, and the choir sang well. Kessler stood next to me, his face drawn, looking extremely pale and worn in the gray light of the church. I knew somehow that he was not praying, but just standing there in awe. He was watching, admiring, and loving the beauty around him, as he always did throughout his life.

After the service was over, we walked up and down the left bank, between Notre Dame and the Pont du Louvre, and he talked about the end of his hopes, his dreams, his life's efforts. His press in Weimar was closed and the furniture of his house was about to be sold. He was beginning to be short of money. His famous pictures and sculptures were gone.

"Now," he said, "I begin to understand what you Russians must have felt when you came to Berlin." And he added softly, as if talking to himself, "This thing in Germany will be long. I will not live to see the end of it."

We parted at dusk, I to my train to Salzburg, he to his homelessness. Now we were both members of the worldwide brotherhood of political *émigrés*. For him the glorious life of a famous patron of the arts was over, for me the life of a "rootless cosmopolitan" was already a habit.

There is a bit of an epilogue. In 1937, in America, I received a letter from a friend telling me that Kessler had died. It did not say what he had died from. That last time I had seen him in Paris he had said, *"Das Leben hat seine Sinne verloren,"* meaning that not *his* life, but *all* life had lost its meaning. Life had gone mad.

"Couldn't he have made an arrangement with them?" someone asked me.

But Harry Kessler could not. The only arrangement possible was jail, or probably extinction. Herr Hitler had no place for Harry Kessler.

I suppose that all his treasures, his art collections, his incredible library, his printing press, and his Weimar villa had been confiscated. But who, precisely, had made off with the spoils? Goering? Goebbels? Hitler himself? Or did they just catalogue all of it and store it away?

Harry Kessler was special in the way *grand seigneurs* tend to be special. They are difficult to define. He was interested in so many things. He would go from taking Pilsudski out of a German jail to be dictator of Poland, to Weimar to check the first proofs of his luxury edition of all versions of *Hamlet* printed by his Cranach Presse, to Vienna in time for Hofmannsthal's funeral.

He was deeply concerned about the arts. On them he spent money, energy, care, and love. But, as Picasso said, "When Diaghilev touched a picture with his eyes, it was like a cook at a market touching a carrot—will it be good for the soup? Diaghilev had to make fresh soup every year. Art, for Diaghilev, went into the soup." For Kessler it was magic, mystery, something to worship and love. Kessler's tastes lingered where they fell in love. There was something fleshy, palpable, and gregarious in the way Harry Kessler loved works of art. To him they were living creatures belonging to the same species as himself. As he said, *"L'art, c'est le prolongement de l'homme."*

He was the last of a breed. Educated and liberal, tolerant and modish, modest and grand, a bit snobbish and yet simple. He was infinitely generous. "If it hadn't been for Kessler, Maillol and many others would have starved," said Derain.

His salon was French in taste, French in its habits. But if it was less brilliant and abrasive than the Parisian salons, it was also less perverse and inbred and infinitely warmer, more humane, and indiscriminately hospitable. I remember once leaving with Gide after a party. *"Vous comprenez, mon cher,"* he exclaimed, making large gestures with his hands, "this here is so much simpler, so much kinder. Paris gives me claustrophobia, with its meanness and it unconcern for people." And Paul Valéry felt the same way, I know.

I hope Kessler died in peace.

"Look, look!" said my mother. "There he is." It was summer 1924 or 1925. In *émigré* Paris, we were sitting in one of those middling Russian restaurants which sprouted all over the world in the twenties, epicurean blessings of the October Revolution. Opposite us, in another corner of the restaurant, a waiter in Russian haberdashery was serving a plate of extinct *hors d'oeuvres* to a big man with a monocle and a flower in his buttonhole. A streak of white cut across his black hair from the right side of his forehead, reaching the back of his large, round head. He talked excitedly to the young man at his side.

I recognized him immediately. By 1924, I, and everyone else, knew the features of one of Europe's famous men; besides, I knew him instantly as the brother of Uncle Valya. Although the Colonel and Sergei Pavlovich Diaghilev were only half-brothers, the size and shape of their heads, the design of their eyebrows, and the form of their lips were so much alike that one could not miss the resemblance.

My mother had been talking to me for some time about the usefulness and necessity of my meeting Diaghilev. Now she seemed elated at the sight of him sitting across the room. "Finish eating, and let's go to their table," she said. "I'll introduce you to him." But I prevailed upon her to wait until Diaghilev and his companion had finished their meal.

All through the rest of the lunch she kept looking at the Diaghilev table, trying to catch his eye, and when she finally succeeded, she beamed at him in such an ostentatious manner that he could not but smile back in that politely irritated way one smiles at people whose faces one has forgotten and who appear to be potential bores (later I learned how terrified Diaghilev was of solicitous ballet mothers, who were constantly asking favors for their daughters).

When they had finished eating and asked for their bill (which my mother duly observed), she pulled my sleeve and said, "Come, it's time now." While we struggled past the crowded tables, Diaghilev rose and started putting on an enormous fur-lined coat.

"Sergei Pavlovich, *ne uznayote?* [Don't you recognize me?]" said my mother as we approached. He dropped his monocle and gazed at her with bewilderment, but before he could answer she identified herself and, turning to me, added, "And this is my youngest son, the one who writes music."

"Oh, *chère amie*, so you are the mother of the second half of Valya's quartet," he said in a gay, high-pitched voice. "Yes, of course I remember, we met in St. Petersburg." His face broke into a charming, benevolent smile. He put his monocle back in his eye and, taking my mother's hand, bent over and greeted her ceremoniously.

"What are you doing here?" he said. "Have you any news from Valya and Dasha? I haven't heard anything since 1921. You know, of course, that Pavlik and Alyosha either were killed in the last months of the civil war or have been executed. Valentin, I believe, is still in prison."

But my mother had no news and, seeing that he was about to

leave, abruptly changed the subject. "Sergei Pavlovich," she said, pointing to me, "I would like you to listen to his music. I want your opinion about it."

His face took on a bored expression and he mumbled hurriedly: "Yes, of course . . . sometime . . . gladly . . . but now I'm very busy . . . rehearsals, you know. Do give me a ring when you'll be back." And fixing me with an icy look, he added: "I'd love to listen to your music, *jeune homme*. I only regret it can't be now. *Au revoir, chère amie, je suis navré.*"

All this was said in such a cutting and final way that even my persistent mother did not dare attempt to delay his exit.

This first encounter was in the summer of 1924. I remember him as he stood flanked by his youthful companion, the fur-lined coat with its handsome beaver collar making his big, tall body and his tremendous head look even more majestic, more lordly, than it appeared in the pictures I had seen. I remember his tired, haughty look, his dark eyes, and the even darker bags under them. I remember the sallow, wasted color of his heavy-set but well-kept face with the neatly trimmed mustache, the protruding lower jaw, and the upturned upper lip, revealing, when he smiled, a row of dubiously new teeth.

There was always a faint scent of violets around him. (He used to chew tiny violet-scented bonbons.) But perhaps what my memory captured best that first time was his voice, his unique manner of speaking. He spoke in a high-pitched, nasal, and capricious tone and he dropped unaccented syllables of long Russian words as if he had swallowed them up.

When I finally succeeded in being presented to Diaghilev as a composer and not as Mama's son and an ephemeral relative (my stepfather's first cousin married Diaghilev's half-brother), I was received with reserve, politeness, and marked skepticism.

This time the road that led me to Diaghilev was the usual road, the same one that composers have traveled for centuries. Mrs. B. learned about me from Mr. A. and passed me on to Mrs. C., an active and kind lady who for many years ran a music salon in Paris. Mrs. C. invited me to a tea party and there introduced me to a Mr. D., who was about twenty-five percent more influential than the original Mr. A. Mr. D. told Mr. E. that I needed help. Mr. E., an elderly gentleman, a hunchback, and a relentless music lover, had a niece of Arab descent, Mademoiselle F., a lady in her middle thirties who was endowed with an extraordinary majestic bosom, a powerful voice, and a wooden leg. Mr. E. bullied his niece into learning three of my songs. Several months later, in the winter of 1925–26, she performed them at a hodge-podge concert of the Société Musicale Indépendante. This organization gave several concerts yearly, consisting of first performances of music by young composers.

The audience, bored and chatty, applauded abstractedly the twenty-odd pieces of music that preceded my songs.

When the time came for Mademoiselle F. and me to march onto the stage, we got stuck in the narrow passage leading to the stage and I unwittingly tripped up my wooden-legged diva. Fortunately she did not fall to the floor, but once onstage she turned to me and under her breath said that if it were not for the fact that we were onstage she would slap my face. This naturally upset me at the very outset of our performance.

After the end of the first song, which was long and tedious, written to poems of Omar Khayyám (translated into French from an English translation by FitzGerald), I saw that Prokofiev, whom I had somewhere and somehow met, was sitting right in the middle of the first row, smiling and quietly but insistently rubbing his chin, which in France means *Quelle barbe!* (What a bore!) I tried to look away, and in doing so caught a glimpse of another very familiar face, in the second row right behind Prokofiev. I recognized the bemonocled, bulldog countenance of Sergei Pavlovich Diaghilev, who, as I later found out, had been dragged in by Prokofiev to hear my music. This discovery made me so jittery that I lost control of myself and bungled the accompaniment of the remaining two songs.

Under those complex circumstances it was only natural that the concert ended as something of a failure, but the reasons for the failure were not entirely musical. I had been living in a small and cheap pension, and naturally the inmates of the pension came in a body to my concert. They had pooled their funds to send me a potted lilac bush with an enormous pink ribbon on each side of the pot. When the blooming bush arrived onstage right after my last Oriental number, the inmates, occupying two middle rows of the tiny Salle des Agriculteurs, burst into thunderous applause. Having, among other things, forgotten to send Mademoiselle F. flowers, and seeing that her temper was reaching an eruptive condition, I tore the card from one of the ribbons and, lifting the bush from the ground, sheepishly handed it to my Arab Polyhymnia. The cloudburst of applause ceased instantaneously. The whole pension in a body stopped speaking to me for several weeks.

But after the concert Prokofiev came backstage and said that Diaghilev was waiting in front in a taxi and wanted to see me.

When we came out, I was surprised to find Diaghilev in a gay mood. He smiled at me as he said, "Your songs were not too bad, not as bad as you think, but tell me, where for heaven's sake did you find that female monster, and why don't you leave Omar Khayyám alone? But you must come and show me your music. I mean your other music."

Thus I was spared any further wanderings through the dreary alphabet of contacts, and with my other music in hand, went to see Diaghilev at his residence in the Grand Hotel.

We sat around an upright piano in what was probably one of the banquet rooms of the hotel. Present besides Diaghilev and myself were Prokofiev; Valichka Nouvel, Diaghilev's friend and collaborator, a small wiry little man with glasses; Boris Kochno, Diaghilev's secretary and official librettist; and the recently discovered Serge Lifar.

I finished playing one movement of a piano sonata and followed it up with excerpts from a cantata I had been working on for a year. After I stopped, Diaghilev raised his eyebrows and said, "*Et bien? . . . C'est tout?*" I said yes, it was all I had to show.

While I was playing, Diaghilev leaned on the silver top of his cane, but as soon as I stopped, he slumped back into his chair and sat there with a bored expression, saying absolutely nothing.

After a while he turned to Boris Kochno and asked, "Boris, when does the rehearsal start?"

"I think it is on already," answered Boris.

"Then let's go." He got up hurriedly and said to me, "Thank you, Nika, for playing your music. When you have written more, come and show it to me. *Au revoir.*"

I felt let down.

"Don't pay any attention," said Nouvel, after Diaghilev had left, "that is his usual manner. On the contrary, if he had disliked your music, he would have been terribly polite and paid you all sorts of silly compliments. Am I not right, Sergei Sergeievich?" said he, turning to Prokofiev.

"Well . . . I think Nabokov should have waited to show him his cantata until he had finished it. This way it doesn't mean much," snapped Prokofiev.

Curiously enough, it was this very same cantata which became my first and only Diaghilev commission.

On a damp and foggy April evening in 1928 I was traveling to Monte Carlo at Diaghilev's invitation and expense. I was going there to work on the production of my ballet *Ode*, my first commission, my first important work. "Tomorrow," I said to myself, "I shall be walking on the warm, crackling gravel of the promontory behind the Casino, looking at the gentle carpet of the Mediterranean and the equally gentle, silky sky. Tomorrow I will begin to play my part in the most famous artistic enterprise in Europe."

I felt exhilarated and proud. I thought of the talks and discussions I would have with Diaghilev and his associates, with the many composers, painters, poets, and choreographers who would be in Monte Carlo with Diaghilev, preparing the new productions for the coming Parisian season. I thought of working with Léonide Massine, the choreographer, and Pavel Tchelitchev, the painter, whom Diaghilev had selected for my ballet; I imagined the excitement of rehearsals, the pleasure of seeing my composition take shape and form.

Valichka Nouvel had come to the station to see me off. He gave me the name of the hotel I was to go to in Monte Carlo and handed me a check—the second installment of my ballet commission. "Don't you get in a row with him," he said with a smile, "and come back in despair. It has happened, you know." But I was sure that everything was going to work out well, and that by the time I returned to Paris the ballet would be in splendid shape for its Parisian première.

On the train from Paris to Monte Carlo, Lyons usually appeared out of the darkness at the deadest spot of the night. As soon as the train stopped at the Lyons station, the corridors were crowded with scores of Moroccan and Algerian soldiers carrying large sacks, metal flasks, and cups hanging low on their leather belts. When the train started moving, these metal objects provided a rattling accompaniment to the guttural and rapid conversations in an Arabic dialect. From Vienne on, the train started playing hide-and-seek with the Rhône River, whose bed gets shallower and shallower as the train moves southward. Dawn overtook the *rapide* somewhere between

Valence and Montélimar, where you were awakened by shouts of "*Nougat de Montélimar!*" By the time the train reached Avignon and was ready to descend into the delta of the Rhône, the sky was all blue, the sun was all gold, and the naked and wintry landscape had changed to a sea of white and mauve, dusty green and bright, bright yellow. The sweet fragrance of the Provençal spring burst through the cracks of the windows into the tired train and chased away the last remnants of yesterday's cheese, wine, garlic, and sulfurous eggs that used to be an inevitable part of a French train trip.

That April, standing in the corridor of the time-worn French carriage amid the African *poilus*, I felt this fragrance pressing against me, invading me, choking me with irrepressible laughter and making the tears come to my eyes; I felt the intense joy that comes from the sight, the feel, the smell of all this mellowness, this beautiful sunlit abandon, this miracle of color and shape which Provence has always been to me and will always be to all men of the north.

Approaching Monte Carlo from Nice, the train started to worm its way past Cap Ferrat and around the Bay of Villefranche. Then, after one last smoke-filled tunnel, it slowed down, and suddenly on the south side of the tracks appeared the life-size version of the famed colored postcard—the Monaco peninsula topped by its medieval castle, with a cluster of quaint houses descending to the lapis-lazuli harbor.

I made my way to my hotel, and from there to the Salle Garnier. After a little questioning and searching I found a path through the labyrinth of gambling rooms, corridors, and rehearsal halls and stepped onto the stage. Diaghilev was sitting on the left side near an upright piano, his back turned to the empty theater. On a chair next to him sat a funny-looking man with thick glasses. Behind him, leaning against the piano, stood the massive figure of André Derain, who, hearing me creep up, turned his head, smiled, and signaled me to come and stand near him. Diaghilev couldn't see me; his back was turned and he seemed absorbed by what was happening on stage. Three ballerinas were clustered around and over a male dancer. The ballerinas were Tchernicheva, Doubrovskaya, and Nikitina, three of the best prima ballerinas of the company. The male dancer was Serge Lifar. That group's pose has since become famous in the annals of choreographic classicism: Lifar knelt among the three ballerinas, who were in an arabesque figure; each had one leg up in the air, their bodies dipped forward and their necks stretched upward so that they looked like three drinking swans whose precarious balance was maintained by a trembling hand firmly clutching Lifar's shoulder. In front of the group stood its inventor, the slight and incredibly young-looking choreographer George Balanchine, Diaghilev's recent discovery, his new choreographic genius.

Suddenly Diaghilev turned around. He saw me, and an ironic smile came over his face. He said in a teasing voice, "Ah, Nika, why are you so late? Where have you been all these weeks? Everybody has been waiting for you to start working." Without waiting for an answer, he pointed at Balanchine and said to Derain, "What he is doing is magnificent. It is pure classicism such as we have not seen since Petipa's." Then he turned his back on us again and continued watching the dancers on the stage.

I was startled, and felt abused by Diaghilev's rude reception. It was unfair and unjust; no one had told me that everybody was waiting for me in Monte Carlo to start working. On the contrary, I had been waiting for more than two weeks to hear from Diaghilev, but no word had come. Finally it had been Valichka Nouvel who decided to send me off. As I stood there getting madder every minute, Derain bent over and murmured, "Don't worry about it, he is in a bad humor."

Soon the rehearsal came to an end. Diaghilev got up and told me to come along with him to the hotel.

As we came out into the sunshine and started walking toward the Hotel de Paris, Diaghilev said, "Come on, Nika, I have to talk to you." He began by telling me that *Ode* was getting to be a problem, that no one really cared about it, and that everything was being mishandled from the very start. "Boris doesn't know what he wants to do with it and Massine knows even less. As for Tchelitchev, I can't make head or tail of his experiments, but I do know one thing: they have nothing to do with the original conception of *Ode*." He reproached me for showing no interest in my own work. "You should be here all the time and you shouldn't think that once the music is written your task is over." He said that the only reason he had decided to do *Ode* against his better judgment was that Lifar liked the music and wanted to have a second ballet for the coming season—"to satisfy his enormous vanity. You know, Seryozha hasn't a brain in his head, and the fact that he likes your music is therefore nothing to boast about."

While he was talking he grew more and more irritated and the adjectives he used became more abusive and unprintable. Finally, as we reached the doors of the Hotel de Paris, he said in his most exasperated tone, "If all of you continue to be indolent and lazy, nothing will come of your *Ode*. I can't do anything for you. I simply won't. I will wash my hands of the whole business. You had better go and find Boris and Seryozha and start working at once." Then abruptly he turned his back on me and went to the door. But before he started revolving he shouted at me once more, "If all of you finally decide to start working, don't pull the cart in three different directions. It will get stuck and I'm not going to help you pull it out of your mud!" And with a curt *"Au revoir,* I'll see you tomorrow," he disappeared.

It was only natural that, as a result of this monologue (it was the first time I had seen Diaghilev in a tantrum), my first evening in Monte Carlo, in the bosom of the "greatest artistic enterprise in Europe," was a melancholic flop.

Diaghilev's secretary Alexandrina, Boris, and I dined at a tiny restaurant and they tried to cheer me up. They said that it was just another one of those flurries of ill-temper which had become routine that spring. Boris assured me that everything was working out well, that Tchelitchev had invented marvelous sets for *Ode*, Massine liked them and was anxiously waiting for me to start working. "Of course," he said, "all will be ready by the time we leave Monte Carlo. Diaghilev is angry because he doesn't seem to grasp our ideas about the ballet. He isn't sore at you or at me but really at himself."

For the rest of the four weeks I spent in Monte Carlo my life was completely regulated. I worked with Massine from ten to one and sometimes again from three to six. I thumped out over and over again parts of my ballet on the horrible little upright pianos which populated the rehearsal halls of the Monte Carlo theater. Massine was composing the choreography while I played, and in the intervals between sections he would ask me to explain the construction of the music. "Where does this melody end? What instruments hold this chord? Is it correct for me to assume that this is one long phrase?" Then he would take profuse notes in an imposing leather-bound scrapbook which he carried around.

Contrary to what I expected, Massine, who in those years was usually stern and taciturn, was voluble with me, and at moments even gay and smiling. On the whole, our work progressed without a hitch. There was, however, an inherent anomaly in our collaboration. It came from the fact that I had no experience whatsoever in working with a choreographer. To judge choreography in the rough, under the drab conditions of a rehearsal hall, requires experience and imagination. I felt unable to make any valid judgment about what Massine was doing, for what I saw were disconnected bits of a whole which my imagination could not put together. Besides this, there was something disconcerting in having to repeat the same measures at the piano hundreds of times and see the same steps accompany them. At times I felt so completely dulled at the end of a rehearsal that I did not know whether I liked the ballet or not. How could I know whether it was good or bad? I did what many young composers do with their first stage works—I acquiesced in almost everything Massine did with my music. After all, he was a famous choreographer who had been in the business for more than a decade, while I was a newcomer. When he would ask me, "Do you like this?" or "Do you think this fits your music?" I would usually say yes.

Not until the broad outlines of the choreographic whole began to be recognizable (which happened about the third week of my stay in Monte Carlo) did it dawn on me that with the exception of two or three lovely lyrical dances, Massine's choreography, although probably very good in itself, had very little to do with my music and with the eminently romantic mood of *Ode*. Naturally enough, it was Diaghilev who made me aware of it. He came one day to a morning rehearsal and watched Massine compose a dance for Serge Lifar. He sat through half of it, his eyes closed, his head drooping. Then, without saying a word, he got up and left. Astonished, Massine and I looked at each other. Massine laughed and said, "I don't see the point of his coming to rehearsals when he does nothing but sleep through them."

But Diaghilev had not slept. Quite the contrary, he was very much awake and equally upset. At eleven o'clock that evening I was hauled out of bed by a messenger who told me that Diaghilev was waiting for me in the rehearsal room, that he wanted to see Lifar's dance again, and that several messengers had been dispatched all over Monte Carlo to search for Lifar and the librettist Kochno, who were somewhere at a party.

When I arrived at the theater, Diaghilev was all alone in the tiny office next to the rehearsal room. Though angry, he was calm with me and looked genuinely concerned. He said that what he had seen that morning was "utter rubbish," that Massine did not understand anything at all—"not the first thing"—about *Ode*. He said that he wanted to see it now, again, without Massine's presence (Diaghilev and Massine had been at odds since the early twenties), but that Lifar and Kochno could not be found. He then gave me a long, instructive talk about how he imagined the choreography of my ballet. He saw it as romantic, lyrical, with rich, suave, and soft movements, "rather of a Fokinesque" character. "At moments it should be pure pageantry—festive, glittering, and brilliant. At other moments it should be tender, mysterious, and gentle. What Massine is doing is modern, cold, angular stuff that has nothing to do with your music."

We waited for more than an hour, but neither Lifar nor Kochno appeared. Finally he said in a sad, tired way, "Nika, you had better go back to bed. I'm sorry about your ballet, but what can I do? Nobody seems willing to cooperate."

After the night of crisis Diaghilev never brought up the subject of *Ode*, nor did he ever seem interested in Massine's choreography. He stopped coming to rehearsals to see what Massine was doing, and when I would mention my ballet in his presence he would keep silent or change the subject.

Only once did he acknowledge the fact that *Ode* still existed, when he asked me to bring over the score and the orchestral parts because the orchestra had twenty minutes of free time and could read it through. I tried to dissuade him by saying that *Ode* was forty minutes long and that, besides, the parts were still full of mistakes. He replied that Scotto, the conductor, would read it through in a fast tempo, and as for the mistakes, they were not his concern but my funeral.

That orchestral reading was one of the worst musical tortures of my life. Scotto had never seen the score before and was beating the beat in double time as best he could.

The parts, because of my inexperience and the copyist's carelessness, were a sea of mistakes. Diaghilev and I sat in the front row in the dark hall. Every time I wanted to jump up from my seat, the heavy hand of Diaghilev kept me back: "Don't disturb them. They haven't much time."

The piece we heard was a mass of inchoate rumblings and noises reminiscent of the tuning-up period of a school orchestra. At the end I felt limp and beaten. Diaghilev turned to me and said, "You

155

like that?" and without waiting for an answer got up and went out of the theater.

At the same time I began to realize that Diaghilev's earlier prediction was coming true: the "cart" named *Ode*, or what there was of the cart, was definitely being pulled in several directions. I did not know what Tchelitchev was doing (he was guarding his work from any intrusion on my part), nor did I quite like or understand what Massine was doing with the choreography.

Only once was I permitted to attend the ritual of Tchelitchev's experiments—he needed me to time some film shots he had made for *Ode*. I saw some extraordinary pictures of young men wearing fencing masks and tights diving in slow motion through what seemed to be water. I could not understand what this had to do with my ballet, but I was told by Kochno (Tchelitchev wouldn't speak to me), who had, in default of Diaghilev, somehow assumed the responsibility for the production of *Ode*, that this represented "the element of water."

Much as I respected the "element," I still could not understand what connection it had with my music and the whole conception of the ballet. All in all, when I left Monte Carlo, a successful production of *Ode* seemed hopelessly remote. Massine's choreography was only half finished, Tchelitchev's decor was a total mystery to me, but I knew that it was largely still in an experimental state and that Diaghilev had had several tantrums about it. Worst of all, so far as I was concerned, was my own orchestration (my first attempt at writing for a large orchestra), which in part did not "sound" at all, and which needed intense overhauling. I left Monte Carlo filled with apprehension and dark forebodings.

I arrived in Paris only a few weeks before the ballet season was to open. The press had already begun to print anticipatory articles about the new productions. I was pestered by so many social calls, interviews, and dinner invitations that my friends Sauguet and Desormière decided to hide me in the apartment of a musical friend, where I could quietly reorchestrate certain sections of *Ode* and correct its orchestral parts.

Finally, ten days before the start of the season, Diaghilev and the ballet troupe arrived in Paris and the rehearsals began again. Massine and I renewed our long morning sessions and in a few days he completed the choreography. The Tchelitchev side of the project, so far as I knew, remained on the same equivocal plane as ever. But this time I was shown some of the drawings for the sets and costumes. Kochno even showed me a complete little model of the stage, with the opening scene of the ballet. For the first time I began to realize what Tchelitchev wanted to achieve.

The model was all in blue tulle, which when lit with a tiny flashlight became strangely alive and acquired an extraordinary mysterious and ephemeral beauty. I also understood that Tchelitchev's whole project depended on many intangibles.

It required mechanical perfection and virtuosity in the use of lighting equipment (then still in its infancy), perfect coordination between light and movement, between the camera (for many of the "light sets" were achieved by means of motion-picture projections) and the music, between the choreography and the changes of scenic effects.

To all this, up to the last two or three days before the first performance of *Ode*, Diaghilev remained completely indifferent. It seemed as though he had abandoned all of us to disaster.

On the morning of June 2, 1928, the telephone rang very early, despite the warning I had left the night before at the hotel desk not to disturb me until ten. I had returned late that night after a full day of rehearsals, an orchestral reading of *Ode*, and a grueling choral rehearsal. Diaghilev had come to the theater with Prokofiev, but had left brusquely before it ended.

At first I thought of just letting the telephone ring, but the thing persisted. I picked up the receiver and was about to bark a curse into it when to my utter surprise I heard the voice of Diaghilev shouting at me.

"Why don't you answer your phone? Why are you sleeping when you should be in the theater? Get up right away and come to the theater. This mess can't go on any longer. I have ordered a full stage rehearsal at ten, a full orchestra rehearsal at two, a full chorus rehearsal at five, and all evening we will rehearse the lights." He hung up on me just as abruptly as he had started shouting.

From that moment on, and for the next three days, until the last curtain had fallen on a highly successful performance of *Ode*, I lived in a state of frenzy. Like everyone else connected with the production, I worked day and night, in an agony of sleeplessness and exhilaration the like of which I never experienced before or since.

157

Diaghilev had taken over in the fullest sense. He gave the orders, he made the decisions and assumed the responsibilities. He was everywhere, his energy was limitless. He ran to the prefect of police to have him overrule the fire department's decision forbidding the use of neon lights on stage, which Tchelitchev wanted for the last scene of the ballet. (Neon lights, a novelty at the time, were considered unsafe.) He supervised the dyeing, cutting, and sewing of costumes. He was present at every orchestra and choral rehearsal and made the conductor, Desormière, the soloists, and the chorus repeat sections of the music over and over again until they blended well with the choreographic movements and the light-play of Tchelitchev's scenery. He encouraged the leisurely and sluggish stagehands of the Théâtre Sarah Bernhardt by bribes and flattery. He helped all of us paint the props and the scenery.

But above all else he spent two whole nights directing the complicated lighting rehearsals, shouting at Tchelitchev and at his technical aids when the delicate lighting machinery went wrong, at me when my piano playing slackened and became uneven, and at Lifar when his steps ceased following the rhythm of the music and the changes of lighting.

On June 6, the day of the opening, I was exhausted, stunned and shaking with the kind of precarious excitement which comes after long exertion and sleeplessness. But when, fifteen minutes before the curtain went up, I saw Diaghilev come in through the backstage door in full evening dress, bemonocled, his famous rose pearl shining on a snow-white shirt, I knew that it was only thanks to this man's incredible drive and energy that *Ode* had been pieced together and that the curtain could be raised at all.

Until the last minute I had been painting scenery, and I had seen Diaghilev leave the theater an hour before the performance was to begin. He had looked worn, gray, and sallow as he crossed the stage, his face covered with a two-day growth of beard. Now he was his usual self, calm, confident, and resplendent.

He stopped before me and told me to go out front into the theater. I mumbled something to the effect that I hoped all would go well and that the performance would be a success.

"Well," answered Diaghilev nonchalantly, his face changing to a charming, affectionate smile, "it's up to you," and he opened his arms and moved them backward in the suave and deliberate gesture of a virtuoso conductor, by which in apparent modesty he raises the orchestra musicians to their feet and makes them acknowledge the public's applause.

I saw Diaghilev for the last time in July 1929, a little more than a year after *Ode*'s first performance. We met briefly at the Baden-Baden music festival. He was in the company of his old friend the Princesse de Polignac (Paris's greatest music patron of the time) and his new youthful composer-find, the bird-like and brittle Igor Markevich.

Diaghilev did not look well; his face was puffy with the glazed yellow quality of diabetics during or after an attack. He had come to Baden-Baden to hear a new work by Hindemith, "his" new composer-collaborator. After the performance of this work I walked him back to his hotel. Despite his appearance, his mood seemed happy. He talked gaily about his plans for the rest of the summer and for his autumn season. "I am going to take Markevich to visit Richard Strauss and to a few Wagner performances at the Munich Opera," he said. "Then I'm going to the Lido, as usual. Why don't you come with us?"

But, much as I would have liked to go, I was bound for Berlin on the morning train.

I asked Diaghilev how Hindemith's ballet was progressing. He answered that he had spent a day with Hindemith in Berlin and that very little of the ballet music was actually on paper. "But I'm not worrying. I know what an extraordinary craftsman he is and how fast he works."

He asked me what I was writing and when I told him that I was in the middle of my first symphony he grew interested and wanted to know all about it—what it was like, whether it was going to be as lyrical and romantic as *Ode*, how many movements there would be, and how soon it would be ready. "Splendid!" he exclaimed. "As soon as I'm back in Paris you will play it for me, won't you? I also want you to look carefully at the music of young Markevich. It's exceptional stuff—still very green, but enormously gifted."

Three weeks later I was returning from Berlin to my summer home in Alsace. As usual, I took the night train, which left Berlin at six or seven p.m. Around ten o'clock the train stopped at Halle. I went out and bought the Halle evening paper. I couldn't read in the compartment, the lights were down, so I went to the men's room. There, in the dim light of its twenty-five-watt bulb, I peered at the front page of the paper. At the top, in the right-hand corner, I saw a two-line message from Venice. It was dated August 19 and read: "This morning at five a.m. the famous Russian dancer Diaghilev died here."

The shock, the loss, and the feeling of emptiness were overwhelming. Why did he have to die? What would happen now to his work? And what would happen to all of us, his friends, his artistic collaborators, his troupe of dancers? I went to the post office and sent incoherent telegrams to Kochno, to Misia Sert, to George Balanchine, to Prokofiev.

Gradually the circumstances of his death became known to me. He died of an attack of diabetes, his old neglected illness. He suffered a great deal, physically and morally. All his life he had been afraid of sickness, of loss of power and consciousness. When the attack began, he must have known that his days, his hours, were counted. Near him were two close friends, Lifar and Kochno. Later, during the last few days of his life, three other faithful friends arrived, Misia Sert, Coco Chanel, and the Baroness d'Erlanger.

He died at dawn on August 19, at the age of fifty-seven, after a long, tormented agony. He died as he had lived all his life, in a hotel room, a homeless adventurer, an exile, and a prince of the arts.

And just as his life had been a strange and exotic pageant, so was his death. On the morning of August 21 a procession of four gondolas took his body to the Russian cemetery on the tiny San Michele Island. The coffin was covered with tuberoses, tea roses, and carnations. A Russian priest and the small choir of San Georgio dei Greci sang the doleful chants of the Slavic funeral service while the procession moved to the cemetery through the still waters of the Venetian lagoon.

It was a gray, soggy, and damp day in October 1927, a typical Paris sneezer. I felt uneasy and apprehensive about what was in store for me within the next few hours.

Finally Diaghilev and I heard steps on the winding staircase and two diminutive figures surfaced from below; first the familiar form of Nouvel, and behind him, also familiar from portraits and photos, but wrapped in shawls and mufflers, Stravinsky's head, hidden by a wilted black felt hat. What caught my immediate attention were the neat light-gray spats and, when he took off his raincoat, the gold chains that crisscrossed his waistcoat.

I had known that Stravinsky was small, but I was startled by his size, perhaps because he was so wiry—the opposite of the usual little fat man of France—but also because his egg-shaped head on its stem-like neck was so large in relation to the body. There was something ancient, Assyrian, in Stravinsky's face, something bird-like and beaky. And at the same time, something of a fairy-tale magician from out of the dark Russian woods, a *lesovichok,* a forest imp of Russian lore, went through my mind.

The lunch was long and dreary. I sat in a daze, feeling unwanted and, at the same time, unable to speak. I only hoped that I could soon get it over with, not only the lunch, but the whole day with its afternoon "examinational torment"—my playing my music for Stravinsky.

But as we walked outside and waited for a taxi, something happened that has stuck in my memory. A young man and a girl darted at Stravinsky and timidly asked for his autograph, holding in their hands old concert programs.

Stravinsky bent over the programs, asked for the date, and signed his name and the date. Then the taxi came and we were off.

"You see," grumbled Diaghilev mockingly, "I am much older than he and, heaven knows, have done many more things here in Paris, but they do not ask me for an autograph, they want his."

Oh, how gloriously kind and charming Stravinsky was that afternoon after the gloomy lunch *chez* Prunier, and, God, was I scared to play my music for him!

Diaghilev stood behind me breathing down my neck, flanked by Kochno and Nouvel. Lifar sat on my right to turn the pages, although he could not read a note of music. Stravinsky sat very close to me on my left, his spectacles raised onto his forehead.

"Must you write so sloppily?" he said, looking at my untidy, penciled manuscript. "One can barely read it!"

I was glad when Diaghilev tapped my shoulder and told me to start playing. I played the introductory chorus to *Ode* and then one of its lyrical ariettas, singing it in a mixture of bass and falsetto.

Suddenly I saw Stravinsky lean forward and start helping me with his left hand, playing the bass part. His frown had given way to an amused and what seemed to me a pleased smile.

When I stopped at the end of the first arietta, Stravinsky said, "Continue, continue, this is quite good. I did not expect *ce truc là.*"

And so, with his help, I played another air of *Ode,* a duet, attempting to sing both the soprano and the bass parts.

But Stravinsky stopped me and said, "Sing just the soprano, I'll figure out the bass myself."

Suddenly I saw another hand move to the keyboard and a goat-like bass joined my castrato-like soprano. That was George Balanchine, who had squeezed himself between me and Lifar and with his usual deftness was hammering out the treble part and singing the bass.

When we came to the end of the piece, everybody laughed. Stravinsky turned to Diaghilev and said in a happy tone of voice, "You know what it's like? It's as if it were written by a predecessor of Glinka, someone like Gurilyov or Alyabiev." And then smilingly at me, "From where do you know all this Russian salon music of the 1830s? It is unmistakably and naïvely Russian."

I did not know what to answer. Stravinsky got up and, turning to Diaghilev, said, "Of course you should perform this music."

A few minutes later we walked down the narrow staircase of the Diaghilev studio and Stravinsky offered to drive me back to the place where I lived.

Once in the taxi, Stravinsky started to ask me questions as if I were the center of his interest. He wanted to know everything. He asked me where I had lived in St. Petersburg, who my parents were, what they were doing, where I had studied music and with whom. He laughed when I told him stories about my teacher Rebikov. "I knew him," Stravinsky said. "He may have been *un original*, but his music was not. But I hear you are a friend of Seryozha Prokofiev. Are you?"

I replied that I had met Prokofiev two years earlier and that we had become close friends. "I always go and show my music to Prokofiev, and he shows me his," I added.

Stravinsky's face grew stern. "I do like Seryozha Prokofiev," he said, "but as for his music . . . it is so uneven . . . not only uneven, there's something *primaire* about it . . . and at times uncouth . . . its spirit is alien to me."

After a pause he added, "I advise you not to let yourself be influenced by Prokofiev. It is not quite healthy for your own music. From what I heard of it, yours is delicately lyrical. His is also lyrical, but never gentle . . . not nostalgic, like what I heard in your music."

When we arrived at my hotel, Stravinsky let me go with a warm handshake and a broad smile.

"I hope to see you soon again . . . and let me call you Nika, may I?"

These were the last years of Diaghilev's Ballet and of its founder's life. While in Monte Carlo in the spring of 1928, when George Balanchine was working on Stravinsky's *Apollo* and Léonide Massine on my *Ode*, I received glowing reports about *Apollo*'s music. I was told that it was classical and yet, in a tongue-in-cheek way, ironic.

But not, of course, ironic in the sense of a spoof, not funny in the slightest bit . . . quite to the contrary, it was often tenderly lyrical and all the time profoundly earnest . . . yet it represented an ingenious and typically Stravinskyan amalgam of nineteenth-century ballet genres from Adam through Delibes to Tchaikovsky and even to such second-raters as Minkus.

Balanchine, on the other hand, spoke of the inherent difficulties of translating this limpid and pure music into an adequate ballet style. "You understand, it's like Mozart," he exclaimed, implying that Mozart is about the most difficult music for a responsible choreographer to deal with.

As I think of it in retrospect, I realize what a work of choreographic genius *Apollo* was in its time.

Classical ballet did not exist in pre-Balanchine, pre-Stravinsky days. What passed under the trademark of "classical ballet" (and still is being peddled as such) was in fact romantic stuff based on a dance vocabulary and syntax—an inventory of steps, movements, and figures—derived from past centuries of classical tradition. Purely classical ballet and classical choreography had probably been extinct since the time of Gluck and Vestris. What nineteenth-century ballet masters did, right up to Balanchine, was to put at the service of romantic subject matter choreography based on traditional classical techniques. And these techniques had been developed long ago, during the early classical centuries of Italy and Medicean France, to suit the allegorical and mythological needs of court ballets.

Most if not all of nineteenth-century ballet was therefore romantic in content and only derivatively speaking "classical" because of its technical vocabulary. And maybe its charm and its success resided in the inherent antinomy between content and form that it exhibited.

The romantic movement, despite all of its glory, was a nonchalant and lazy movement so far as technique was concerned. To invent a technique of its own was not one of its major concerns. The romantics were not patient enough, nor had they a sufficient regard for any kind of logical (and hence rational) system. Especially not when it dealt with such a "minor art" as ballet.

This is why it is hazardous to oppose the terms "romantic" and "classical," at least as far as ballet is concerned, as it is wrong to call a ballet such as *Giselle* or *Les Sylphides* anything but a romantic ballet. Anything else would be a misnomer.

When Balanchine was faced with the music and the subject matter of *Apollo*, he had to invent a classical ballet style from scratch. The result was an astounding work of unsurpassed perfection in which every step, every movement, every pose and structural device grew out of musical needs, and was at the same time a reassertion and sublimation of classical technique and its ancient vocabulary and syntax. And one felt as one feels when one watches the Spanish Riding School in Vienna—the famous Lippizaners—that it was not a rebirth, but the birth of a truly new classical style. One also felt, as with most works of intuitive genius: How did no one think of it before?

And this assertion of Balanchine's *Apollo* (that classical technique is not just a vocabulary but the "ground" of an art form) is what Diaghilev perceived when he called it a *"ballet blanc"* or *"blanc sur blanc."* It was to ballet what the invention of Mondrian's white-on-white and Malevich's black-on-white square was to the rise of abstract art.

From *Apollo* onward one can—and indeed one *must*—speak of a new true classicism in ballet as one of the extraordinary artistic inventions of the twentieth century and of its protagonist, George Balanchine.

But *Apollo* was only the first step in this new direction, or at least the first recognizable one. From it gradually arose the new classicism of George Balanchine which is now the glory of America and of several generations of American dancers. In more ways than one, George Balanchine turned the tables of ballet's fortune and its future. He relegated the musty romantic stuff still pervading some dance companies of Europe (and still the source of lucrative business for art merchants) to past history and replaced it with something which is not only attuned to our time but parallel with the currents that prevail in other arts. He also reflects the true attitude of a ballet master for whom technique and art are inseparable, showing that classical dance means nothing more nor less, but also nothing else, than a faithful translation of heard music to visual music.

Yet the rise of George Balanchine's new classicism would never have been possible had there not been Stravinsky's own new classicism.

To me it seems there can be no doubt that soon, much sooner than one thinks, Stravinsky's new classicism will be fully vindicated and considered a necessary and sound historical development if only because it gave birth to the new classicism in ballet, which would never have been born had there not been the forty-year-long collaboration between Stravinsky and Balanchine. Like a sleuth, Balanchine entered into the innermost core of each one of Stravinsky's compositions. And, as if reconstructing a crime, he translated it into the language of dance, his visual music. No one had ever done that before, nor could anyone do it again. Not with the music of Stravinsky. It is Stravinsky's music, with its classical style, with all its ironic over- and undertones, that gave birth to Balanchine's new classicism. The shrewd and discriminating musician that Balanchine is found a way to penetrate into the essence of Stravinsky's art and to translate into bodily movement all of its intricacies and complexities.

Did I, in 1928, grasp any of it? I do not think so. Somehow, darkly in the mists of memory remains the feeling of having been made uncomfortable by the music of *Apollo* when I first heard it. For even by comparison with Stravinsky's preceding compositions it seemed to me to be too artificially restrained and stylistically "quotational." It was only much later that I learned to love the music of *Apollo*. Curiously enough, its lyrical beauty appeared to me at a ballet rehearsal, many years later, when Balanchine was working on it with his company in America.

But there were alleviating circumstances for the misunderstanding in 1928. The decors of the French neo-primitive painter Bauchant-Jeune (he always insisted on that "*Jeune*" although he was in his untidiest sixties) seemed appallingly silly to me. I do not know who induced Diaghilev to commission them from that "curio," but they were certainly detrimental to both the music and the dance.

Then there was also the meager quality of Diaghilev's string orchestra stretched out in the narrow orchestra pit of the old Théâtre Sarah Bernhardt, which Diaghilev used to call *"mon pissoir."* Poor Roger Desormière, already one of France's best conductors, could do nothing about improving the quality of the sound arising from that hideously anti-acoustical pit.

But, above all else, *Apollo's* première was just a few days away from the première of my *Ode,* and I was in a justified state of dithers. I could not listen to *Apollo* as intently as I should have. Certain now-celebrated images of the choreography stuck in my mind, but not the music. It was through those choreographic forms that later on I found my way back to Stravinsky's music and was permanently converted by its beauty and its imaginative string writing.

On the whole, those last Diaghilev years did not do anything to further our friendship. There was too much "societal traffic" around Diaghilev's Paris seasons, most of which Stravinsky wisely avoided, but which I then enjoyed. It was time- and wit-consuming, but terribly seductive. To me, at the age of twenty-five, it seemed gay, clever, and amusing. Those were, after all, my own Gay Twenties. I came to them late, toward the very end of the decade, after many lean years of exile. No wonder I threw myself headlong into all of those Parisian pleasures my sudden (but, ah! so relative) fame could provide. I was profligate with everything from time and menus to love-making, passing through the whole spectrum of hedonistic enjoyments.

But what separated us then was the "generation gap." Stravinsky was so much older and very, very famous. I was a beginner and very green. I did not dare approach him as an equal. I was much too much in awe of Stravinsky as a master of twentieth-century music.

"Dammit," I cursed, pushing and pulling on the pedals of a Pleyel harpsichord, unable to obtain from that beastly animal anything but irritatingly buzzing sounds that make one think of flypaper and fly agonies. In 1930 I had been commissioned by the Maison Pleyel to write a piece for the new harpsichord they were putting on the market, and given a studio with a harpsichord in it. Suddenly there was a knock at the door of my studio, and before I could say *"Entrez,"* Stravinsky and his shadow, Arthur Lourié, came in.

"Did you know we are neighbors?" Stravinsky said. And he

pointed to a door on the opposite side of the dark corridor that ran between two rows of studios. "Come to my place."

Lourié unlocked Stravinsky's door and we walked into his studio. From that morning on through the three or four weeks of Stravinsky's stay in Paris, my life was concentrated on being with Stravinsky, waiting for Stravinsky, and spending all the time I possibly could muster at his side.

He lived somewhere in St. Cloud and would come to his studio between nine and ten in the morning. He would peep into my pen and say: "Nika, let's go and have a *petit café arrosé* at the corner and then I'll start working."

The *café arrosé*, meaning coffee with Calvados, which at the time Stravinsky liked, would inevitably be followed by deciphering at his piano, four hands, a cantata or a passion by Bach, or an oratorio by Handel. Stravinsky was a superb score-reader and I a miserable one. He would shout, *"Merde, alors!"* every time I made a mistake. But then when he had enough of playing, he would hug me and say, "Thank you, dear Nika, for playing with me. Now you go back to your room. I have to work."

Usually he went out for lunch, with Lourié or Vera Arturovna de Bosset, whom I had met two years earlier at a Diaghilev rehearsal, or with other friends of his. But sometimes we would walk over to the Russian restaurant across from the Russian church on the Rue Daru. We would drink vodka and eat a *pirozhok* (Russian meat- or cabbage-filled pastry), and then Stravinsky would say: "Now you order whatever you want. I am, you know, on a diet and can eat only raw things."

Then Stravinsky would explain to the disconsolate waiter: "Bring me a plateful of sliced raw potatoes and tomatoes with no salt or pepper, but with half a lemon and some olive oil on the side."

Stravinsky would eat his horrid mixture, saying: "In fact it's quite good. It tastes a bit sour, like earth . . . or like what the pigs eat."

I would order those Russian ovaloid meatballs with the noble name of Côtelettes Pojarsky. Stravinsky would say to the waiter: "Bring him three. He is big, hungry, and needs meat."

And then, when I was full after two *côtelettes*, Stravinsky would pick up the third, cover it with sour cream, and, winking at me slyly, would say, "I want to astonish the raw potato in my stomach."

Those weeks in the summer of 1930 in Paris were to me a gift from heaven. That was the time when the knot of our friendship was tied for good. We started to have intimate talks, exchanges of views, mono- and dialogues, all of which, like everything that came from Stravinsky, were unrepeatably personal, angry or funny, gentle or harsh, but always exciting, always full of meaning, and always marvelously partisan.

Now, nearly fifty years later, some keep coming back.

"I always compose at the piano. I need to hear the physical sound, not an imaginary one. Only then can I imagine how it will sound played by this or that instrument or instrumental combination.

"You see, I was never trained as an instrumentalist, but only as a composer. Piano was *nebenbei*, which, I suppose, is a wrong, nineteenth-century pedagogical innovation. J. S. Bach and his son Philip Emmanuel were trained as instrumentalists. Indeed, in those centuries, to be a composer was incidental. The primary task was to be an instrumentalist. Thus, the two Bachs and, for that matter, Mozart and Diabelli, because of their instrumental training, had a clear and natural perception ever present in their minds as to how a lump of music would sound 'physically.' The sound of their instruments was constantly present in their heads.

"I, alas, and, for that matter, most composers of my generation have had none of this. And to write abstractly, without a precise physical representation of the instrumental sound clear in my mind is impossible, it is even odious to me."

One day when the heat made him leave his studio door open I heard Stravinsky get up, pace the room for a few minutes, go back to his piano, hit the same chord and mutter in French, *"Pas de pitié."* I walked into his studio and asked if I could do something for him.

Without turning around, he said, "No, nothing, Nika, thank you," and continued erasing with a large pencil eraser.

Then he turned to me and said sententiously: "Never have self-pity. Never give in to any kind of self-indulgence when you compose. Approximations won't do in music. To compose is like shooting darts—one has to hit the O right in the middle. All the rest does not mean anything at all . . .

"Music, or rather, sounds and sound molecules come to me from the outside, from everywhere.

"My ear, the inner and the outer one, is always open and greatly enjoys listening to sounds in their state of *matière première*. Sometimes these sounds are useless, but sometimes they excite me and I get, as it were, an erection of my inner ear. Then I start to manipulate these sounds at will and little by little something close to a spermatozoon creeps out of those manipulations.

"Look, for example, at this piece," and Stravinsky pointed at a neat manuscript lying on the table—the sketch of the *Symphony of Psalms.*

"Two years ago I heard somewhere something which I wrote down. Then I manipulated it and it became an embryo of those two minor thirds that make up the main theme of this piece. If I showed you the sketchbook you would not recognize the relation between what I wrote down then and the actual theme the way it is now. But in my memory I can reconstruct the whole process, step by step.

"Art and, in my case, making music is to make order," he said, "to invent orderly structures of sound, in orderly time and space. I must have a root, or roots, as poles of attraction. Call it whichever you want: tonality, modality, root-ality. It must be discernible by the ear in each phrase, in each sentence."

It was a Saturday, the day when the choir of the Russian church opposite had its longest and loudest rehearsal. And every time, at the height of a fortissimo, the choir would stop because the sopranos— perhaps due to a mistake in their parts—would make the same mistake. They would move a half-tone upward, instead of a whole tone.

Stravinsky had been complaining about the coda of the last movement of the *Symphony of Psalms.* "I simply can't find an end for the last movement. Every time I think I have found it, it goes wrong and then, *pas de pitié,* I erase it."

Suddenly I heard him come into my studio and put his hands on my shoulders. "From where comes this singing?"

"Oh," I said, "listen to that, Igor Fedorovich. They have been singing the same phrase over and over again for the last fifteen minutes, and every time, on the third repeat of the phrase, the sopranos make the same mistake. They move a half-tone upward instead of a whole tone."

"Shhh . . . shhh," Stravinsky interrupted and whispered in my ear, "Be quiet, let me listen."

"You see, there it comes again, the mistake."

But Stravinsky grinned from ear to ear and said, still whisperingly: "But this is beautiful . . . this is exactly what I need." And he ran back to his study.

At half past twelve Stravinsky opened my door and exclaimed in a jovial tone: "Nika, come on, let's go and celebrate. We'll have vodka and caviar. I have found the coda."

Two days later Stravinsky played the whole coda of the *Symphony of Psalms* for me. And the chromatic passage in the Alleluia was born out of the mistake made by the Russian choir's sopranos.

One day I asked Stravinsky a question about melody. I must have put the question in too general and unprecise a way, forgetting that he liked meticulous precision in everything.

"I don't understand what you mean," he replied. "Do you mean a tune, a *popevka* [a fragment of a song], or do you mean *melos* in general, the *melopoeia*, the long melodic outline?"

I said that I meant both.

"Well," answered Stravinsky, "a *popevka* is something distinguishable, identifiable, something that sticks like glue to the memory. This, I suppose, is the way I used bits of street songs in *Petrushka*, or invented tunes for *Les Noces*. But this is not the way melody interests me now. Now I am interested in long, melodic lines that will serve my polyphonic needs, and such lines do not necessarily contain—how shall I say it?—identifiable melodical moleculae or patterns. In this piece, for example," and he pointed to the *Symphony of Psalms*, "the melodic moleculae are clearly identifiable, but this is not what matters because those moleculae do not really determine the structure of the whole. What is important is how I hide them in those long, melodic passages with the help of my *libre arbitre.*"

Then, as suddenly and as unexpectedly as Stravinsky had appeared in his Pleyel studio, he vanished. He left Paris, having told me that he was going to take a vacation and travel through France. A few days after his disappearance I started getting postcards from restaurants in the provinces, and realizing that the summer was on, I packed up and left Paris for my refuge in Alsace.

When I came back in October, I heard that Stravinsky was in town and saw posters announcing a Stravinsky Festival Concert. I tried to contact him at his studio, but it was locked. I did not see him. Then both our lives changed drastically, and so did the world. I went to America and began teaching there—he toured and composed.

In 1941 I published an article in the *Atlantic Monthly* about music under dictatorships and got a few fan letters, among them one from

Hollywood which was typed in Russian and signed by Stravinsky.

I knew that after several years of familial disasters (Stravinsky's mother, his first wife, and his oldest daughter had died all in one year, and he himself had been seriously ill) he had reached American shores, married Vera Arturovna de Bosset, and, for strictly climatic reasons, settled in Hollywood, then an unsmogged and un-degraded town, and an attractive intellectual center due to the large influx of talented people from Europe.

Stravinsky had read the article and seemed very pleased, especially about my comparing the form of Shostakovich's symphonies to an oyster taken out of its shell and dangling on the tip of a fork. "When shall I see you?" he asked at the end of the letter. "Could you come and visit us here in Hollywood?"

This started a regular correspondence between us, and every time Stravinsky came to the East Coast, I would rush to him from wherever I was.

In 1947 came a letter:

Dear Nika Dimitrievich,

Yes, of course we will be expecting you for Christmas. You will stay right here with us. You will sleep on the sofa on which slept Nadia Boulanger, Olsen, Auden, and others. Huxley was too long. I hope it will be long enough for you. (What is your height?)

You and Balanchine will probably take the Super-Chief, which gets you into Pasadena at 8:13 a.m. We will meet you *there.* (Pasadena is the last station before Los Angeles and closer to us.)

Please don't disappoint us this time—*come!* Vera sends greetings.

> *Yours,*
> *Igor. Str.*

The letter was in Russian, written on one side of a half-sheet of airmail paper, in Stravinsky's jagged handwriting, and in very black ink. The sentence "What is your height?" was in red pencil on the left-hand margin, with an asterisk following the previous sentence and a red-pencil tracer leading to it. The sentence about Pasadena was in blue pencil, upside down in the top right-hand corner. A blue asterisk and a blue-penciled tracer connected it with the previous sentence. The word *zdes* (here) was underlined with a blue pencil; the word *tam* (meaning there and referring to Pasadena) was boxed in a blue-penciled frame; the word *priezzhaite!* (come!) was heavily underlined in red pencil. The whole little sheet gave the impression of compact and calculated orderliness and with its several colors looked like a gay and nervous drawing.

And so I went to Hollywood and visited the Stravinskys.

I have described the minutiae of that visit twenty-five years ago in a book of essays, *Old Friends and New Music*.

I visited the Stravinskys again in Hollywood in 1951 to arrange for Stravinsky's participation in the Paris festival, *Masterpieces of the Twentieth Century*, which I was organizing.

Both visits were warm, hospitable, and very, very gay.

It was during the first California visit, in 1947, that Stravinsky pulled out a penny postcard covered with tiny scribbling in a nervous, intellectual handwriting. I do not remember the precise content of the postcard, but it showed not only casual, fan-like interest in Stravinsky's music, but made some kind of precise proposal concerning a concert. The writer of the postcard wanted to conduct in New York some of Stravinsky's vocal works. The postcard was unsigned and had no sender's address on it. There was but one clue: the person who wrote it was choir leader at Hunter College.

"What do you think of this strange thing? Is he a *she* or is *she* a *he?*" asked Stravinsky. "The handwriting is a bit effeminate, but the content is not at all. It sounds like a man, and a man who seems genuinely interested in my music and ready to do something for it."

And while I was still deciphering the hieroglyphics of the postcard, Stravinsky continued: "Couldn't you, when you get back to New York, find out the name and address of this choir's conductor and perhaps see him or her and write to me what you make of it?"

I said that I would.

Back in New York, I called Hunter College, but it was vacation time and there wasn't anybody in the Music Department who would tell me what I wanted to know. I left a message and my name for whoever was the choir director.

Several days later I got a telephone call from someone whose voice sounded halting and timid. The voice said that his name was Robert Craft, he had written Stravinsky a postcard, and he offered to come and see me.

But I was leaving for Washington and my chores with the Voice of America. I was then helping Charlie Thayer, Charles Bohlen's delightful brother-in-law, to organize, at the request of the State Department, the Voice of America to Russia. I suggested that Robert Craft write to Stravinsky directly and this time not to forget to sign his letter and give his full address.

The same evening I called up Stravinsky and told him that the choir leader's name was Robert Craft and that he was a man, not a woman.

"Is it Kraft like the cheese or Kraft like our chocolate shop in St. Petersburg?" said Stravinsky's voice on the other end of the line.

I answered that it was different from both and that the American cheese, like the St. Petersburg chocolate, was spelled with a K.

"Are you sure?" said Stravinsky. "Well, all right . . . so long as he'll learn to sign his future letters. Let him be chocolate *and* cheese."

Somewhere between 1947 and 1949 a slight but distinct change took place in our relations. Not that they got worse—quite the contrary. As time went on, they became closer, warmer, and more tender. But Stravinsky started getting interested in musical experiments which he knew I did not know anything about. He started toying with the twelve-tone system of composition which he had so vehemently rejected twenty years earlier.

I knew, of course, that one of the extraordinary peculiarities of Stravinsky's character, and to me its most attractive quality, was the fact that he was both a perpetual neophyte and an autodidact. And in both functions a zealot of genius. This is what kept him and his art young and fresh for so many decades.

Stravinsky was constantly "discovering" something, and though the impulse for those discoveries came from outside and often from quite unexpected sources, the process of the discovery was entirely his own, unrepeatably personal. Whether it would be Glinka or Tchaikovsky, Rossini or Bach, he would "discover" them and in them that which was necessary to his own music. In other words, Stravinsky would take full possession of the discovered domain as if he had bought a house and then remodeled its rooms, walls, and windows and put in new furniture, leaving upon every room the imprint of his personality.

Stravinsky was full of excitement and immensely eager as all neophytes are, to add to his own musical domain new territories gleaned from music's historical past. In a way, he was a musical colonialist, but more like the Portuguese or Spanish colonialists, who left ineffable imprints upon their colonial empires, than Anglo-Saxon colonialists who either reduced the original population to impotence or disdainfully refrained from mixing in the affairs of the "natives" except to extract huge fortunes from their labors.

Only a musical colonialist could have produced out of a territory called Pergolesi so personal a piece as Stravinsky's *Pulcinella,* not to speak of the extraordinary Stravinskyanization of Tchaikovsky in the *Baiser de la Fée* and the orchestrations or, rather, "registrations" of Bach's chorale prelude *Vom Himmel Hoch* (with added Stravinskyan counterpoints), or of those admirable madrigals of Gesualdo.

How often did I hear Stravinsky exclaim: "Nika, do you know Bach's A cappella motets or Rossini's Mass or Handel's opera *Rosamunda?*" Always in the eager tone of an explorer relating his discovery of an unknown waterfall in Africa or of a dead city in Tibet.

And twenty years later he would ask: "Nika, do you know Guillaume de Machault and Meister Isaac?"

I would nod acquiescingly, remembering those days of boredom in Berlin when my teacher Paul Juon would have me write a fragment of a mass imitating precisely the style and technique of Machault or of the "isorhythmic" motets of Meister Isaac (and how stilted and lifeless were the results of my labors).

And Stravinsky would continue excitedly: "But this is extraordinary music! One should shout about it from the rooftops! I got myself the scores of Machault and Isaac. I find all of it so near to me, so close to my present-day concerns."

And sure enough, in one of Stravinsky's next works there would be an unrepeatably Stravinskyan, but stylistically and technically recognizable bit of Machault or Meister Isaac.

All of music's past, so to speak, was virgin territory for Stravinsky's exploratory instincts. And he was never satisfied unless he had explored it in depth, learned the style, the technique, and the form of each of those new territories he was discovering. Only then did the territory become his own so that he could attach a new colony to his crown.

And also: what other composer, since the times of the Great Flemings has composed music to so many tongues? Stravinsky had always loved "language" as such. He was surrounded by dictionaries, searching for precise equivalents and laconic definitions. At times he would correct someone who misused a word in whatever language he was speaking and would stop the conversation until the precise equivalent could be found.

To play with language, to make a "charade" with language, to pursue the hidden semantics of a word was to Stravinsky the source of continuous pleasure and interest.

First of all, Stravinsky used three different Russian tongues: The contemporary poetic Russian of the nineteenth century (*Rossignol, Balmont Songs, Japanese Poems*). Then the nonsense-rhyme Russian of the *Pribautki*. And finally the *patois* Russian of *Les Noces*. He set texts in French (*Perséphone*); in Latin (*Oedipus Rex, Canticum Sacrum*, etc.); in English (*The Rake's Progress, The Shakespeare Songs*, etc.); and in ancient Hebrew (*Abraham and Isaac*).

Curiously enough, Stravinsky did not compose in the two languages most frequently composed in, Italian and German. But he was not overscrupulous about the translation of his texts into other tongues. I suppose that consciously or unconsciously he felt his music was invented strictly to suit one tongue and hence should not be sung in any translation.

After the early 1950s, Stravinsky got gradually converted not only to the understanding of serial music, but to the actual adaptation of serial techniques for his own compositorial needs.

Gone were the statements of the thirties: "Serial composition inevitably leads to atonality, and atonality is disorder, while art is order," "Music must have a root, a center, a gravitational pole," etc.

Now Stravinsky exclaimed to me: "Nika, do you know Anton Webern? This music is a miracle of structure and precision. I feel so close to it now."

And Stravinsky met Boulez and they became friends, and I remember lunching with Stravinsky and Boulez in Paris and then going to Boulez's tiny walk-up flat and Boulez showing Stravinsky and explaining to him how to play an "aleatoric" piece by Stockhausen, whose title I have forgotten, but whose structure consisted of combining at will one central element with six or eight others for an indefinite duration. All of it was printed on one large sheet of paper which we had to hold open on both sides while Boulez with extraordinary skill and dexterity played it, combining the "theme" printed in the middle of the huge page with various elements surrounding it. And while he played, he continued to explain with didactic precision how the piece had been worked out by Stock-hausen and what all the "aleatoric" variations represented from the point of view of polyphonic technique.

Stravinsky stood in back of Boulez with a frown on his face and watched intently what Boulez was doing, occasionally interrupting him with pertinent, eagerly interested questions.

Then, as we walked down the winding staircase, Stravinsky said to me under his breath, "*M-da eto shtuchka neprostaya!* [Yes, this is not so simple a trick!]"

It turned out to be a great boon for Stravinsky because it aroused in him the appetite to dominate and make completely his own that new system of composition. Though now, of course, "music matter in the raw" could not "float freely" to Stravinsky's musical conscience from "the outside" and be refashioned by his *libre arbitre.* Now Stravinsky was in a self-imposed straitjacket. But, however illusively, Stravinsky suddenly felt young again and was excited by the needs to invent and to conform to "Ground *Gestalts*" of his own and then work with them like a goldsmith, developing them meticulously according to the principles of serialism, and of serialism that affected not only the *Gestalt* and it convolutions, but also serialism of tonal intensities, of rhythmic patterns, of dynamics, and of intricate polyphonic structure.

It took Stravinsky several years and a few important compositions to achieve complete domination of that new style. But that had always been the aim of his life: to discover a new domain and then to dominate it completely with all of its stylistic and technical possibilities. And Stravinsky succeeded. His *Movements for Piano and Orchestra* and his *Requiem Canticles* bear witness to a complete Stravinskyanization of near-total serialism.

What was amazing was the simple fact that Stravinsky's "Great Leap Forward" into "*Mare Serialisticum*" took place at a time when he was an old man and not, like Schoenberg or Webern or Boulez, in youth or middle age. Furthermore, Stravinsky in more ways than one "overleaped" them. Those two last works I mentioned represent a complete command of the intricacies of serialistic style and its technique, but also an equally total Stravinskyanization thereof.

It also gave Stravinsky the additional invigorating feeling of being a new leader, if only in an illusory fashion, of the postwar generation of composers. It was they who became Stravinsky's friends. There were new faces around him, new and younger minds sought his company, he made peace with old enemies like Schoenberg, he became friends with that delightful person Edgard Varèse, who had admired Stravinsky so much, for such a long time, but in the past could not approach him for fear of being rebuked.

But most of the old friends dating from the days of Stravinsky's life in Europe, those years of insecurity and torment of the so-called Frivolous Twenties, for one reason or another moved to the "pen of enemies" or at least became indifferent to Stravinsky. Only a few faithfuls remained, like Nadia Boulanger, Vittorio Rieti, myself. But we seldom discussed "in depth" Stravinsky's new aesthetics, his new approach to musical composition and its techniques.

All of this was, I believe, an egocentric necessity of Stravinsky's genius. He had to be constantly phoenixoidal. It often made me think of European politics of past centuries, when allegiances changed abruptly and a German Protestant prince would suddenly find himself an ally of the Catholic League.

From a glamorous cinema capital, Hollywood was rapidly becoming a polluted antheap with more days of smog than of sun and with an ever increasing absence of friendly faces. Despite the advice of friends, Stravinsky refused to move eastward—for example, to a flat in New York and a house in Connecticut or somewhere in the south of Europe.

"But what will I do with all this?" Stravinsky screamed, pointing to the racks full of books, scores, papers, archives, the walls pasted with pictures, the tables and drawers filled with gadgets, trinkets, bibelots, mementos. "Where will I put all this? No, no, *non, merci!*" and he would stamp his feet. "Don't talk to me about moving. I have moved enough in my life, thank you! And enough is enough!"

Instead Stravinsky started moving all over the world. He went on extended tours to the East, all over America, and at least once a year to Europe, where his center became the Bauer-Grunewald Hotel in Venice with its *table d'hôte* and its irreplaceable concierge, Tortorella. Stravinsky had always liked to stay in a comfortable suite in a European luxury hotel. It is a nostalgic trait common to most of us "rootless cosmopolitans." My cousin Vladimir has been enjoying life in the old-fashioned Palace Hotel in Montreux since *Lolita*. And the first thing Ivan Bunin, the émigré writer, did when he received the Nobel Prize was to move into a *hotel de luxe* in Stockholm.

I persuaded Stravinsky to come to Paris in 1952 to the festival I organized then, called Masterpieces of the Twentieth Century.

It was a glamorous affair. *Oedipus Rex* was produced with decors designed by Jean Cocteau. And the Boston Symphony Orchestra performed the *Rite of Spring* under the same conductor who had conducted it thirty-nine years earlier in the same hall, Pierre Monteux. And he performed it in Stravinsky's presence.

Then started a series of collaborational activities between Stravinsky and me. He came to my second festival in Rome in 1954 called *Music in Our Time* and conducted his music there.

A few years later I arranged a meeting in Venice between him and my friend, the composer Rolf Liebermann—then the director of the North German radio, and later the celebrated director of the Hamburg Opera. It resulted in two successive commissions—the first was *Threni* and the second, *Noah's Flood*.

The late Hungarian conductor Ferenc Fricsay approached me and asked whether Stravinsky would be interested in writing a piece for piano and orchestra for the pianist-wife of a wealthy Swiss merchant. I passed the information on to Stravinsky. He accepted the commission and wrote his *Movements for Piano and Orchestra*.

I also introduced Stravinsky to Sir Isaiah Berlin of Oxford, and to A. Z. Propes, the director of the Israel Festival, and he wrote for the Israel Festival his oratorio *Abraham and Isaac*.

Then in 1962, when he reached his eightieth year, it was I again who took the initiative, through my friend Arthur Schlesinger, Jr., of proposing that the President and Mrs. Kennedy give an anniversary dinner for Stravinsky.

And in 1964, when he was already ill and deprived of the free use of one foot, I arranged a triumphal concert for him at the Festival of Berlin in the presence of Mayor Willy Brandt and in the beautiful new Philharmonic Hall.

I followed Stravinsky everywhere, except, alas, to the Soviet Union. I went to London, to Hamburg, to Munich, to Rome, to Berlin, to Copenhagen, and even to Japan, always trying to fit my own schedule to his, to be with him as much as I could, and to attend most of his premières. And throughout all of those long decades of his life there was nothing but warm and tender friendship between us.

But we rarely discussed his new music, nor did he show me, as he used to before, his "work in progress." He never again spoke to me about my own music. We talked about a million things, we laughed together, ate and drank together, I listened to most of his new music at rehearsals, but he never asked my opinion of it. It was as if we had tacitly agreed to avoid some corpse in a closet.

I did not, I could not, at least not fast enough, and not as whole-heartedly as I would have wished to, learn to love Stravinsky's new "serial" compositions, whereas I did spontaneously and instinctively love *all* of his music up until *The Rake's Progress* and *Agon*. I did admire, of course, the phenomenal craftsmanship, but with a few exceptions these latest works of his seemed remote and forbidding to me.

I remained, and I'm afraid will always remain, deeply rooted in the "tonal" tradition of Russian music and am quite unable to acquire and exercise even to an infinitesimal degree Stravinsky's phoenix-like gifts of change and rebirth without betraying my own Russian self.

Thus, while we were becoming closer and closer to each other as human beings, and while I played the role of a kind of "middleman" for some of Stravinsky's latter-day musical commissions, I was helping to promote that particular music of his which I least understood. Its technique, its structural devices, its style were the most remote of all of his music to my own natural instincts.

Toward the very end of Stravinsky's life something changed. He wrote a piece, his last grand piece of music, the *Requiem Canticles*. Though in it he used the novel devices of serial technique, he somehow overpowered them. It was immediately, instinctively, totally lovable to me. I was able without any effort to penetrate into the essence of its tragic beauty. I was as fully taken and shaken by it as I used to be in the thirties and forties by every new composition of Stravinsky.

In the last two years of his life, when he could not compose any more (and how bitterly he wanted to compose!), he turned his back on nearly all of contemporary music.

He would ask Bob Craft to play for him records of Handel and Mendelssohn oratorios, which he would follow attentively, reading the scores. And he himself played as best he could, over and over again, Bach's *Well-Tempered Clavier*, and transcribed several of its preludes and fugues for groups of solo instruments. But, above all, he discovered an affection for Beethoven. Of Beethoven's *Fidelio* he told me, "Beethoven catapulted all his symphonies into this opera." And he especially loved Beethoven's late string quartets.

"This music," Stravinsky whispered to me, "is now so close to me, Nika . . . Ah . . . so very close. . . ."

One of the last times I saw Stravinsky, he was sitting in his little wheelchair at the Essex House in New York, thin and transparent, his profile of an extraordinary ancient Oriental beauty. He was holding my hand and whispering. "Nika, don't go away. Stay with me. Don't leave me *avec les femmes de chambres*."

But Vera had invited my wife and me for dinner with Bob Craft and the composer Yannis Xenakis. She came toward Stravinsky's wheelchair, all dressed up, and said hurriedly, "Nika, we are late, we must go."

"But where are you going and why?" Stravinsky whispered, looking at Vera.

"We are going to dinner at the Pavillon."

And suddenly from inside his tiny body came a booming voice: "*Et qui va payer?*" And Stravinsky grinned maliciously.

That took place, as far as I remember, on February 12, 1971, less than two months before Stravinsky died.

The posters announcing Stravinsky's funeral in Venice were printed by the Venice municipality, and said: ". . . *Che con gesto di squisita desidero in vita essere sepolto nella citta che amo sopra ogni altra. . . .*" Small crowds of Venetians stood in front of the posters and smiled.

It was too obvious. "*Desidero in vita essere sepolto*" could so easily be misread as meaning that Stravinsky had expressed the wish to be "buried alive" in his beloved Venice. How he must have laughed at this last dart of irony, from wherever he was!

III

To America

ON AUGUST 9, 1933, my first wife, Natalie Shakhovskoy, whom I had married in 1928, and I embarked at Le Havre on the smallest *paquebot* of the French Line, the S.S. *de Grasse*, and sailed to New York via Lisbon and the Azores. How did it come about?

It was, all of it, a plot masterminded by Natasha and it took several years to mature.

We had a friend in Paris in the early 1930's called George Keller, who with a partner, Monsieur Bignou, owned an art gallery on the Rue la Boétie. Bignou et Keller were big-time art dealers. One of their principal clients was the famous Dr. Albert C. Barnes from Philadelphia. Natasha learned from Keller that Dr. Barnes invited artists and scholars to come to America as his guests and to give lectures at his highly private institution, part art gallery, part art school, called the Barnes Foundation in Merion, Pennsylvania, a suburb of Philadelphia. Natasha persuaded Keller to suggest to Dr. Barnes that he should invite me as a lecturer, or at least put me on Dr. Barnes's list as a candidate.

Things weren't going well in France. *La crise* was reaching into everybody's pocket, and we Diasporatic Russians were the first to feel it. Sources of income, such as private "commissions" or composing incidental music for plays or for films, were rapidly drying up. The Pleyel firm was about to discontiue publishing its monthly journal, *Musique*, where I worked as an assistant to its director. The outlook for the future was hazy. The only salvation, thought Natasha, would be to move to America. To follow up the Barnes trail

183

as a tangible possibility seemed to her not only reasonable but indispensable.

Needless to say, to me, Natasha's scheme seemed loony. Why
should Dr. Barnes invite *me* to America? I thought. I had never
given lectures. I did not know anything about painting, and the
only thing I could offer the doctor from Pennsylvania was a weak
knowledge of English and a vague love for telling stories. Besides,
I was not at all sure that I was ready to leave France. Somehow, I
thought, we would muddle through. America seemed remote, un-
attractive, and forbidding.

But Natasha believed in her plot and kept prodding George Keller about it.

It must have been May or early June 1931 when Keller tele-
phoned and said that Dr. Barnes had arrived in Paris, that Keller
had spoken to him about me, and that he intended to take him to a
concert at which my music was being performed. If the good
doctor liked my music, said Keller, he would introduce me to him
and we would see what happened.

The concert was one of the Parisian *avant-garde* medleys of the
1920s and early 1930s at which "young" composers had their latest
works performed to a friendly *public mondain*. Mine was a song
cycle, *Chants to the Virgin Mary*. It came second on the program
of eight to ten items.

The songs went off well. In the intermission I went backstage to
congratulate the singer and the conductor of the little orchestra,
Roger Desormière.

As I was returning from the greenroom, I saw George Keller
leading two strangers toward me. One of them was a stocky fellow
with a bulldog's face, tousled hair, and spectacles perched on a
purple-plum nose. The other was pale and noodle-like.

Keller introduced me, and the bull face asked: "Parly vous English?"

I said that I did.

He barked back at me a sentence that for some reason stuck in
my memory. "Your stuff's okay," he said, "it has *balls*. But the rest
of the program is dreck and horse piss." My English was not yet
up to the last synonym.

He turned and introduced me to his companion: "This here," he
said, "is Mr. Dribblebees, a trustee of our foundation, he'll be in
touch with you."

184

Natasha and I laughed at the "balls," the "dreck" and "horse piss." Then I forgot about America and Dr. Barnes.

But from that concert onward, whenever a piece of mine was being performed in Paris, Mr. Dribblebees would pop up backstage, smile, shake my hand solicitously, and say that he would report the "event" to Dr. Barnes.

Except for these periodical encounters with the noodle man of the Barnes Foundation, all was quiet on the American front.

It remained quiet for two years until mid-May 1933. Then, one day while Natasha and I were in the country in Alsace, the postman appeared with an express letter for Natasha from George Keller. Dr. Barnes, said the letter, was in Paris; he wanted to see me as soon as possible. "I believe *cela va marcher*. Nicolas should come to Paris at once. I'll arrange a luncheon in the basement of the gallery."

At that time the three of us, Natasha, our infant son, Ivan—not yet a year old—and I were staying in a sweet little house in Alsace, next to a beautiful *château* called Kolbsheim.

The *château* and the little house on the edge of Kolbsheim's village belonged to lifelong friends of mine, Antoinette and Alexandre Grunelius, and to Alexandre's mother.

When in 1923 I moved from Berlin to Paris, Kolbsheim's *château* became a haven for me. My friends, and especially Alexandre Grunelius's sweet and gentle mother, adopted me as a member of their family. She surrounded me with affectionate care and with generous hospitality. I could come to Kolbsheim whenever I wanted. I was always welcome. I could spend my summers there, compose, read, write, and rest, partaking of the intimate spiritual beauty of the place and of the civilized, tender friendship of Mrs. Grunelius and her son.

The pink stucco *château*, a sprawling eighteenth-century country mansion, stood on a hill overlooking the Alsatian part of the fertile Rhine valley; the valley was framed on the west by the indigo-blue Vosges Mountains and on the east by the largely invisible Black Forest. The *château* had about it an air of leisurely spaciousness and of gracious, tranquil beauty. It exuded peace and sweet repose.

Its terraced gardens descended to the valley's floor, its trimmed ewes and evergreens, its hornbeam hedges, box-framed greens and flowerbeds, its sparse but adroitly placed classical statuary had, all of them, a nostalgic hue of Italy. But a kind of unreal, dream-like

Italy, the one the great Flemings used to paint in the hidden backgrounds of their portraits.

It was in this pink *château*, at Mrs. Grunelius's bountiful table, that in the early 1920s I met Dr. Albert Schweitzer and his two musician-cousins, Charles and Fritz Munch. It was at Kolbsheim that I wrote most of my music and read or reread my French, German, and English classics. It was there that I acquired my love for mountain hikes, for Romanesque architecture, and for nature tamed by man's mind.

Later on, when Natasha and I got married, the Kolbsheim *chatelains* offered us the little house on the edge of the village as a summer residence.

Between 1928 and 1933 we spent happy and peaceful summers there. We were visited by a swarm of friends. Fellow composers like Darius Milhaud, Sergei Prokofiev, Henri Sauguet, and Paul Hindemith came to see us. Writers like Cocteau and cousin Vladimir and many, many others.

But most important of all visitors turned out to be the gentle and saintly philosopher Jacques Maritain. My *chatelains* became deeply devoted to him, to his wife, Raissa, and her sister, Vera. And Kolbsheim gradually became Maritain's second home.

I went to Paris right away and called George Keller from the railroad station.

"The lunch is today," he said, "at twelve thirty. Dr. Barnes is anxious to see you. Don't be late."

When I arrived, Dr. Barnes was already at the gallery, with his wife and the noodle-man, Mr. Dribblebees.

Dr. Barnes was as laconic as the first time. When he saw me, he turned to Mr. Dribblebees and asked for a "letter."

Mr. Dribblebees produced an envelope from his breast pocket. Dr. Barnes read its contents and handed it to me.

"Now look, Nick," he said, looking at me sternly, "read this letter and if you agree with it sign the copy and give it to me. Keep the original." He frowned. "But if you do not agree, forget about it. We'll tear it up and have lunch. Okay?"

I read the letter very carefully, asked for a pen, and signed it. Natasha was right. For some irrational reason her plot had worked. I was invited to America to lecture at the Barnes Foundation. I felt elated and disturbed at the same time.

"Oh, never mind about that," said Natasha, reading the letter at Kolbsheim. "The main thing is to get out of here. What will we live on in the next months? The only hope is America. And as for those lectures you'll have to give, you just have to prepare them . . . and that will do you good."

Dr. Barnes's letter contained, so far as I remember, the following points:

1. I agreed to come to America at the invitation of the Barnes Foundation and to stay there for nine months.

2. I agreed to give twice a month a lecture at the Barnes Foundation. The precise subject of the lectures was to be discussed later on, but the general idea should be a comparative study of the aesthetic trends in music and in painting in the last hundred years.

3. The travel expenses for me and for my wife would be paid by the Barnes Foundation. I would also receive a monthly honorarium of $200.

4. I could live wherever I chose, but I'd have to turn up every other Saturday in Merion, Pennsylvania, and give my Sunday-morning lecture at the foundation.

And so, carefree and happy, we sailed to America on the slow and tidy *de Grasse*, a single-class liner, via all those pretty southern ports. We were surrounded by the pleasant and gay company of academics and students and a few "returnees" of quite a different order.

Earlier that year Mr. Roosevelt had devalued the dollar. Life in Europe and especially in France suddenly became very expensive. Quite a number of Americans who had settled in France after the end of World War I started trekking back. The ones who led the trek were intellectuals. There were a few of them on the *de Grasse* —the poet John Peale Bishop with his wife and two boys, Edgard and Louise Varèse, and a few others. As usual on trans-Atlantic liners, we all became friends.

In the course of our leisurely cruise, the Bishops and the Vareses indoctrinated Natasha and me as to what to expect in America, where we should settle in New York, whom we should meet, and whom and what to avoid.

I remember *not* being surprised or overwhelmed by New York. I found it the way I expected it to be: a kind of immense vertical mess (Edmund Wilson used to call it real estate gone mad) set upon a square horizontal order.

I *expected* the quaint elevated railroads, of which I had seen reproductions since my tenderest childhood, and I also expected them to be noisy, filthy, and dilapidated. I *expected* to see shabby three-story brick houses rubbing shoulders with smart skyscrapers. I *expected* the comfy drugstores with their milkshakes and banana splits on each street corner, the commodious taxicabs and the funereal monsters of private cars clogging traffic. All of it was the way I had seen it in films, read about it in books, and heard about it from the few Americans I had met.

What *did* overwhelm me, after the highly *cloisonné* European society, was the extraordinary openness of America—the egalitarian readiness of its inhabitants to help each other and especially help the newcomer, the immigrant.

No sooner had we debarked from our voyage than we were overwhelmed by dinner and cocktail parties, by weekend invitations, and by offers of tickets for theaters or concerts or gallery openings.

The ominous lectures at Dr. Barnes's institution turned out to be harmless. I had prepared three or four of them, but soon realized that the subdued creatures, fellows of the Barnes Foundation's Art School, that I had to address every other Sunday expected from me something other than a scholarly lecture. They expected amusing talk, peppered if possible, by anecdotes.

"What we want to know, Nick," said Dr. Barnes, "is how *you feel* about Debussy and Cézanne, and not what some art charlatan says or thinks about them."

Dr. Barnes had established for himself the reputation of being an inveterate "original," at times mannerless and nasty, whom everyone feared. But during the first months of my stay in America he was extraordinarily amiable to me. He was solicitous, hospitable, and compassionate. Then brusquely, for no evident reason, just a few months before the end of our contract he turned against me. He severed his relations and wrote me nasty pornographic letters.

But later on I learned that sudden reversals of this kind were frequent with Dr. Barnes. Insulting people had become a well-established habit of his.

Bertrand Russell, who followed me on the Merionite lecture trail, had the same experience with Dr. Barnes that I did. Only, unlike me, he went to court and won his case. And many other people had similar experiences with the quarrelsome doctor.

Dr. Barnes was an American eccentric, an "oddball." He combined a streak of genius with a petulant, near-schizophrenic character.

Soon after reaching New York I was introduced to the poet Archibald MacLeish and his wife, the singer Ada, and encountered the lovely couple Gerald and Sara Murphy, whom I had met fleetingly in Paris. Both the MacLeishes and the Murphys were, like the Bishops, recent returnees from France.

On the *de Grasse* during our crossing John Bishop had talked to me about Archibald MacLeish and given me his poem, *The Conquistador* to read. At that time I knew very little about English or American poetry, and though I plowed through the poem with difficulty, I could not make head or tail of it.

When I met Archibald MacLeish, I was overawed. He seemed the image of the noble American from New England. He was handsome, manly, courteous, and quick-witted. "This is the way all Americans should be," I thought.

Gerald and Sara Murphy were much more Europeanized and worldly. In fact, when I first met them I thought they were English.

The MacLeishes and the Murphys had seen my ballet *Ode* in Paris and they knew that the Paris Opera was preparing to produce another ballet of mine, *La Vie de Polichinelle*, for 1934. It was natural, therefore, that our first conversations turned to the subject of ballet.

MacLeish deplored its absence in America. At the same time he spoke of an American ballet libretto he had thought of for some time. It had to do with the construction of the Union Pacific Railroad.

At first I did not pay much attention to MacLeish's suggestion. But then a succession of coincidences brought MacLeish's ballet theme to the forefront of my preoccupations.

I do not remember where, when, and under what circumstances I had met Sol Hurok.

I do remember seeing him at a concert at Carnegie Hall late in September 1933. He told me then that he was importing to America from France the so-called Ballet Russe de Monte Carlo.

The Ballet Russe de Monte Carlo was a new enterprise. It had been started by George Balanchine in 1932 and its manager at that

time was M. René Blum, the brother of the ex-Premier Léon.
Soon Balanchine and René Blum stepped out of the picture.
Léonide Massine took over as the company's chief choreographer,
and a curious character, an ex-Russian who called himself Colonel
de Basil, became the company's proprietory manager.

At first Hurok's Ballet Russe de Monte Carlo tour did not seem
to be a success. I met Hurok on a train to Philadelphia late in November. He was going south to meet the ubiquitous Colonel de
Basil for an opening somewhere beyond Washington.

Hurok was sour. He complained about the American public. "All
they want is big names," he said. "You tell them that this is the
best ballet company outside of Russia, but all they want is Pavlova
and Nijinsky! And where am I going to get them Pavlova and
Nijinsky?" In the course of the conversation he mentioned that
Léonide Massine would like to do a ballet on an American subject,
but had no idea what to do. Would I speak to Massine about it?

Back in New York I called up Gerald Murphy and told him
about my conversation with Hurok. I knew that the Murphys knew
Massine from Paris and I suggested that he and MacLeish get in
touch with Massine and talk to him about MacLeish's idea for a
Union Pacific ballet.

Gerald Murphy owned a large collection of cylinders with recordings made by Thomas Edison or one of Edison's assistants at
the turn of the century. He wanted me to come and listen to them.
"You'll be surprised by those recordings," said Murphy. "They're
sung and played by old people remembering songs and dances of
their youth. Some of the music goes far back into the 1870s."

In December I went to hear these extraordinary documents of
vanished America. They were poignantly authentic. Not only their
tunes, their harmonies, their rhythms, seemed fresh and real, but the
manner of playing or singing and the choice of instruments.

After a long evening of this music I promised to get Massine to
listen to it. I was sure that he could get an American composer of
the young generation, someone like Aaron Copland or Virgil
Thomson, interested in taking this American treasure and making
out of it a score for MacLeish's libretto.

"And you know," said Gerald Murphy as I was on the doorstep,
"if MacLeish does the libretto, it is going to be easy to raise the
money to produce the ballet."

I do not remember if it was me or Natasha or someone else who broached the subject of the Union Pacific as a ballet to Hurok and to the crooked Colonel.

At first their reaction was a firm no. But when they were told that there existed this unknown record collection and that if Mac-Leish's name was to be associated with the ballet, money might perhaps be raised, Hurok suddenly warmed up and said: "Then . . . vai . . . not . . . try?" The Colonel immediately calculated that the amount needed would be $25,000.

From mid-December 1933 onward, the idea of MacLeish's ballet on the subject of the Union Pacific was bandied about by the Murphy circle as a *fait accompli.* Yet whenever someone confronted Hurok and Colonel de Basil with the suggestion of a "serious" American composer (as opposed to "popular" ones), they would wince and turn sour. In other words, they did not wish to risk a new production with someone as little known as Copland or Thomson, someone of the avant-garde, not even if it was done with other people's money.

Thus things stood until the turn of the year.

It was at Christmastime, somewhere in snowy New England, with those bright, shivering Christmas trees in front of the houses, that MacLeish, while driving to someone's home for a Christmas party, asked me: "Nick, why don't you yourself write the music for *Union Pacific?* We've been running in circles chasing a composer like a bluebird! Why can't *you* do it?"

I laughed. "Fancy," I told MacLeish, "me, a Russian from France, writing the first American ballet!"

"So what?" snapped Archibald MacLeish. "Maybe it'll have to be this way and nobody will mind."

Shortly after New Year, Massine came to New York. We went together to the Murphys' and listened to the old recordings. We stayed many hours. Murphy also showed us other recordings, Chicago and New Orleans jazz and older ones of black music made in the Deep South.

He told Massine and me that he had kept up contact with old black folk in Virginia and Georgia, people who could dance all those forgotten "bear steps," "wolf steps," "fox trots," and true pre–Civil War "cakewalks."

Massine was completely taken with this mass of forgotten musical material. When we left, he looked at me, smiled sheepishly, and said: "Nika, don't you want to try your hand at it? It could be a fascinating job to work with all those tunes and dances. Why don't you try?"

But still I was not sure I wanted to. A few days later I went back to Gerald Murphy. This time I came with pencils and music paper. I spent a long afternoon listening to the old Edison machine and writing down the tunes in my own musical quickscript.

That same evening I called Leonide Massine. "Do you think you can persuade Hurok and the Colonel to let me compose the music for the ballet?" I asked.

"I think I can," he replied.

The next morning I called MacLeish in Massachusetts and told him that, if he still wanted me, I was ready to compose the music for *Union Pacific*. "We must get together with Massine at once," I added, "to plan the whole story minute by minute."

But nothing moved for quite a while. I decided not to start composing until I was sure that the venture would really take place.

Nothing moved because it turned out that money was not so easy to get as Gerald Murphy had thought. Although I stayed out of the money-raising campaign, I knew that the going was rough, especially since Colonel de Basil's original estimate proved to be too low. Every remote acquaintance of mine had been approached for money. Even Dr. Barnes promised a share and bought all the seats in the balcony for the première of the ballet.

MacLeish, Massine, and I worked out the details of the libretto. Someone proposed a young designer by the name of Johnson to design the sets. The rising star Irene Sharaff was to design the costumes, and Efrem Kurtz was to conduct the orchestra.

The première had been tentatively scheduled for March 6, 1934, in Philadelphia. All seemed to be set while I was still waiting for a signal from the two *compères*, Sol Hurok and the Colonel, to start writing the music. The signal came on February 11, when the money had been finally guaranteed. I had now twenty-three days to compose the music for what was supposed to be the season's great event, the first truly American ballet.

I asked Hurok to find me an aide—someone who could spend the next three weeks with me and, while I composed, orchestrate the music page by page under my supervision.

The young man who turned up was sheer delight. His name was Eddie Powell, one of the best orchestrators in town. Incredibly musical besides being quick, gay, and never tiring. Later on he became the head of a powerful orchestration outfit in Hollywood.

I worked day and night. I wrote down bits of music on subways and buses, waiting for lunch or breakfast, and banging at the piano in my shabby little flat on West 55th Street.

Though the plan of the ballet was simple enough, one had to satisfy a number of appetites. The company had pretty young ballerinas and Massine wanted to show them off. Each one had to have a solo, followed possibly by a *pas de deux*. The amount of music to be written was far greater than I had anticipated.

Not much happened in the libretto of *Union Pacific*, nor do I clearly remember its details. I remember that there were two main scenes. One took place in a railroad workers' tent where all kinds of exotic people were exhibiting their respective dances. The highpoint of that scene was Massine's "Barman's Dance."

Then there was a scene in which dancers played rails and were laid one on top of another until two steam engines arrived, driving upon them from both sides of the stage, "spanning the globe" in the famous postcard sight that enlivens so many albums of nineteenth-century photographic Americana.

We left New York for Philadelphia on the 3rd of March. The day before, Massine called up to say that Tamara Toumanova, one of the ballet's best and prettiest dancers, was having a tantrum because she did not like the number we had masterminded for her. Couldn't I cook up a Mexican number?

I ran to the Public Library, got myself a handbook of Mexican lore, and copied out a few tunes.

Next morning Eddie Powell, several copyists, and I occupied the smoker half of a Pullman car. Between New York and Philadelphia I was composing the Mexican dance and Eddie Powell was orchestrating it while the copyists wrote out the parts. I finished composing the seemingly endless piece that afternoon in a smoke-filled hotel room in Philadelphia. The copyists sat at folding card tables, Eddie Powell on the john, and I on the bed.

There were supposed to be two orchestra rehearsals on the 4th of March, another rehearsal on the 5th, and a general rehearsal on the morning of the 6th.

By the time of the third rehearsal, nothing worked. Massine was in a frenzy and so was I. The parts were peppered with mistakes; the orchestra played like pigs; Efrem Kurtz complained that the penciled score was illegible; the dancers did not remember their steps; the group scenes did not work; the sets weren't dry and could not be hung; none of the sizes given to Johnson proved to be correct; props were falling down; the curtain was too short; the tent was too small. The costumes weren't ready or did not fit.

On the 5th Massine demanded two extra rehearsals with orchestra. The Colonel and Hurok threw up their arms in despair. We worked until midnight of the 5th and still it all looked and sounded like inevitable disaster.

Then, after midnight, I had to trail and rescue Johnson, who went out on a drunken binge. I had to walk him all night in the frozen and morbid suburbs of Philadelphia. A depressive drunk, he cursed and yelled, whined and ranted, and tried to throw himself into the first bit of water he saw.

When I came back to the hotel, having dumped Johnson at a YMCA establishment, I found glum Eddie Powell sitting on my bed, chain-smoking and correcting orchestra parts.

On the morning of the 6th, fresh and rosy as if they were coming to a first communion, arrived the Murphys, the MacLeishes, Natasha with a whole caravan of friends, and a dozen creatures from the Barnes Foundation. Yet not very much had improved during the night. The orchestra still played wrong notes and the dancers still did now know what to do on the stage.

During the intermission I asked Hurok, "How do you like the music, Sol?"

He looked at me with surly eyes and said, "What d'you mean, the music? Everything about the goddam thing is lousy! Especially in the first act, you have there one sour note. Take it away!"

In the evening at the première the unexpected happened.

The ballet started well, and after the first two numbers one could sense that it might work out after all.

I sat among the public, more dead than alive, expecting a flop. But the applause went on rising, number after number, until Massine's Barman's Dance stopped the show.

Instinctively we all knew that the game had been won and that something spectacular would come at the end. It was a triumph, but an awkward one for me.

The terrible Dr. Barnes had distributed five hundred seats in the balcony to his foundation members, and when the ballet came to an end, he led them in a chorus, shouting, "We want Nick! We want Nick!"

When I appeared on the stage to take a bow, Massine's face was at his nastiest. I heard his rasping whisper in my ear: "A fine claque you organized for yourself!"

Union Pacific became for the next two years the most successful ballet of the Ballet Russe de Monte Carlo's repertoire. It was played all over America. It toured throughout Europe and through most of the world. Almost everywhere it had the same rousing success.

Alas, neither MacLeish nor I profited by it. Partly because of the crooked ex-police colonel, partly because of my own carelessness.

In the constrained weeks before the production of *Union Pacific*, neither MacLeish nor I, but mostly I, thought of drawing up a proper contract with the ballet company and its boss. Somehow it simply did not occur to me. I was so busy composing the voluminous score, constantly adding new music and supervising its orchestration, I had no time to think of contracts. Besides, I somehow had the feeling that it was a one-evening affair, a *divertissement* that could not possibly have a follow-up. Never did I dream of a success. I did not even have time to make for myself a copy of the orchestral score, or even of the piano sketch. The piece went on public performance totally unprotected by copyright. All that I obtained from the Colonel was an "oral promise" to pay me a $500 fee for composing the music. Then, once the ballet started being performed on the average of four times a week, I raised with Hurok and de Basil the question of royalties to the authors. The Colonel promised. I wrote letters, registered ones, but nothing happened. The company was en route all the time.

Nor did I have a publisher who could handle the matter for me. My Paris publisher, the Russian house of Serge Koussevitzky, was not the least bit interested in an American ballet of mine.

The crooked Colonel continued to reap benefits from MacLeish's and my ballet without paying us anything. We started a lawsuit. But by the time we won it, two years later, *Union Pacific* had petered out of the company's repertoire.

Still I did not get back either my orchestral or my piano manuscript score.

Only when the Colonel died, someone unknown sent me my old penciled orchestral score. I had no use for it and gave it to the Princeton University Library.

As for the piano score, I was told it had been lost. Another five years later a former stage director of the Colonel found it and returned it to me.

Even that wretched $500, the fee the ex-colonel promised to pay, was doled out in homeopathic doses. The last dose, some £25, was paid to me in June 1934, backstage at the Royal Covent Garden Opera House in London.

I put the neat white £5 notes in my side pocket and drove straight to the last boat train to Falmouth and onward to Boulogne and Paris. The sea was rough and I gave back to Neptune what I had been given at the grill room of the Savoy. Still in dinner jacket, still terribly wobbly, I boarded the grimy third-class compartment in Boulogne. I needed the bathroom quickly. Alas, in those years third-class toilets in France often lacked paper.

Fortunately I produced out of my pocket lovely soft and clean British paper. Only when I saw it whirling down to the roadbed did I realize what had happened.

Early in 1936 my American lady patrons, Dorothy Chadwick, Edith Fincke, her sister Marion Dougherty, and Zocia Kochansky, the widow of the Polish violinist Paul Kochansky, decided that I should stop leading a wayward life and get myself a steady job.

At that time the ways of compositorial flesh were limited in America. And for an unfamous imported composer there were only a few choices of how to earn a living. To teach in a college was one of them. Trustees of provincial colleges at that time believed that imported composers, like wines and cheeses, are of necessity superior to, or at least more glamorous than, native ones. Another choice was lecture tours. For a person with an exotic background, lectures could fetch fair fees. Giving private lessons was the least secure way of making money.

Looming brightest on the money-making horizon were the worlds of Hollywood and of Broadway. One could join these American dream worlds, but only if (and the if was a big one) the joiner had the talent and the adaptability for those glamorous worlds.

Vladimir Dukelsky—alias Vernon Duke—when I met him at Prokofiev's in Paris in 1926, raved about the fathomless chances to make quick "big" money in Hollywood and on Broadway. "One *can* do both," he claimed, "one *can* move from one chair to another, from 'popular' to 'serious' music, but, of course, 'serious' music should be foremost in one's mind."

Dukelsky was a gifted composer with a genuine lyrical talent. Yet he never achieved a success with his "serious" music, despite

196

Diaghilev's and Koussevitsky's patronage. In his "popular" garb, as Vernon Duke, he is still remembered for his cozy song "April in Paris." But Vladimir Dukelsky and his alter ego, Vernon Duke, never sat securely on either of the two chairs. Vernon Duke never made "big" money with his "popular" stuff and Vladimir Dukelsky's "serious" music remains unperformed.

The only two composers I knew who succeeded in moving from chair to chair were Kurt Weill and George Gershwin. But Weill had left the serious-music chair in a closet in Berlin long before he came to America, and George Gershwin was quite another kettle of fish. He was in a class all by himself. Still I do not think that his attempts to move *beyond* the world of his genuine song talent with its strands of the Lower East Side of New York, the Russian Jewish Diaspora, and black America into the world of "serious" music had so lasting a value as one usually assumes. The ones that deal with *song*, like *Porgy and Bess*, are as lovely as Offenbach and Johann Strauss, but the purely instrumental concert compositions suffer from an abundance of secondhand rhetoric and outworn harmonic clichés.

As for "imported" contemporary "serious" music fetching any kind of money in those mid-1930s, it was beyond anyone's expectations unless, of course, the imported composer was already famous, like Richard Strauss, or Rachmaninov, or Stravinsky. And even then the composer had to be *also* a "glamorous" performer of his own music in order to "make" the market controlled by powerful concert agencies.

I had missed my chance to go to Hollywood after the "triumph" of *Union Pacific*, and was too frivolous, too carefree, and much too eager to participate in New York's *strudel* of variegated amusements and pleasures, to try my hand, or rather my bottom, at sitting on the "popular music" chair. George Gershwin urged me to go to Hollywood and exploit *Union Pacific*'s success at once, but, alas, I did not heed his advice. I remained on the East Coast.

I cannot remember what I lived on during those first years in New York, once my corrosive adventure with Dr. Barnes came to an end, but then, what had I lived on in France or before that, in Germany? Or, indeed, ever since we had left Sevastopol in 1919? What had we, all of us, lived on once the contents of Mother's *nécessaire* had evaporated and the income from Lubcza's forests had been squandered?

Occasionally I did "hack jobs" in New York, orchestrating pop songs for what used to be called "big bands," but this was rare. Well-paid professionals attached to publishing houses were in command of that market. I also tried to give private lessons. But the good students, like the delightful pianist-composer Leo Smit, were rare and poor; and rich ones were unreliable. They would cancel their lessons at the last moment or not appear at the appointed time.

Very often I had to rely on the generosity of rich friends. Foremost among them were my lady patrons and a new friend, Raimund von Hofmannsthal, the son of the Austrian poet. I met Raimund in February 1934 and we became friends at once. He was then married to Alice Astor, who was rich and generous. Alice had a country estate near Poughkeepsie, the large and grand Rhinebeck mansion overlooking the Hudson. I went often to Rhinebeck for gay and happy weekends.

Raimund was by nature a *grand seigneur*, immensely thoughtful and generous to his friends. He was lovable and amusing and, like me, enjoyed life as a true hedonist. He loved good food and drink, but, above all, the company of pretty and clever people.

In addition to Rhinebeck, the Hofmannsthals shared a luxurious castle in Austria with Eleonora von Mendelssohn. They invited friends to their castle, entertained them lavishly, and gave brilliant parties. The castle stood on a promontory on the Attersee, a mountain lake in the Salzkammergut. In the summers of 1934, 1935, and 1936 I spent several weeks at Alice's and Raimund's castle and in nearby Salzburg. I had my full share of musical pleasures and the other amusements it offered.

And in America my lady patrons helped my by commissioning me to write music which they arranged to have performed. They also invited me to stay at their country homes and arranged for me to meet important people and make useful contacts.

Still, I never knew how I was to pay next month's bills or whether I would have enough money to pay the fare to Europe. In those pre-aviational years, boat fares were ridiculously expensive. And yet I had to go to Europe, not only to see my mother and my relatives but essentially because in Europe I had a permanent haven at my friend's little house at Kolbsheim in Alsace.

One of my patrons was Ambassador Myron Taylor. On his advice, I went to Boston to see a Wells College trustee who was in charge of selecting a new head of the college's Music Department.

He, in turn, promised to come and see me with the President of Wells College, whose name was Dr. Weld.

President Weld must have had the shock of his life when he and the Bostonian trustee came to my studio on 39th Street near the corner of Lexington Avenue one Saturday at noon in late May 1936.

The room I lived in alone (already separated from my first wife, Natalie) was a spacious studio. It had four windows, a high ceiling with a skylight, a bathroom, and a large open closet. It was a one-flight walk-up above an architect's study.

Soon after I had moved into that studio in the early autumn of 1935, I was given two pots of tropical creepers by Cecil Beaton. The two plants started to climb toward the skylight. In a few months they covered one of my walls and part of the ceiling. I made a makeshift netting to keep them from falling on my bed and tied small water bottles to their loose roots. By October my room looked like a jungle.

Being moneyless, I lived largely on fruit and coffee. I bought cheap fruit in large quantities and stacked it on the mantelpiece, the windowsills, the piano, and the shelves of my closet. As a result, my room smelled permanently of oranges, bananas, pineapples, apples, of rotting pears, and of coffee. I had read somewhere that Schiller cured his stomach upsets by eating rotting pears. I tried it, and found that *one* rotting pear was a convenient laxative, and ate one foul pear daily.

Pavel Tchelitchev, the painter, had the idea of holding a photographer's exhibit in my jungle. He and I were friends of Cecil Beaton, of Carl Van Vechten, Hoynigen Huehne, and of Horst. The four of them gave us several dozens of their portrait photographs. Tchelitchev, his friend Charlie Ford, several pretty models, and I hung them on the foliage-covered walls of my huge jungle room. We held a boisterous *vernissage.*

Raimund provided it with drink and a caterer's buffet, and with an Austrian band that played waltzes, polkas, and the stuff one danced to at that time in America. After the *vernissage* all of them danced with the pretty girls until the early hours of the morning. Two large cops appeared around three a.m. and wanted us to stop the noise. But we got them drunk. They took off their uniforms and joined the ball. In the graying light of dawn the band went into 39th Street and, flanked by the two uniformed policemen, played soft Austrian lullabies to soothe the wrath of my neighbors.

* * *

Early in March 1936, Tchelitchev called up to say that Henri Cartier-Bresson had arrived from Mexico with no money and no place to stay.

"Could you put him up in your jungle?" he asked.

I told Tchelitchev to send Cartier-Bresson over.

I had met him a year earlier in Paris, but only fleetingly. He was as yet unknown except to a small circle of close friends. He was very young and handsome, with a blond and pink head and a gently mocking smile playing around his lips that I have always liked in Norman French faces. But what was astonishing in Cartier-Bresson's face were his eyes. They were like darts—sharp and clever, limpidly blue and infinitely agile. "Henri has the fastest eyes I know," Pavel Tchelitchev used to say. Indeed, there was the quick spark of a shrewd *voyeur* in Cartier-Bresson's eyes.

Cartier-Bresson installed his cot on the opposite side of my room, catty-corner from my day bed. We moved the chest of drawers into the bathroom and borrowed a folding screen to separate our sleeping quarters. Then we started living together in delicious harmony, sharing whatever money we could muster.

Cartier-Bresson loved to eat apple pie *à la mode*. He found it to be the cheapest and most nourishing dish. I ate skimpy drugstore hamburgers, and both of us consumed a huge amount of fruit.

Cartier-Bresson was enamored of Harlem. He spent days, evenings, and nights there. Sometimes I would accompany him. We would trudge from club to club and listen to marvelous bands. Some of Cartier-Bresson's friends belonged to Harlem's radical elite. They were extraordinarily bright and educated people, and nearly all of them immensely open and hospitable.

But with some of Cartier-Bresson's intellectual black friends I used to get into scraps about the Bolshevik Revolution. To them, Lenin was a hero and a saint whose role in history was not supposed to be challenged. But then, not only blacks held such views in the early thirties; some of the most dedicated future anti-Communists were at that time in or close to the Communist movement.

Henri was carefree, gay, and immensely companionable. He was, like me, totally unconcerned with America's main profession—money-making. He spent his time going for long walks, snapping photographs, but, except for our small circle of friends, no one saw them or seemed to be interested in them. His quick and admirable *voyeurish* "eye art" was not yet *à la mode*. Most photographs of those years were posed ones, carefully arranged, not snapped. The snapping belonged to the domain of hack newspaper reporting. It was not yet considered an art. I suppose that it started to be an art during the Spanish Civil War and grew to be a respected art form with World War II. In a way, Henri Cartier-Bresson was the great "snapper pioneer."

Oh, how good and how meaningful were those weeks that Henry Cartier-Bresson shared my jungle with me! Not only did we become friends forever, but his intransigence, his *droiture*, his instinctive sense of justice and compassion, his single-minded devotion to his craft were a much-needed lesson to me, the shifty, wayward, and insecure.

We had long talks mostly on morals and on politics. I suppose that both of us were radicals. But to Cartier-Bresson the Communist movement was the bearer of history, of mankind's future—especially in those years, when Hitler had saddled Germany and when a civil war was about to explode in Spain. I shared many of Cartier-Bresson's views, but, despite the gnawing longing for my Russian fatherland, I could not accept or espouse the philo-Communist attitude of so many Western European and American intellectuals. I felt that they were curiously blind to the realities of Russian Communism and were only reacting to the fascist tides that were sweeping Europe in the wake of the Depression. To a certain degree I felt that the philo-Communism of the mid-thirties was a passing fad, cleverly nurtured by a mythology about the Russian Bolshevik Revolution shaped by the Soviet Agitprop Apparat.

Fortunately, Henri Cartier-Bresson was never dogmatic or didactic about his beliefs or his leanings. He listened attentively and trusted the sincerity of my own views. He did not argue with me or contradict me. I believe that in the course of time he came to agree with me, although we have never talked about it since.

Dr. Weld and his Bostonian companion were urbane and amiable. If they had been startled by the sight of my jungle, they did not show it. The meeting turned into a lunch at the Harvard Club.

From the very outset I sensed that their minds had already been made up in my favor and that Ambassador Taylor's recommendation had played the decisive role. During the luncheon it was agreed that the Bostonian trustee would drive me up to Aurora at the end of the spring term to enable me to visit Wells College and decide whether I would like to teach there.

We drove to beautiful but intensely melancholy Aurora in mid-June 1936. There, with qualms but without hesitation, I signed a contract with the college. I was to be head of the Music Department, teach courses in music theory and history, and conduct the college choir. Never before had I done any of these things, but I knew that somehow I could live up to them.

I joined the Wells faculty in September 1936 and stayed five long, frustrating academic years in that boring, provincial college.

In the early spring of 1939, still at Wells, I got married for a second time. My second wife, Constance Holladay, was very young, good-looking, high-spirited, and bright.

I thought that maybe now things would turn for the better. Life would become less lonesome, less dull. We spent the summer on the Cape, in Wellfleet. We met dozens of new friends, some of them brilliant and interesting, other just gay and pleasant. In the early autumn we moved into a comfortable, spacious house, surrounded by ancient elms, limes, and maples. Many more friends came to visit us. Besides, I knew all of the visiting concert artists and most of the scholars, writers, and poets featured by the college's concert and lecture series. We replaced the traditional receptions with parties of our own. And our parties were fully "wet" and often very gay.

By trial and error I learned to cook. I remembered recipes of George Balanchine and refrained from the use of cookbooks.

I composed choral music for my college choir, which by 1938 had become first-rate, even by professional standards. I enjoyed working with it and transcribing for it a great quantity of early Renaissance music.

The only thing that did not improve, but progressively soured, was the teaching routine. Not the individual theory teaching, but the courses in music history. I grew more and more restless in Aurora.

In May 1940 came the French disaster. All contact with friends and relatives in Europe was severed. *Emigrés* continued to pour into New York from Lisbon, England, the south of France, and Morocco. The Milhauds arrived, and Vittorio Rieti, and Paul Hindemith, and cousin Vladimir with his wife Vera and their son Mitya; a bit earlier came the Maritains—to name but the closest.

I used my strategic academic position to be useful to some of the arriving friends. I got Paul Hindemith and Jacques Maritain partial appointments to the Wells faculty, so as to enable them to obtain American visas. Both came and stayed for a while in Aurora, enlivening its continuous boredom.

A year later came that fatal night of June 22, 1941. That long, hot, miserable night! I sat at my incompetent radio trying to get Moscow on shortwave and instead getting nothing but static. Finally I fell straight into the triumphant boom of Berlin: "The enemy's air force has been destroyed on the ground. All resistance is broken. Our victorious troops are advancing unopposed. *Heil Hitler! Sieg Heil!*"

The next morning, unkempt and unslept, I drove to Wells. I had to keep myself busy in order not to think of what was going on. We were to move to Annapolis in a few weeks and lots of packing had to be done.

I stopped at the filling station to get gas, and asked the attendant if he had heard the news.

"What news, Mr. Nicolas?" he asked sleepily.

"About Russia getting invaded," I said.

He was watching the meter. "Well," he said after a while, scratching the back of his head, "well . . . I'll tell ya, Mr. Nicolas, that's what's gonna happen to all them small countries. They all get invaded some time or 'nother." He glanced at the meter. "It'll be a dollar and fifty-eight cents."

That same year, 1941, came Pearl Harbor. And again the same perplexed feeling, the same question: How could it have happened?

Jacques Maritain had introduced me to Scott Buchanan, the dean of St. John's College in Annapolis, Maryland, and after an interview he had offered me a job.

Little did I know what I was in for when in the summer of 1941 I moved with my wife and my newborn son, Peter, to sweltering Annapolis.

The St. John's College Liberal Arts curriculum in those years was a strange affair. It was a jet odyssey through 2,500 years of Western intellectual history. All of it was based on the reading, the discussion, and—hopefully—the understanding of "One Hundred Great Books," as the college curriculum was then advertised. These "One Hundred Great Books" were supposed to be the rock upon which stood our "great Western Judeo-Graeco-Roman civilization."

203

The "Great Books" were selected and arranged in chronological order to fit the needs of a four-year college curriculum by the powerful Liberal Arts Committee of the University of Chicago.

Besides questioning the validity of some of the choices of these "Great Books," I never could find out what were the criteria by which the selection had been made and why these hundred books alone formed the grand civilizatory rock. "Liberal Arts," "Great Ideas," "Fundamental Knowledge," "Watersheds in Thought" were some of the cliché answers. But why, for example, was *War and Peace* included in the select hundred and *Anna Karenina* (by far a better novel) not? Why anyone had to waste anybody's time on reading and discussing an obscure medieval essay, *On the Breadth of Forms* by Grosseteste, Bishop of Lincoln, and not, for example, the much more entertaining but equally obscure *Horoscope of Wallenstein* by Kepler, remains beyond comprehension. Surely, so it seemed to me, the "lighthouse" that was supposed to shed its Jewish, Greek, and Latin light upon our dubious civilization and make us feel "rockbound" was, to say the least, incompletely and arbitrarily "fueled" by those hundred chosen books and their authors.

Nor could I find out why these *fundamental* "Great Books" fell so conveniently into the even number of 100 and not, for example, 97 or 103. Was it perhaps, I thought, in order to elicit the same psychological response or conditional reflex that haberdashers aim at when they advertise the sale of three ties for ten dollars?

Yet, here I was, in the autumn of 1941, about to start a pedagogical flea race (with obstacles), skipping merrily from Homer (*The Iliad* and *The Odyssey* in three weeks!) to Plato, from Thucydides to Aristotle and onward through Greek and Roman poets, dramatists, historians, and mathematicians, and scientists—all of it, fortunately, in English—to the Bible! Two-thirds of it, mind you!

Yet, despite all this, I enjoyed my first year at St. John's. I was forced to read or reread books I would never have read otherwise. It bothered me to read them in such haste, because since the age of consent I have been a meticulous, slow reader. But on the whole, it provided me with the opportunity of re-awakening my mind's discriminatory faculties, which, with the advance in age and the dustbin world that surrounds our lives, had inevitably got dulled.

Reflecting now upon the St. John's pedagogical flea circus and its whirlwind "One Hundred Great Books" reading acrobatics, I cannot but think of the last scene of Alban Berg's *Wozzeck:* A child, a waif, jumps back and forth on a wooden horse and singsongs: "Hop-hop . . . hop-hop." Hop-hop from Plato's *Republic* to the Book of Kings. Hop-hop from *Faust* to Freud. Hop-hop from Dostoevsky's Karamazovs to the Communist Manifesto. and hop-hop lightly and swiftly through the cumbersome expanses of our 2,500-year-old "cultural heritage"—to where? For what purpose? Surely not for the sake of a profitable humane education in the so-called Liberal Arts.

Fortunately, the St. John's College community was bright and even brilliant, and the human relations I established with some of its members, both teachers and students, led to lasting friendships. But above all else, the proximity to Washington and in a lesser degree to Baltimore was exhilarating, and in more ways than one, that period became a turning point in my own life's progress.

It was during my first visit to St. John's that I met Chip Bohlen, that thoroughbred American who spoke elegant Russian and had spent time in Russia from the first post-Revolutionary Embassy on. Little did I then suspect that it would be the Bohlens who would make America a true home for me.

In the beginning, all went well at St. John's. The colleagues were nice and helpful, the students far superior to the Auroran maidens. The president, Winkie Barr, was charming, and Dean Buchanan seemed to approve wholeheartedly of Elliott Carter's and my approach to the problem of fitting *la bella musica* into the Liberal Arts curriculum.

Elliott Carter and I had devised a plan whereby we would offer several stylistic prototypes of "Great Works of Music" arranged in chronological order. We would start with a monophonic Gregorian Mass followed by a polyphonic one by Guillaume de Machault (fifteenth century). We would go on from there to Monteverdi's *Orfeo,* then to J. S. Bach's B Minor Mass, to Mozart's *Don Giovanni,* to Beethoven's C Sharp Minor Quartet, and end it all with Stravinsky's *Rite of Spring.* This musical menu would be spread over the four academic years as a kind of *table d'hôte* for all students and for the members of the faculty.

Our idea was simple and practical. These works existed in recordings. Students could listen to them as much as they wanted to, individually or in groups, with scores in hand. We would give a precise, fully informative, and aesthetically objective lecture about each one of these "Great Works of Music" and answer questions concerning them, avoiding, of course, anything which could be construed as a personal opinion. Then, once these works had been lectured about and listened to and, we hoped, at least to a degree digested, we would discuss them in seminars with records and scores at hand, as we discussed the "Great Books."

Parallel with this the students would be required to do experimental work on tuning and acoustics in laboratory, and read excerpts from theoretical masters: Aristoxenus, Descartes, Kepler, and Helmholtz.

In the course of his first year at St. John's (1940–41), when Elliott Carter was alone there, he had had sonometers built. When I came in 1941, there were two or three one-string sonometers on which to experiment with the so-called Pythagorean system of tuning by dividing the string into various lengths, and several thirteen-string sonometers so one could tune a full chromatic scale as well as all kinds of eight-tone modes. Both of us wanted an electronic gadget that would measure frequencies, but it turned out to be too expensive.

Elliott thought and I fully agreed that these laboratory experiments could give the students an insight into the complex theoretical evolution of tuning, from the Pythagorean one, as described in the first chapter of Plato's *Timaeus,* through the Ptolomean and the so-called "mean-tone" tuning, to the Keplerian *Gamut,* and to the equal temperament as it was developed at the time of J. S. Bach. It would also enable them to experiment with tuning empirically. Few people realize what an influence the changes in tuning systems had upon the evolution of musical techniques, musical structures, and musical thinking in general.

At the time I came to St. John's there were altogether about 250 or 300 "Great Books" guinea pigs there. Only about five percent of them could read a piano score and perhaps one in a hundred a score for a string quartet. We were not in nineteenth-century Germany, where all schoolchildren were taught to read music at the age of ten or eleven. We were in musically illiterate, or at best half-literate, America.

Elliott and I both believed that there was not much sense in talking earnestly about a piece of music without being able to discuss its structure, its technical intricacies, its form and style. For that purpose, the ability to read musical symbols, however minimally, was essential and indispensable. We decided therefore to give several technical and to a certain degree historical lectures on the evolution of musical notation. These lectures were to be obligatory for the students and for the faculty, like all other so-called "formal" lectures at St. John's College.

Actually, it was like asking the college community to learn the ideographic signs of an Asian language, or the Hebrew alphabet. But, to my surprise, there was very little grumbling when we announced those obligatory lectures on musical notation. We tried to make our lectures as lively as possible, by drawing parallels with developments in paleography.

The first lectures (Elliott and I gave them alternately) were well attended and the questions asked showed real interest on the part of the students. We were both pleased. All in all, I had the feeling that we were on the way to finding a more intelligent, more pragmatic way to teach laymen something about the art and the craft of music then the slipshod "Music Appreciation" courses that flourished in colleges all over America in those remote years.

Besides these curricular activities I had other "elective" chores. I had formed a choir and an orchestra. The first was all male and consisted of students. The second was a hybrid of students, amateur Annapolitans (male and female), Midshipmen from the Naval Academy, and two or three professionals from the Baltimore Symphony Orchestra. We practiced regularly and gave several concerts a year. We sang and played all kinds of good music, with a goodly number of false notes. But we did it all with dedication and enthusiasm. And our public liked us.

One day Dean Scott Buchanan sat in on one of my lectures on musical notation, and afterward called me to his office. There was a battle of wits, during which I tried to explain to him that you couldn't teach anything about music before teaching its language. We agreed on an experiment in which together we would expose some students to a Beethoven quartet without the preliminary explanations, "goading" them to learn—Buchanan's favorite method. The experiment quickly revealed the error of Buchanan's method. It turned into a comic fiasco, and Buchanan never forgave me what he called my foolish, gratuitous joke. In April 1942 I knew that my days at St. John's were counted.

But Scott Buchanan was a kind and generous man. Knowing that I was in financial difficulties, he suggested that I try to get a part-time teaching job at the Peabody Conservatory in Baltimore in addition to my jobs at St. John's.

In 1943, with his approval, I took over at the Peabody Conservatory its History of Music courses. I liked to teach there. At St. John's I always felt a bit of an impostor. But at the music school I taught the stuff I knew.

On a spring day in 1943 Kay Halle called from Washington, her voice as eager as ever.

"Nicky, I'm here with sister Betsy. We share an apartment. Why don't you come next Sunday? We'll have lunch at a Greek place around the corner."

"Not this Sunday, Kay," I replied, "I can't."

"Oh, but you must come. Just for lunch. I want you to meet an *extraordinary* man!" And the tone of her voice became flamboyant. "He's just arrived here in Washington. He works at the *British Embassy*, but actually, like you, he's a *Russian*. And he's a don at *Oxford* and he's a specialist on Marx! And—"

"Couldn't I meet this personage some other time, Kay?" I said, trying to tame Kay's burst of enthusiasm.

"No! No! You've got to come Sunday! You must meet this man! *Ab-so-lu-tely!* He's only in his thirties, but he's already *famous*. And he's a philosopher and a historian and a marvelous linguist. And here at the Embassy he's kind of Churchill's 'eye' in America and a *marvelous* wit. Believe me, Nicky. He's the *most remarkable* man I've ever met!"

I wanted to interrupt, but she went on from superlative to superlative. Finally I shouted into the receiver: "Listen, Kay! Will you, please? If I *can* make myself free, I'll come.

"But what's the man's name?" I asked as an afterthought.

Kay giggled. "You won't believe it. It is kind of unexpected. But it's true. His name is: *I-s-a-i-a-h* BERLIN," and she spelled out each letter, pronouncing the "a's" like diphthongs.

Then she started again: "Believe me, Nicky, he's *fantastic!* A linguist. A historian. He's Russian, but actually he's an Englishman. He's a philosopher, but a diplomat. He's Churchill's 'eye.' Still young, but so clever, so witty, and so wise. A real scholar . . . and yet so amusing."

I waited for the end of her superlatives and asked: "Are you sure, Kay, that this man isn't pulling your leg? Or maybe you're pulling

208

mine? That kind of combination—a Hebrew prophet with the Nazi capital—at this time of the war sounds odd."

Kay interrupted: "What do you mean, *odd?* Come and see for yourself! And don't be silly! He's perfectly real and he's *here*—in *Washington.* I saw him yesterday. And his name is Isaiah Berlin! Randolph Churchill told me about him some time ago. He's the *most* brilliant man in England. And he's coming to lunch on Sunday with Betsy and me and you'd better come along. 'Cause you got to *meet* him, you simply must!"

I had known Kay, or Katherine, Halle for quite a while. I do not remember where we met, but it must have been through or with George Gershwin, probably in 1934, or maybe even earlier, in 1933, shortly after Natasha and I landed in America. I do remember that a whole bunch of us—George Gershwin's friends—traveled together to two premières, one at Hartford, the other in Boston, and the one in Boston in 1935 was the première of Gershwin's *Porgy and Bess.* After the glorious première in Boston, the next morning the unshaven and underslept George, Kay, Martha Rousseau, Mary Cushing, Martha's brother Teddy, a friendly fellow called Spivacke, and I had large, bowls of creamy oyster stew at the Oyster Bar of New York's Grand Central Station.

But this took place in New York before and during the first years of my Auroran exile, before I stopped commuting to New York City.

Once I went to Wells College, I dropped out of Kay's sight for a while. When I came to New York I had chores to do, and my visits were rare, passing ones. I came in a breeze, on the way to Europe or, later, to the Cape. Then after I moved to Annapolis I was fully immersed in my unwanted reading-and-teaching bath.

On Sunday I pressed the doorbell of Kay Halle's flat. It sounded a quaint third. "Major third—good omen," went through my head.

"Come in, Nicky, come in," said Kay, hiding behind the door. "I'm not quite dressed and Betsy's gone to get the paper."

It was a large duplex studio flat. Very little furniture and everything plain, spotless white.

A few minutes later Kay came down in a light summer dress and Betsy returned with the paper.

Precisely at one o'clock the major third sounded again. Kay ran to the door, and someone came in. He appeared in the studio room in a light summer suit bearing a thin cane *s nabaldashnikom* ("with a top") and a small Victorian bunch of flowers. There was a gently embarrassed, shy smile on his pale face. The don started speaking at once, as soon as he came into the room. He spoke ostensibly to the three of us, but so *fast*, so "lippingly," and in such an Oxonian way that neither Betsy nor I nor even Kay could quite understand all of his words. I had never before been faced with this kind of performance and was unprepared for it acoustically and mentally.

"A fine luncheon it will be," I thought, imagining Oxonian cascades interrupted by Kay's superlatives throughout the meal.

After a while Kay and Betsy put on large straw hats and the four of us marched first to the lift—the don still speaking—down in the lift—still speaking—and into the glaring sunshine of the street. Once outdoors, we started walking in pairs, the sisters holding their hats in front, the don and I trailing them.

Within moments something very simple but to me utterly unexpected took place. In an absolutely unblemished, moderately fast, bassoonish-sounding, and perfectly articulated Russian, the don asked me for my first name and my patronymic.

From that moment onward, the fortunes of the luncheon turned around. Not Kay or Betsy or the kebab would be the victor in the midday "engagement," but rather the Oxford don and *me*. We would certainly turn the sails of the conversation in the direction of Russian winds. Especially since in the course of the brief walk to Kay's Greek neighborhood restaurant I discovered in Issaiya Maximovich—for this was the proper way to address the don in Russian —an ever-ready, incredibly agile, more Slavic than Anglo-Saxon gift for huge guffaws of unquenchable laughter.

Not that we misbehaved at that luncheon by switching off altogether the *Ruisseau Anglais* and being rudely and exclusively Russian, as Russians are apt to be. We kept the two sisters happily entertained, but did lapse occasionally into Russian "asides."

The lunch was long and relaxed. After it, I had to rush back to Annapolis by streetcar and bus. But before I left, the don and I exchanged addresses and telephone numbers, and quite early the next morning the phone buzzed in my ear and a gay voice said: "*Noo-Zdrastye*, how are you? When shall we meet? Can you come here? Tomorrow? Wednesday? Or shall I take the bus and come and visit you in your 'Great Books' reservoir? Ha-ha!"

A few years ago I asked Chip Bohlen in Aspen, during those sad summer weeks so close to his death, whether he remembered our luncheon with his cousin Edith at the Mayflower in the spring of 1940. So far as I am concerned, our friendship reaches back and forth in time and makes me feel as if there was never a time when it did not exist. As there has never been a time without Mozart's *Don Giovanni* or Stravinsky's *Rite of Spring*. And when I say "it has always existed," I mean all of it, the whole wonderful friendship —I do not mean in some moot Platonic way, but rather that it had been written in our stars by a generous genie, the protector and furtherer of human friendships.

Because this is the way lifelong friendships are, or at least have been with me: immutable and permanent, whether their protagonists are together or on opposite sides of the globe. I could count at most a score of such friendships in the course of a long life. Not more.

And they were all of them "tea with jam under an apple tree," as we say in Russian—cozy, warm, and peaceful. There are, of course, quick-flash ones that are like glowworms or lightning. They come and go, moments of gladness followed by quest: Where is he or she? What happened? What is she or he doing? With the Bohlens, from the very start it was, and has remained, tea with jam.

I remember the first time I saw them together: Avis and Chip entered the room, she in a smart organdy dress, he in a dark suit. A vision of *noblesse et beauté*.

"So you're here, comrade? I'd like you to meet my wife." And while introducing me, he added smilingly in Russian, "She also speaks a bit of Russian."

Avis blushed and smiled again, producing those dimples. "Very little . . . we'd better speak English."

During that dinner party I told Chip that once a week, on Tuesdays, I came to Washington for war work at the Justice Department.

"You mean to say that Justice is in the war racket too?" Chip laughed.

"Then why don't you come to dinner next Tuesday?" said Avis.

A small, simple, modest house. Cozy disorder. Absolutely no pretenses. Nothing "rich." Guests, frequent but rarely numerous, mostly close friends. Often colleagues, collaborators. Among the closest from the Department, George Kennan, Tommie Thompson, Durbrow, Freddie Reinhardt (future Ambassadors). Englishmen— John Foster, Johnnie Russell, and, of course, Isaiah Maximovich, Don Berlin, known already as "the Prophet," the closest of all.

Conversations, topics: mainly politics, with Russia as the center.

211

The tenor and character of the conversation is at times fast, sometimes laconic and caustic.

These new friends had few if any illusions about "Uncle Joe," about Russian Communism and the future shape of the Socialist Motherland. In more ways than one, they were an anachronistic group in the Washington of those years, perhaps even in all of America. America was in a state of Sovietophilic euphoria, which none in the house on Dumbarton Avenue shared.

The bulk of American public opinion had switched twice in three years in its feelings toward Russia. First it was *against*—after the partition of Poland and the "fiendish" Finnish war (1939). Stalin in newspaper cartoons looked like a nasty mixture of a wolf and a bear. Then, as abruptly, opinion was *for* Russia: after the Nazi invasion of Russia in 1941. Stalin was suddenly beautified, represented as a knight in armor defending the Kremlin against a horde of Teutons, or reproduced from Margaret Bourke-White's slenderized and idolized profile photographs. And then, in 1943, the pro-Russian feeling was enhanced by Stalingrad.

"You will see," argued trusting Americans, "Communism will never come back to Russia the way it was. It will be a different country after the war. Didn't Stalin bring the Patriarch back from exile? And the writers and poets? And didn't Stalin re-establish officers' ranks and reinstate the historical national heroes, and even some of the tsars and saints, like Alexander Nevsky and Peter the Great?"

Not so the skeptics at Dumbarton Avenue. They knew, as Kennan once said, that Stalinism is irreversible.

By the spring of 1943 my work at the Department of Justice had shifted from evening to noon. Every Tuesday morning I would take my little boy Peter to his kindergarten in Annapolis, perform my tutorial duties at the college, and flee to Washington. There I would descend to its Hades, a stuffy, dank basement where I would sit until six o'clock in a plywood stall, confronted by a microfilm-reading monster. It was an eye-breaker and a migraine-inducer. I would read the weekly "fly-ins" from overseas. They consisted of newspapers and journals published in those regions of Russia that were under German occupation. The material was "procured and processed" by our Embassy in Sweden and flown via Britain to Washington. I was supposed to read all of it and the next morning prepare a "comprehensive résumé with appropriate quotes" from the week's catch.

Most of it was drab Nazi agitprop stuff in abominable Russian (worse than *Pravda*'s) or in technocratic German. I never quite understood the point of my microfilm ordeal or the need for it, but I was told that professional "evaluators" (I never saw one, and computers did not yet exist) could, by "reprocessing" my "processed" résumé, evaluate or estimate the social and economic shifts in those regions to which the papers and journals referred.

Occasionally there were juicy bits in those publications. For instance, in the late summer of 1943 a town in the southern Ukraine was visited by Reichsmarshal Goering. The captive paper wrote: "Because of intensive harvest work *not all* [sic!] of the native population turned out to cheer its liberator from Bolshevik tyranny."

At six o'clock the work of the Department's day shift ceased, a night-shift colleague took over my stall with its eye-breaker, and I hurried to the nearest tram stop. Then, for one long evening, life became a delight. Soon, very soon, I was a regular Tuesday addendum to the family and a member of the Dumbarton circle. Imperceptibly my own interests changed.

My political perspectives, which until then had been "simplistic," gradually acquired a degree of sophistication. I began to perceive the basic nature of the twentieth century's political scene: that the evil spirit of this century was double-headed. Hitler and Stalin were two parts of the same phenomenon. Stalinism was the opposite side of the same coin as Herr Hitler.

Yes, the charmed house in Georgetown, its family, its circle of friends soon became my "home" in America. But when I say "home" I do not mean it in the habitual sense of the word. Not as a place to which one belongs either by birthright or by matrimonial and parental ties. I mean rather as a center of friendship and of intellectual affinity. There is no one so much in need of a home and of belonging as an exile. And a matrimonial or parental abode always smells of a dog's chain. Especially to an inveterate (but consecutive) polygamist like me. The only real and longed-for home is an elective one—only to such a home can one belong.

In Europe I had found one such home, in Alsace. I had none in America before the advent of the Bohlens.

How much of my affinity with Chip and Avis and with their circle of friends was due to the fact that the center of their interests was my former motherland, I cannot tell. I rarely thought about it. But most probably it had more to do with the original impulse of our friendship than either of us realized.

As I have said, the discovery of an American home led to a broadening of my interests. From being a composer and an academic, I became someone deeply interested and involved in the political scene around me and in political action. No wonder! At that time it was in the air. It was the concern of intelligent people all over the world. Men and women of good will and integrity readily abandoned their professional occupations, their private lives and interests in order to help win the war against what seemed to be obvious evil.

But were it not for the fortuitous meetings with Chip Bohlen and with Isaiah Berlin, I might have lingered much longer in what would have become the "grooves" of Academe.

Instead, from 1943 onward my life changed. First imperceptibly, then radically. For nearly twenty years I became involved in politics and in political action. Not that I abandoned my basic profession; I became politically involved *within* that profession. Indeed, never was art (including music, of course) so misused and abused by politics as during those fearsome last years of the rule of Messrs. Zhdanov and Stalin.

But whether I was in Berlin in American uniform as advisor to the U.S. military government or, later, had become the ubiquitous Secretary General of the Congress for Cultural Freedom, Chip Bohlen was always my model, my source of advice, and often my comforter.

From the time Chip, Isaiah, and I met, and especially during the last two war years, we were a homogeneous, congenial trio. We had a deep bond in common: our interest in Russian culture, Russian politics, Russian destiny. Not that I played an active role in that trio. Actually it was more of an Anglo-American duet with an occasional peep coming out of me. But many years later, in Paris, Chip explained to me what my role in that unequal trio had been.

By virtue of his experience and of his training, Chip Bohlen was the only one of us three who could be legitimately called an expert on the Soviet Union. He had lived there for many years. He had met and dealt with Soviet leaders and average bureaucrats. He had studied their ideological literature, and could quote their classics. He had followed with diligent attention the sinewy paths of Soviet internal and external policies. He had witnessed numerous phenomena of Soviet Communist repression—the liquidation of the Kulaks, the 1937–38 purges and trials, the macabre horrors of Zhdanov's "cultural policies," and the ghastly mores and manners that had established themselves in what once was on the way to becoming a civilized European land.

Yet in all of it, as Chip readily admitted, he was concerned mainly with the present, with what was going on in the secretive top hierarchy of the party and its complex, infighting caste system. Who stood next to the supreme boss during the May Day or October Day parades? In what order did they stand on top of that dark mausoleum and why was X absent and Y in the second row? These were the kind of questions diplomats asked themselves during those Stalinist years in Moscow.

Little time was left for the study of Russian culture as such, and there was very little opportunity for direct contact with Russian people, Russian scholars, writers, and artists. Besides, only those whose brains had been appropriately streamlined by the party apparat were allowed to have contact with foreigners. Hence Chip did not and could not have either the leisure or the opportunity to acquire a comprehensive scholarship of Russian civilization. In fact, Chip and his colleague and friend George Kennan were, so to speak, the founders of a novel branch of modern scholarship that goes under the name of Kremlinology. But both Kennan and Bohlen did it in the line of duty and not for any dividends. They did it as a service to their country, and this, I believe, is why they were supreme in their Soviet expertise.

Isaiah Berlin, a Russian-speaking native of Riga, but fully English by adoption, by scholarship, and by training, had never been in the Soviet Union before December 1945. He did not have the firsthand knowledge of the U.S.S.R. that Bohlen possessed. Yet he was and still is, without the slightest shadow of a doubt, one of the most erudite scholars of Russian culture, especially of Russian political and social thought of the last two centuries. He is also a lover and a connoisseur of Russian letters and of Russian music.

In all these capacities Isaiah Berlin was indispensable to Chip. But Chip in turn was indispensable to Isaiah when a clear answer had to be found as to the reaction of the Soviet bureaucracy to a given situation or to a particular problem.

Yet neither Bohlen nor Berlin was even in the remotest sense Russian by *instinct*. How could they be? One of them was English, the other American. As Chip once said, "The only one among us who is gut-wise Russian is you." In other words, their reflexes, their intuition, their unconscious instinctive reactions were of necessity non-Russian, whereas mine could be gauged as such. Thus the duet occasionally turned into a trio. Although I never thought of myself as a "hearty Russian," Chip believed and insisted that I was one. "You've remained just as Russian as they come, brother," he would say. And this to him was a psychological asset. An asset to our friendship.

It would be presumptious of me to try to assess Chip Bohlen's achievements as a diplomat. Others have done it better than I ever could. Their verdict has been unanimous: he was one of the best diplomats America has ever had. He himself has reported on his work modestly, truthfully, and with his usual candor and understatement.

What I do want to say, if only to honor his memory, is something quite different. And maybe it is the protoplasmic Russian in me that feels the need to say it. Maybe, deep down, I am also saying it on behalf of those who were true Russians. I want to express to Chip Bohlen's memory my deep gratitude for his compassion and kindness to Russians in distress. Few people have been so compassionate as was Chip in dealing with Russians, few have been so understanding and have taken their problems so close to heart. If it hadn't been for Chip Bohlen, the cruel and wanton shipment of Russian DPs from West Germany to Stalin's concentration camps would have continued unabated for many more months. There are many examples of Chip's compassion and goodness. And like all true compassion and goodness, his kind deeds were done modestly, intelligently, and with no publicity whatsoever.

Wystan Auden slid into my life thunderlessly in the late autumn or winter of 1943. I met him through Isaiah Berlin, in Washington.

He had a handsome, very Anglo-Attic profile. It was a noble profile, almost classical, its parts in measured proportion to each other. The large ear shell, the gently curved arch of the brow and of the nostrils, the willful, ample chin, and the broad forehead half concealed by unruly, short-trimmed hair—all of it a coherent, harmonious whole. But what gave life and identity to that whole were minor traits which at a cursory glance went unnoticed. A poutingly protruding upper lip that failed to cover a fleshier, sensuous lower one. Two wrinkles. A long one descended in a wave from the edge of one nostril all the way down to the chin. The second, much shorter and straight, was tangent to the mouth's corner. But if one looked more closely at those wrinkles, they said something more—something about compassion and grief, about anger and irony, and about a strange kind of lassitude. And then there were those eyes of his. They did not see, they reflected. They seemed turned inward, concerned with something that was going on in that person's own self. Maybe remembering. Or maybe helping the mind's eye to tend to the game of taming words and sentences, finding the clearest, the most articulate way of stating a thought, expressing a feeling, describing a landscape, a face, an object.

This was not a dreamer but a maker, and the maker's mind was keen, his wit sharp, his senses aglow.

I still hear through memory's wilderness the first sounds of Wystan's nasal, noisy voice, his clumsy laughter, his assertive way of telling not quite exportable (English parsonage) jokes, and can recapture my astonishment at seeing the dirt of his fingernails, his sartorial neglect (in childhood Russia I imagined all Englishmen as romantic but elegant Lord Byrons or Beau Brummells)—but also being startled by his quick mind, his staggering erudition, the ebullient sense of humor, and his dogmatically funny prejudices.

With persons like Wystan, relationships either click at once or they never do. Ours did. We started seeing each other, not very often but at least three or four times before he left for Europe in the early spring of 1945.

Before the early forties my ignorance of contemporary English poetry was near total. All I knew was Joyce's *Chamber Music* and T. S. Eliot's *Ash Wednesday* and those only because Marguerite Caetani had given them to me and had bullied me into reading them. In my childhood, German and French winds were blowing far stronger than English ones. Later on, the German and French Diasporas were not propitious to the learning of English verse. Thus, until midlife my poetic love affairs remained basically Russian, with a few promiscuous excursions into Teutonic and Gallic territories.

But one day Edmund Wilson gave me a thin book of *Selected Verse* by W. H. Auden.

"Nikolai Dimitrievich," he said with a chuckle, "now that you are an American citizen, you cannot continue to ignore the existence of English and American verse! *Pozhaluista*, read this." He opened the book and turning its pages, added, "This is the best English-language poetry since early Tom Eliot. It is very, very musical. I'm sure you'll like it."

From that day onward I not only read Auden's poems, but, as Russians are apt to do, learned some of them by heart. I liked his poetry at once. I liked its laconic sense of humor and pervasive wit; I liked its bitter-sweet irony, its skillful way of toying with familiar images, metaphors, and quotes. I liked its prosody, its lilting meters, its games with inner rhyme and clever assonance, its extraordinary lyrical temper. I do not know whether this particular 1940 selection contained Auden's long poem *The Sea and the Mirror*, a poetic commentary on Shakespeare's *Tempest*. But I do remember that *The Sea and the Mirror* was one of the first long poems by Auden I fell in love with. When I met Auden in 1943 I knew large bits of that poem by heart. I remember how pleased he was to hear me quote from memory. ("Imagine, Nicky, a total stranger quoting my poetry!") It is still as fresh as ever in my memory, and as loved.

On a Tuesday evening in January 1945, Auden appeared in Isaiah's living room in Washington in an American military uniform. He looked snappy and incongruous, very pleased with himself.

"What does this mean?" I asked, perplexed by the masquerade.

Auden explained that he had joined a government wartime outfit. "I'm a member of the Morale Division of the U.S. Strategic Bombing Survey. It is known as *USBUSS*. I'm an Usbusster," and he roared with laughter. "I am to be shipped overseas, perhaps in a few days. In fact, I've come to say goodbye to Isaiah. I'm glad Nicky is here. I can say goodbye to both of you."

I asked the freshman Usbusster how one could join his outfit. I had been trying for over a year to go overseas in some capacity, but to no avail.

"You just call them on the telephone," said Auden, "go there, and apply for a job. Here, I'll give you the number," and he wrote down a number on a yellow pad. "Call this number and ask for Miss Katz. I know that they are looking for people like you—people with languages."

A few days later Isaiah told me that Auden had left for England. "Did you call that Jewish outfit at the Pentagon?" he asked.

Indeed, I had called Miss Katz and gone to see her at the Pentagon. She received me like an old friend. She introduced me to Mr.

Kohn. Mr. Kohn interviewed me and introduced me to Mr. Kalksteen. Mr. Kalksteen cross-checked Mr. Kohn and added a few questions of his own. Both gentlemen spoke English with a massive German accent.

I went back to Annapolis, having signed and countersigned a dozen application forms. Then for two months there was silence. I concluded that Auden's outfit had forgotten about me.

Suddenly, in April, I was called out of my class at the Peabody Conservatory in Baltimore. "There's an urgent call for you from Washington," said the operator.

Miss Katz was on the other end of the line: "Remember me, Mr. Nabokov?" she asked in a Mae-Westish tone of voice. She told me to come to her office the next day and suggested that I bring with me a change of clothes and my "toiletry."

Four days later, pumped full of vaccines, dressed in uniform, I was flying toward the Azores aboard an Air Force DC-4. I was tied to a bucket seat and surrounded by twenty-five-odd men, all of them, like me, in Army fatigues.

On June 25, 1945, the Usbusstian morale outfit to which I belonged was transferred from the north of Germany to Bad Homburg near Frankfurt—the European headquarters of USBUSS.

That famous spa used to be referred to by GIs as "*bad* Homburg," probably because of its meager supply of "frat" or, more commonly, "pieces of tail."

It was an ice-cold June evening and we had a great deal of mileage to cover before we'd reach that fratless, or whoreless spa. It was an arctic journey. No drink and no coffee stands on the highway.

My T-4 driver, Himmelstoss, was quite bitter. "Vai do we haff to drife thru die night, I ask you? I'm frozzen, aren't you?"

We reached the Kurhaus Hotel of Bad Homburg at *three* a.m. in a state of frozen pork. We had been told that this was the place we were to be billeted in. "But ofkors die fucking Army" had decided otherwise. The hotel was packed with other outfits of our far-flung organization. We were invited to spend the rest of the night in the hotel's dining room.

"Is there any coffee?"

No!

"Whiskey? Gin?"

No! . . . and the no's were definite.

The sight of the dining room was forbidding. The floor was strewn with debris: empty beer and pop cans, gin and whiskey bottles, broken glasses, filthy paper napkins, and moist cigarette and cigar butts. The air stank like a pigsty.

I did not waver. I wiped glasses and liquids from the bar, spread my sleeping bag on top of it, crawled inside, and, conforming to the bar's configuration by turning into an L-shaped khaki caterpillar, I dropped into immediate oblivion.

The next thing I knew, a face was leaning over me and saying: "Why, for God's sake! What are *you* doing here in this place?"

Auden was clean-shaven, freshly washed, and on the lookout for breakfast, furious that the dining room had *not* been tidied up and instead invaded by corpses in sleeping bags.

Toward noon everything and everybody got sorted out, billeted, washed, and fed. I shared a room with the disgruntled Himmelstoss and another USBUSS driver. Auden was on the same floor with a colonel and a Midwestern professor.

The weather turned fair, sunny, and warm. Syringa was in full bloom and the little spa did not look "bad" at all, but pleasant, neat, and untouched by the war, yet unfortunately invaded by a pack of noisy Americans.

We had nothing to do except wait to get paid and attend debriefing sessions led by Ken Galbraith and other "inventors" of the USBUSS operation. Auden said that at these sessions "a lot of dim-witted folk talked dim-minded trash in bogus socio-political jargon. All of this is *waste*, my dear. But it better remain that way. It is none of *our* concern."

USBUSS was being disbanded. Its leadership was hurrying home to well-upholstered jobs. Auden had handed in his report and was going back to America via England, where he was to visit his family.

"This 'Morale' title still makes me squirm," he remarked. "It is illiterate and absurd. How can one learn anything about *morals* when one's actions are *beyond* any kind of morality? *Morale* with an e at the end is psycho-sociological nonsense. What they *want* to say, but *don't* say, is how many people we killed and how many buildings we destroyed by that wicked bombing."

Most of the daytime at Bad Homburg Auden and I spent taking long walks in the pine woods that surrounded the little Middle

German town. Or else we sat on the terrace of the hotel having drinks and trying to avoid our gregarious USBUSStian colleagues.

"Most of them," explained Auden, "are crashing bores, my dear. They have *no* or *wrong* ideas about everything and belong to the world that neither you nor I can possibly like or condone."

What did we talk about during those walks or sitting on the hotel's terrace? Or rather, what do I remember now of our talks?

I know that we talked a lot about the war and its consequences. Auden, like so many of us, was shocked by the desolation of German cities and the disarray in which we found German citizens.

"I know that they had *asked* for it," he would say, "but still this kind of total destruction is beyond reasoning. It seems like madness! Don't you feel that way, my dear? It is absolutely ghastly!"

He did not like those "obtuse *Krauts*," as he called Germans at this time of life, "but still, Nicky, are we justified in replying to *their* mass murder by *our* mass murder? It seems terrifying to me, don't you agree? And . . . I cannot help but ask myself, was there no other way?"

He would drop into silence and add in a quieter tone: "Well, I've done my do, and I'm glad to leave. It is, all of it, a sorry mess."

We talked about the extermination camps we had seen in the course of our inspection tours—the horror of them, and especially what Auden referred to as "the horror of their meticulously systematic organization."

"I knew that the Krauts could be cruel. But none of us could have imagined that degree of cruelty. They applied to all of it the same pedantic organizational skills a piano tuner does when he tunes a virtuoso's concert grand," and Auden would shake his head.

But we also talked about music and poetry and read or recited to each other verses, he in English, I in German and Russian. He asked me questions about Stravinsky. Like me, he did not like Stravinsky's so-called Russian period as much as he did *Oedipus Rex* and the *Symphony of Psalms.* "That Russian stuff, Nicky, is folksy haberdashery—haberdashery not much different, except in degree of quality, to those Hungarian *bores* Kodaly and Bartók." And he asked whether I had heard Stravinsky's opera *The Nightingale* and how did *it* sound—"Did it make sense?"

He thought that ballet was a "very, very minor art, despite what Lincoln Kirstein thinks about it," but that "I suppose, within the limits of ballet, Balanchine is its only genius—at least, he strikes me

as if he were the only one to make something muscially sensible out
of ballet choreography."

But, as he soon proved, he was a true lover and a potential connoisseur of opera. And I say "potential" because real knowledge of
opera came to Wystan Auden through Chester Kallman in the years
to come. In fact, in that future collaborating team Kallman played,
I am sure, a determining role.

Auden had two projects he wanted to tackle some time soon, he
said. One was to make a *pertinent* and *palatable* translation into
English of Goethe's *Italienische Reise;* the second, to write a longish
essay on Kirkegaard. He did both a decade later.

To Auden, Goethe's travel book was a masterpiece of observa-
tion and imaginative description. It stood at the fount of the romantic movement, more so, he believed, than either *Werthers Leiden* or
Rousseau's "crashing bore" *Emile.* "And then, my dear," he would
say excitedly, "Goethe's prose style is admirable. It is still pre-
Hegelian, unencumbered by all those prefixes and postfixes and
page-long verb forms."

I knew nothing about Kirkegaard and was intrigued when Auden
said that Kirkegaard was the only nineteenth-century thinker, next
to Nietzsche, worth talking about. "He's the inventor of existentialist philosophy, but he remained—as is proper—a Christian existentialist," explained Auden. It all seemed a mystery to me until, several years later in New York, Auden presented me with a plump
volume of *Either Or* and read parts of it aloud to me. Only then—
but still faintly—did I understand what Auden had meant by calling Kirkegaard a Christian existentialist.

The sun had disappeared again as Auden's stay at Bad Homburg
was coming to a close, and a gray mist enveloped our hotel from
morning to night. We sat indoors reading, doing crossword puzzles, and, "after sundown," drinking.

One evening, past the dinner hour, Auden and I were sitting in
an empty room adjacent to the bar. For some reason, the bar was
closed and therefore its surroundings were deserted. There was only
one other couple in another corner of the room, a British officer and
his American WAC girlfriend.

We had brought down our own provision of drink from our
rooms—Auden gin, I bourbon whiskey. I found a bucket of melting
ice and we were set for the night. Auden was supposed to leave the
next day.

Suddenly, looking straight at me, Auden asked: "And what are your plans, Nicky? Are you being demobbed like me and returning to America? Or are you staying here in Germany with all the American brass?"

In a way, I had been expecting Auden's question. Had he not asked it, I would have induced him to do so. I needed his advice. I was in a quandary. I knew that his advice would be sound and compassionate, but also strictly impartial. It would, I thought, help me make up my mind.

Although I had known Auden for over two years, I had never spent any length of time in his company. The eight or ten days at Bad Homburg were like a boat trip—we were together every day and had nothing to do but enjoy being together. To me it was a blessing, not only because I discovered Auden as a person and re-discovered him as an extraordinary mind and as a great poet, but because he helped me solve what to me at *that* time appeared a riddle.

I had just gone through a traumatic experience in northern Germany, an experience that in more ways than one affected my future life.

Nowadays, after people have spoken and written about it, it may seem "old hat." But at that time it was new and odiously fresh. It was fresh to me, a newly baked American of Russian extraction, in military uniform, projected into one of the most sinister aspects of the disarray that followed the collapse of Nazi Germany.

It had to do with two evils—with Nazism *and* Stalinism. But it also had to do with a third one, with the Western Allies (and mainly America) playing into the hands of Russian Communists by committing the *sin* of sending back to Soviet Russia hundreds of thousands of people who had either willingly or unwillingly been imported from there by the Nazis.

I was projected into the ugly mess the week after I reached Germany. I soon discovered that *nothing* had changed in the Soviet Communist empire, and that what was going on in my motherland was a hell as vast as, if not much vaster than, the one we had just laid bare to public inspection in Germany. I felt pangs of conscience and a kind of helpless misery at not being able to do something about it—something to help Americans, especially the American leadership, realize the plight of these Russian, Ukrainian, and other DP's gleaned from Soviet Russia, *now* being shipped by *us* into slavery and certain destruction.

"How can one stop this policy?" was the thought that went through my head all the time after I started visiting DP camps at Hanover, at Hamburg, near Lübeck, and farther north, close to the Danish border. I still see those outstretched hands reaching out to me bits of crumpled paper with Cyrillic hieroglyphs upon them: "I have a cousin in Tampa" . . . "I have a friend in Chicago" . . . "I have . . ."

I decided—or rather I began to come close to a decision—to forgo my desire to return to civilian life and instead try to find myself a nook in what was being established in Berlin as the Allied Military Government of Germany.

I knew that the realization of what I believed in was difficult. One would have to bring a number of influential people to "see the light," to understand the sin we were committing. But I thought that if a few zealots would start a campaign for that purpose and work toward that aim, we would be able to convert enough American and British brass and enroll them in a kind of collective protest against our established policy. In other words, I thought that I ought to stay in Germany with the American Occupation Government as an anti-Stalinist and stay precisely for that *single* purpose.

There were, of course, private reasons that, so to speak, "co-motivated" me. I had a father in the Soviet Zone of Germany who had been displaced there from Poland. I had a sister and her family in Berlin. I had friends who had remained steadfastly anti-Nazi and needed help in those ghastly postwar years of cold, hunger, and misery.

There was at Bad Homburg another illustrious American outfit, called Psychological Warfare. It was run by a group of people, some of whom I knew from New York. Most of the outfit was being demobilized. But some of it was being transformed into what was to become the Information Control Division of the U.S. Military Government in Germany. I had heard that they were recruiting personnel for one or two years of service overseas. I went to see them and applied for a job. But I was still uncertain about it. My plan, or rather my aim, seemed ephemeral and quixotic.

I explained my dilemma to Auden, speaking in a low monotone in order not to be overheard by the love-couple in the other corner. I told him why our encounter in that illusionist's spa was to me providential, and asked his advice.

Auden looked serene, gazing into space. The love-couple had started gathering their coats and hats and were leaving.

Auden waited until they had gone. Then, very gently and quietly, in the embarrassed, timid way he sometimes had, he said: "Well . . . Nicky . . . couldn't we wait until tomorrow? Could I answer your question at breakfast? . . . I'm leaving the hotel at seven. Let's have coffee . . . say at six thirty. Is that okay?"

Next morning Auden was in the breakfast room before I was. I could not fall asleep for a long, long time. Himmelstoss and his companion snored like a chorus of Cossacks and my head buzzed with unanswered riddles.

Auden looked disgruntled. "You're eight minutes late," he said and plunged back into a crossword puzzle he had been working at. We sat in silence, sipping tepid, transparent coffee.

Then Auden looked at his watch again and remarked: "I'm supposed to be off in six minutes, but I don't see the bus, do you?"

No, the bus wasn't there. "*Noch nicht da,*" said the German waiter. "*Odder* officers are *vaiting* in the *lounch.*"

"Now about your question, Nicky." Auden's voice was matter-of-fact, impersonal. "My answer to it is neither yes or no, or rather neither stay nor go—it is *entirely* your own business. I'm sorry, Nicky, you've got to make up your own mind. No one can, or should, make it up for you. It would be improper and wrong." Suddenly he smiled broadly. "But if you do go to Berlin, I may perhaps come and see you there. May I?" He got up, picked up his gear, and started dragging it to the "lounch" through a labyrinth of chairs and tables.

The bus had arrived and was loading Usbussters in fatigues, each one with his huge, sausagy duffel bag. The light was gray and misty, but there was a faint June scent of syringa and bird cherry in the air.

"As for the substance of your question," said Auden before he mounted the bus, "it is indeed horrid and monstrous! It is barbarous to send people back to hell without even asking them for their consent! But then, what humans do to each other is usually messy . . . and a *sin* against God's laws." He stepped into the bus and waved at me from inside. He pulled down a window and hailed me: "Nicky, whatever you do, keep well . . . and drop me a line."

For many years I had toyed with the idea of setting T. S. Eliot's *Ash Wednesday* to music. But then I discovered *The Sea and the*

Mirror, and, having produced and directed *The Tempest* twice, I was naturally attracted by this commentary on *The Tempest*. Yet I could not make up my mind which of the two poems to choose, *Ash Wednesday* or *excerpts* from Auden's commentary. Each had its attractiveness but also its seemingly insoluble problems.

When in January 1947 I came back from one and a half years of service with the U.S. Military Government in Germany, I turned to safer and much more familiar poetic territory, replacing Eliot and Auden with Pushkin and Dante. I composed in succession two cantatas (both of them were commissioned by the Boston Symphony Orchestra).

Many years later, in 1963, when Auden was staying with me in Berlin, where I was director of the yearly festival, I started toying again with the idea of setting parts of *The Sea and the Mirror* to music. I spoke about it to Auden, but as I wanted to make extensive cuts in his commentary, he was not amenable. He shrugged his shoulders and said in his crankiest tone of voice: "But why, my dear? Why should you cut it? *The Sea and the Mirror* is a reasoned whole. No, no! It won't work . . . forget about it."

Fortunately (and quite unexpectedly) a much grander collaboration with Auden and with Chester Kallman was in store for me. It came seven years later, in 1970, and turned out to be Auden's and Kallman's last major enterprise for the lyric theater.

I think it was February 1969 when Lincoln Kirstein first said to me, "Why don't you compose an opera with Wystan and Chester? It would be good to bring them together again and have them work on a libretto. They haven't done anything since Henze's *Bacchae* and, as you know better than I do, they are master librettists. It was you, after all, who first talked about Auden to Stravinsky."

"I don't even know whether Wystan and Chester know and like my music," I demurred.

"Oh, yes! Oh, yes, they do!" exclaimed Lincoln. "Wystan must like your music precisely because it is melodic and because it does not conform to fads or fashions."

And after a while he added in a different tone of voice, "You know, only recently Wystan told me that the only Shakespeare play that is written like an opera and can readily be turned into an opera libretto is *Love's Labour's Lost*."

And as he said it, something clicked in my mind. I remembered Peter Brook's production of that strange and beautiful comedy. I asked Lincoln, "Would you speak to Auden and ask him whether he and Chester would be willing to work with me on an opera? I mean, prepare for me a libretto from *Love's Labour's Lost?*"

Lincoln agreed. He would call Auden the next morning, he said, and let me know. "But don't put it off, Nicky," he grumbled as I was climbing out of the cab at my street corner. "Get the play at once. Read it carefully and call Wystan . . . I'll let you know!" and he slammed the cab's door.

I had never read *Love's Labour's Lost*. I got an Arden copy, and at first sight the play seemed forbidding. Its language was cumbersome, with many antiquated word forms, obsolete jokes, and puns which seemed hopelessly obscure. That first reading left me numb and bewildered. I could not help but be stung by the complex beauty of certain parts of the play, but I was unable to fathom how it could ever be turned into an opera libretto.

Was it right for me, a foreigner, to try to enter that self-contained world of Shakespearean fancy, so closely knit with the very essence of the English psyche? Would I ever be able to move freely about in this world? I knew, of course, what a challenge Shakespeare had been to all composers since the seventeenth century. So tempting but so terribly risky. And yet the only ones who seemed to me to have done justice to Shakespeare's plays on the operatic stage and hence dealt with the Shakespearean challenge successfully, were the two nineteenth-century *maestri* Verdi and Boito. They gave the *"illustrissimo e glorioso bardo"* (as Boito called Shakespeare in one of his letters to Verdi) a thoroughgoing, bare-to-the-bone Italian rubdown, transforming his theatricals into operatic equivalents and giving his characters, although coarsened and modified, a new life on the lyric stage.

But could we, in our self-conscious and hopelessly epistemological century, deal as nonchalantly with Shakespeare's plays, with his *dramatis personae*, his plots and subplots, his lyrics, his meter, and his grand meditative poetry, as did Boito and Verdi? Yet I felt for some reason that only this kind of approach was possible and needed, particularly in the case of *Love's Labour's Lost*.

Having spent a week in conscious-stricken torment, I decided to accept the Shakespearean challenge, and instinctively I decided to rely upon the experience and judgment of my double-headed team of poet-librettists. Knowing them to be men of total integrity and extraordinary talent as well as uncompromising fundamentalists in

227

matters of opera libretti, I thought I could not go wrong.

As it turned out, I did not go wrong. The composing of *Love's Labour's Lost* became a continuous pleasure, thanks to my master librettists. I worked at the opera with a compositorial gusto I had rarely experienced.

"Yes, of course, Nicky," said Auden that first day as I sat down in his dimly lit, smoke-filled workroom on St. Mark's Place, "*Love's Labour's Lost* is the only Shakespeare play that will do as an opera. It is structured like an opera and so much of it is already rhymed verse."

I told Auden about my struggle with the Arden volume and with the *Love's Labour's Lost* word forms, puns, and jokes.

"Well . . . I don't think we should worry about that," he said. "Some of those words can be changed, others can just as well remain. That isn't the problem. What needs to be done is to trim the play down to opera requirements. A number of secondary characters should be eliminated. Most of the comic scenes with their banter should be cut—they won't do for opera. Maybe some of the verses could be shortened, and all of the play must get leaner. I see it," he continued, "as an *opera buffa* in a fast tempo, a kind of perpetual allegro going through to the last scene. Then everything must grow solemn and slow—that is most important," and he emphasized the word "most." "The morality-play ending of *Love's Labour's Lost* and its meaning should remain quite clear and intact."

We agreed that he should write to Chester, who was in Greece. If Chester consented to collaborate on the libretto, we could meet later that summer. Ten days later I received a postcard from Auden. It said that Chester would be glad to collaborate and that we should meet in Austria.

We started to correspond. Usually it was Chester who replied in great detail to my letters. When I arrived in Kirchstetten in July, Auden and Kallman had done the whole first act. They had also prepared an outline of the second and third acts.

In the autumn, when I passed through Vienna, we met between planes at the airport and they gave me the complete libretto. By mutual consent we reduced all parts to ten, cutting out most of the comic characters and scenes. At Auden's suggestion, Moth, the messenger boy and page to Armado, was turned into a major character. He became a synthesis of Ariel, Cupid, and Puck. He was to sing all the songs, behave as if he had plotted the play, miscarry the letters with their love sonnets, and poke fun at the courtly fools and their games.

I started reading the libretto on the plane. Then I read it carefully over and over again in Paris. Only very gradually did I realize what a remarkable job my librettist friends had done. They had turned Shakespeare's comedy into a perfect opera libretto.

I did not start to compose the music for *Love's Labour's Lost* right away. I waited for a stretch of time free from other obligations so that I could devote all of it to *Love's Labour's Lost*. This came only in the summer of 1970. Meanwhile I had shown the libretto to the directors of the Deutsche Oper of Berlin, and soon thereafter they commissioned me to write the music for *Love's Labour's Lost*, to be produced by that opera company.

I used a number of traditional operatic forms and devices, but I did not compose, properly speaking, either a comic opera or an *opera buffa*. What I did was to set a comedy to music. I used extensively one particular device for which there is no term in English except the ill-transferable French term *persiflage*. *Persiflage* implies making fun of a style or of a stylistic "prototype." Closest to it is the English term "take-off." But a take-off suggests improvisation, something passing and superficial. *Persiflage* does not have this passing connotation. On the contrary, it implies pinpricking a model, jokingly but harshly. I used *persiflage* as a "comedy method," a method of mocking characters and situations.

For example, I used the Tristanic chord in a jazzed-up way for Berowne's love aria at the end of Scene II of Act I, ending it "foolishly" with Beethoven's beginning of the Fifth Symphony. I "persiflaged" Renaissance forms of polyphonic music, dear to English hearts, like the catch and the madrigal. In the "Discourse About Love" in Act II, I thought it attractive to pinprick Messrs. Weill, Eisler, and Brecht, and in Moth's songs I "persiflaged" American croonery of the 1930s. I thought it appropriate to use tidbits of Orientalia for the Aragonese court throughout the play. I believed it justified by the fact that most of Shakespeare's comedies are set in what were then to Englishmen "exotic lands." And Shakespeare's Aragonese kingdom of King Ferdinand (alias Henry IV) lies close to the Moorish borders of Spain. I thought that this kind of Orientalia might add a comic note to the academico-erotic enterprises of the Aragonese gentlemen. And of course, Don Armado was an obvious butt for slightly phony nineteenth-century musical espagnolisms. In the masquerade scene of Act III, the libretto gives the following stage direction: "All Gentlemen, except Boyet, appear dressed up as Muscovites." (According to W. H. Auden, it is the only time Shakespeare mentions my former compatriots.) Here a *persiflage* of Moussorgsky and Glinka in coincidental counterpoint seemed to me the obvious thing to do.

But I respected my librettists' (and Shakespeare's) wishes scrupulously as far as the end of *Love's Labour's Lost* was concerned. After the news of the King's death is announced, the tone, the character, and the style of the music changes. It becomes serious, serene, and solemn.

At the end of the opera when Don Armado sings the last words of the famous sentence, "Harsh are the words of Mercury after the songs of Apollo," he sings them on a theme from Stravinsky's *Apollo*, and this is not *persiflage* anymore. It is in memoriam to a beloved friend and a master who was at that time dying in New York.

The music of *Love's Labour's Lost* is tonal, non-experimental, and consistently melodic, in the sense of trying to be "tuneful." I like to invent melismatic patterns that enter readily into the secret folds of the listener's memory.

I do not belong to any school of aesthetic ideology, but I suppose that, quite beyond my conscious control, the music that comes out of my mind and my heart belongs to my generation of composers, and sounds Russian to foreign ears.

In writing *Love's Labour's Lost* my aim was twofold: first, I wanted to serve with all my capabilities the admirable libretto of my poet friends, and through them Shakespeare; and second, as Ariel says at the end of *The Tempest*, "I wanted to please."

The première of *Love's Labour's Lost* took place on February 7, 1973, at the Théâtre Royal de la Monnaie in Brussels. It was a guest performance given by the Deutsche Oper. It was a splendid performance. The costumes and the decor by Filippo Sanjust were admirable, the direction by the young Berlin director Winifried Bauernfeind was able and imaginative, and the conducting by Reinhard Peters superb. But what was supreme was the young and dedicated cast of American, German, and English singers. I could not have dreamed of a better one and only hope that the next time the opera is given, they will sing it again.

Auden and Kallman arrived the day before the general rehearsal.

They liked the music, the scenery, the costumes, and the singing, but disagreed with the direction and with the fact that the orchestra was too loud and covered much of the poetic text.

The performance was a success. But I did not feel quite happy about *Love's Labour's Lost* myself. I realized—alas, much too late—that *Love's Labour's Lost* should never have been given on a large stage and orchestrated for a large orchestra. The nature of its libretto required intimacy and the concomitant ability to understand every word of what is being said (i.e., sung). The sound of the large orchestra and the separation of the public from the stage by the wide pit drowned out too much of what happened on stage.

Shakespearean comedy needs immediacy of perception and intimacy between the actor and his public. Auden's and Kallman's libretto accentuated that particular quality. Furthermore, *Love's Labour's Lost*, by its androgynal structure, a comedy that turns sour at the end, bewilders the average opera-goer. It starts like an *opera buffa*, then suddenly, toward the end, it slows down, becomes reflectively introspective and bitterly real. Yet this is precisely what attracted Auden and Kallman, and certainly me, to *Love's Labour's Lost*. It is an old man's and a wise man's tale, and not a tale for a bourgeois audience that wants to feel young and gay.

I keep dreaming of a production of *Love's Labour's Lost* in a small, intimate opera house. I firmly intend to reduce *Love's Labour's Lost's* orchestration to a small chamber orchestra. My only regret is that when it is done the way I would like it to be done (and, I hope, in England and in America) Auden will not be there to hear it. But then . . . but then during the last years of his life he "heard" so little. Only end-game voices: *Auden . . . Auden . . . Auden . . .* Getting older, crankier, lonelier. Cracking the same jokes, repeating himself: "Had I chosen the orders, I would now be a bishop"—five times in two days. Finding life absurd, wanting to get out of it, yet working as hard as ever and remaining endowed with the same great mind, the same gift, the same fathomless knowledge. Auden was waiting for the end. Like my other Christian friend who died the same year, Jacques Maritain, he was, I am sure, longing and praying for it.

"Look what I found," said Mary McCarthy and handed me a sheaf of crumpled mimeography.

It was a dank, slushy evening—January 1949. Mary with her husband, Bowden Broadwater, and a few other friends had come for dinner.

Since 1946, while in Berlin with military government, I had divorced Constance Holladay, had settled in New York in 1947, and had remarried in 1948. My new wife, Patricia Blake, was a thoroughbred intellectual, brilliantly intelligent and good-looking. Having spent part of her childhood in France, she spoke French as well as English and was soon to add Russian to her linguistic treasure.

Patricia and I had moved to a flat in an old-fashioned apartment building opposite a brick crusader's castle, with the quaint French inscription BOUTTEZ EN AVANT, that stood on the corner of 95th Street and Madison Avenue.

After two years of service with our Occupation Government in Berlin and six months of helping Charlie Thayer to shape the Voice of America to Russia, I had quit government service, vowing never to return. Returning to Baltimore and the Peabody Conservatory, I resumed teaching music history, music theory, and music composition.

I would leave New York on Monday morning and return on Tuesday night, having done twelve to fourteen hours of teaching. I would feel content and relieved, free to compose, to go out, to see old friends and meet new ones, and eventually to write a book, my first one, called *Old Friends and New Music*, splendidly edited by Patricia.

I looked at Mary McCarthy's "find." It was an announcement of a Soviet-American Cultural Peace Conference to be held in March 1949 at the Waldorf-Astoria Hotel.

"They must have spent ages preparing for this kind of thing," exclaimed Patricia. "How in the world didn't we know about it?"

"That's what interests me," said Mary. "Why did they keep it so secret? I mean, why did they shun advance publicity? Were they scared? And of what, I wonder."

"But shouldn't we do something about it?" Patricia looked at us questioningly.

There was little doubt in anybody's mind that we should react, but we didn't know how or in what way.

Someone proposed picketing the Soviet-American affair around the clock. But this seemed much too innocuous and smacked of labor-union procedures. "We need something that resembles a political gesture," said one of our group. Somebody else suggested "infiltration."

We agreed that whatever we did should have public appeal and the support of the press, but at the same time it should be authentic. It should not look as if it were government-sponsored or—as Mary said—"staged by Joe McCarthy."

Toward the end of the evening we had worked out a sensible plan of action.

We decided that within the next few days a small action group should be formed, made up of liberal, leftist, non-Communist, and anti-Communist intellectuals. This action group should become the core of a nationwide and perhaps even international, or rather internationally supported, committee. We should solicit membership in this larger committee among the same kind of people that appeared on the Soviet-American conference list. We should contact our potential membership at once by phone, wire, and cable. We should draft a brief statement of purpose and make it as clear and as urgent as possible. I do not remember who found a name for the larger committee: American Intellectuals for Freedom. Curiously enough, the name stuck.

The next step would be to rent rooms at the Waldorf-Astoria Hotel for the duration of "their" conference, establish in those rooms the headquarters of our large *ad hoc* committee, and undertake from there whatever protest activities we would deem useful or necessary.

"In fact, we must build up for just that one week a kind of agitprop apparat of our own," said another friend.

I felt elated. After so many years of frustration, something useful was in the making. At least there would be an earnest attempt to expose Stalin and Stalinism.

The action group was formed. Meetings were held. The plans, as worked out at our flat, were adopted. Mary had obtained the full program of the Soviet-American cultural affair with its impressive list of participants and sponsors. I was introduced to Sidney Hook, who sent me to David Dubinsky, the head of the Ladies' Garment Workers Union, to get from him a subsidy of $1,500. He in turn introduced me to Arnold Beichmann, a pleasant and clever fellow on the staff of the now extinct afternoon daily *PM*, who appeared with a thin, sad-looking person called Mel Pitzele. "We'll need him for PR," said Beichmann. Pitzele at once found an efficient, bright lady who was ready to volunteer as secretary.

In less than a week our anti–Waldorf-Astoria Conference operation was running smoothly on the road to success.

Our chief engineer and self-appointed commander-in-chief was Professor Hook, seconded by Messrs. Beichmann and Pitzele and followed, somewhat grumpily, by members of our action group.

The remaining weeks of March were spent in frenzied activity. Rooms at the Waldorf-Astoria were reserved. Wires and cables were sent. Phones rang uninterruptedly. Programs of action were discussed. The "enemy's" preparatory activities were observed and the task of reacting to them was divided among the ever growing membership of our larger *ad hoc* committee, whose name was now definitely established as American Intellectuals for Freedom.

Since my return from Berlin in 1947 and the six months with the Voice of America, I had stopped meddling in politics. I composed. I wrote my Second ("Biblical") Symphony; two other major works commissioned by Dr. Koussevitzky for the Boston Symphony Orchestra, *La Vita Nuova* and *The Return of Pushkin;* a smaller piece, *Studies in Solitude,* for Dr. Ormandy and the Philadelphia Orchestra.

Though I was not active in politics, it had pleased and amused me to watch how not only "middle America" but the leftist American intelligentsia had swung from wartime Stalinophilia to various degrees and natures of anti-Communism.

The astonishing thing was that, as if by a miracle, the suggestion of the need for an agitprop apparatus of our own produced one. I do not know whether it was from the outset masterminded by our generous "donor," Mr. Dubinsky, or by Field Marshal Hook and his aides, Messrs. Beichmann and Pitzele, but by the time we moved into the Waldorf-Astoria premises and established there the headquarters of the *ad hoc* committee of American Intellectuals for Freedom, we were operating as efficiently as any Communist governmental outfit.

Many of us objected to the way Sidney Hook ordered, or at least tried to order, some of us around, telling us what to do where and at what time. But the ultimate PR and press success of our sabotage operation was largely due to his efficient handling of our inchoate and heterogeneous, but intellectually enlightened group of protestors.

It was the third Tuesday of March 1949 when our forces invaded one of the Waldorf-Astoria's plush bridal suites. There was a perpetual flow of visitors. "Freedom lovers" of varied sizes and genders squeezed their way in and out of the cluttered premises. Some chatted excitedly, others buried their faces in reading matter that the two secretaries or the attendant of the mimeograph machine provided from its bathroom-paper heap.

Since 1947 and especially since the Berlin blockade of 1948, the foreign policy of the American government had taken a sharp turn. The Cold War was breathing hot upon everyone's neck. But that foreign policy had its unfortunate domestic counterpart. And while *few* non-Communist, or anti-Communist American intellectuals— whether conservative, liberal, or radical—disagreed with the need to resist Stalinism (indeed, quite a few thought that the government was sluggishly slow and much too hesitant in its reaction to it), most of them, especially the liberal and radical wing, resented the turn of events inside the country. The witch-hunt had started, the spy trials were on, and some of the activities of government agencies that participated were, to say the least, dubious.

It was especially hard for those among us who, though recent converts to anti-Stalinism, had been brought up on a deep distrust of modern American capitalism and could not, therefore, fully give up their attachment to Marxism as a philosophy of history and as a social ideal. To them Stalin was someone who had betrayed an otherwise genuinely noble revolution, and Lenin remained firmly fixed upon his historic pedestal as a revolutionary hero.

But what was the fuss all about at the Waldorf-Astoria Hotel in March 1949? What were we protesting against?

Surely not against the twelve Soviet sacrificial lambs—scholars, writers, and composers—who were performing their sycophantic duties under the vigilant eyes of KGB "nurses" and party *apparatchiki.* Those, at most, had to be exposed. They were tortured, innocent creatures saying things they did not mean and could not believe.

All of this most of us knew. We knew that the genuine Soviet scholars, writers, and composers who took part in the ghoulish farce at the Waldorf-Astoria were *not* free agents. (In fact, eighteen years later, meeting one of the participants of that conference at a *dacha* in a Moscow suburb, I was told how he had been "ordered" to be a member of the Soviet delegation and how he had to read a paper "prepared" for him by his KGB supervisors.)

What interested me then, and still puzzles me, was the abysmal misinformation and misunderstanding of America's mood and political climate on the part of the Soviet Union's leadership. The fact that they were ready to co-sponsor the Waldorf-Astoria peace conference right in the midst of the Cold War (only months after the end of the Berlin blockade) showed a total ignorance of America and of American society.

That the Soviet organizers of the peace conference found American patrons and moneybags to pay for the circus at the commodious hotel (tax deductible, of course) did not astonish me. Conscience-stricken merchants of Tsarist Russia had paid large sums of money to revolutionary causes. Thus, when I learned that the American-Soviet cultural peace ploy at the Waldorf-Astoria was, at least in part, being subsidized by Mr. Corliss Lamont, I found it not surprising at all.

The next few days were spent in total tumult. Our headquarters operated day and night, vigorously and efficiently. The response to our appeal was overwhelmingly positive. It seemed as if American and European intellectuals were ripe for an opportunity to express their anger and their condemnation of Stalinism. We received hundreds of phone calls, wires, and cables, all of them expressing support for our protest action.

An international committee of sponsors was formed. Among its members were Benedetto Croce, T. S. Eliot, Karl Jaspers, André Malraux, Jacques Maritain, Bertrand Russell, and Igor Stravinsky. Even the ubiquitous Alsatian from Africa, Dr. A. Schweitzer, sent us his blessings, although his name also appeared among the sponsors of the Waldorf-Astoria peace conference.

All of this information was transmitted with alacrity to the press. Messrs. Beichmann and Pitzele fed the press constantly with a flow of releases, statements, and replies to whatever statements or speeches were made by the other side. By midweek ours looked like an efficient, professional PR job.

Slightly perturbed by the cost of the enterprise, I asked Beichmann, "Who's going to pay for the extra days in the hotel?" and I added, "And what about the extra secretary and the machine attendants?"

Beichmann grinned. "Didn't you hear the boss [Dubinsky] say

that I'll be taking care of the money? So why d'you bother?" I was glad not to bother so long as I knew that the union would pay the bills.

The press took an amusingly clever tack on the whole Waldorf-Astoria to-do: it played it as if it were a battle of the wits, and in its course gave our side increasingly larger coverage. By the end of the week it became clear that public–opinion–wise we were winning the engagement and the Soviet agitprop and its unwitting American colleagues and supporters were losing it.

The Waldorf-Astoria peace conference had established several discussion panels. They took place simultaneously in different halls of the hotel. There was wrangling among us as to how we should react or, rather, behave at those public panels. We agreed that all of them should be visited or infiltrated. But should we obstruct and disrupt their proceedings and thus create an atmosphere of scandal —as wished by Field Marshal Hook and I suppose some of our press friends—or should we use civilized methods of public debate as advocated by Mary McCarthy, Dwight Macdonald, and most of us? Finally it was left to each one of us to do as he pleased. In the end, the civilized method won and worked better than if we had behaved like hoodlums.

I, for one, decided to stay strictly within my profession. There was a panel where Dimitri Shostakovich was to be one of the speakers. I decided to go to this panel and to none of the others.

The question I wanted to ask Shostakovich was simple and straightforward, but obviously embarrassing to him. I knew in advance what his reply would have to be, and I also knew that his reply would expose him as being not a free agent. I knew that his American colleagues on that panel would also be embarrassed by his reply. Yet this was in my opinion the only legitimate way to expose the internal mores of Russian communism.

Among the musicians on the podium were friends. I waved at them and they waved and smiled back sheepishly. The Russians marched in just before the chairman was to call the meeting to order. There were four or five of them surrounding the frail and strangely myopic figure of Shostakovich. The public and the members of the panel rose and gave the Russians a hearty welcome. Shostakovich and his KGB nurse-interpreter took seats to the left of the chairman, Olin Downes.

The session was long and verbose.

When I was finally able to ask my question, it was: "On such-and-such a date in No. X of *Pravda* appeared an unsigned article that had all the looks of an editorial. It concerned three western composers: Paul Hindemith, Arnold Schoenberg, and Igor Stravinsky. In this article they were branded, all three of them, as 'obscurantists,' 'decadent bourgeois formalists,' and 'lackeys of imperialist capitalism.' The performance of their music should 'therefore be prohibited in the U.S.S.R.' Does Mr. Shostakovich personally agree · with this official view as printed in *Pravda?*"

There was suddenly a bewildered expression on the faces of the Russians. One of them, near Mr. Downes, muttered quite audibly, "*Provokatsya.*"

The nurse-interpreter was whispering something in Shostakovich's ear.

Shostakovich got up, was handed a microphone, and, looking down at the floor, said in Russian: "I fully agree with the statements made in *Pravda.*"

Then there was our own meeting organized by the Committee of American Intellectuals for Freedom. We held it in the small hall of Freedom House on March 27.

The hall was packed. Our team of promoters—Beichmann, Pitzele, and the fiery Hook—had done a splendid publicity job. The block on 40th Street between Fifth and Sixth Avenues had been roped off. A dense crowd listened attentively to two loudspeakers planted on Freedom House's balcony.

The speakers that evening were nearly all good. Only a few lapsed into what Churchill called "unbridled oratory." The rest were forthright, factual, and made a forceful indictment of Stalin and of Stalinism. Indeed, what our speakers were saying then in March 1949 (and what our opponents at the Waldorf-Astoria peace conference were concealing) was to a large degree the same stuff Khrushchev "revealed" seven years later in his "secret" speech to the Twentieth Party Congress and what Solzhenitsyn has been writing about ever since.

I made a short speech about the plight of composers in the Soviet Union and the tyranny of the party's *Kulturapparat*. I deplored the use that was being made of Dimitri Shostakovich by our antagonists at the peace conference, especially since Shostakovich had been a recent victim (and the main "culprit") of Mr. Zhdanov's purges.

After my speech I saw a familiar face rise from the back row of the hall and come at me. It was an acquaintance of mine from Berlin who, like me, had worked for OMGUS. He congratulated me warmly. "This is a splendid affair you and your friends have organized," he said. "We should have something like this in Berlin."

I do not remember when, where, and through whom I heard rumors about a grand, or even a grandiose, cultural conference being planned for June 1950 in Berlin. I was told that the American government had agreed to offer financial help to the Mayor of Berlin from what used to be called "counterpart" funds, to pay for that enterprise.

Sometime in the autumn of 1949 Mel Lasky, the editor of a German-language journal, *Der Monat*, published by our occupation establishment in Berlin, held a press conference in New York at the New School on 12th Street.

The gist of his announcement was: Yes, there would be a grand international cultural conference in Berlin in June 1950. It would be an anti-Stalinist or, rather, an anti-totalitarian (i.e., also anti-fascist) gathering.

The host of the conference would be the Mayor of Berlin, Ernst Reuter, and invitations would be issued in his name. The intellectuals invited to the conference would represent only "themselves"— in other words, representatives of political parties, clubs, or committees would not be invited. The host would pay for the travel of invited guests and for the sojourn in Berlin.

In an exchange with a questioner, Lasky confirmed the rumor that the U.S. Military Government in Berlin was "helping" the Mayor financially from "counterpart" funds.

Since 1949 Patricia and I had spent our summers in Europe. We rented a cottage on the edge of Fontainebleau's forest and traveled around a great deal by car. Patricia loved being in Europe, while I . . . I enjoyed trips to Aix-en-Provence's festival, to Switzerland, to Italy, to England, and to Salzburg—all of them places I had visited rarely or never before. But I felt uneasy in Paris. Postwar Paris seemed glum and alien to me. I felt as if I had come back to an old house and found it oddly remodeled. Most of its former tenants were gone and the new ones were indifferent, unsmiling, or frankly hostile. The few old-timers looked somewhat seedy and sour, prone to evoke "the good old times" and having nothing new to say.

There was also in the back of my cerebrum the nagging question:

239

what had he or she done during the arduous years of occupation? The gossip was persistent and nasty. It lasted until late into the 1950s and poisoned France's societal climate, especially for those like me who had been a part of it in the 1920s and early 1930s.

As for Germany, I had had my fill of it during its hardest and hungriest postwar years. Now it was on its way to a febrile economic recovery. I felt superfluous in it. Besides . . .

Besides, it had taken me sixteen-odd years to get acclimated to America and thirteen of them to worm my way back to the capital from the bleak American provinces (including America's postwar establishment abroad). And now I was not any more a jobless immigrant, but a composer and a teacher, a resident of the world's capital, and a member, however modest, of its bounteous intellectual aviary. Why go back to live abroad, I thought, when at long last America was holding out promise for me and I was having my second, far more stable, and by now nearly "native" romance with New York?

In May 1950 Patricia and I flew to Europe on a thoroughly insecure charter plane run by a company called Youth Argosy. It was cheap, packed with guitared college youths and subdued professorial couples. Somehow we made it to Luxembourg without our plane falling apart.

In my pocket I carried an invitation to the Berlin conference signed by Mayor Reuter. It was to take place early in June and last for five or six days. A "tentative" list of participants was enclosed in the Mayor's letter. Among them quite a few glamorous names: Reinhold Niebuhr, Alfred J. Ayer, Ignazio Silone, Arthur Koestler (whose unconvincing novel *Darkness at Noon* I finally read on the argonautic airplane). But besides myself there wasn't a single musician, painter, sculptor, or even a poet.

I was of two minds about accepting the Mayor's invitation. On the one hand I asked myself, what will I be doing *dans cette galère;* on the other hand, I was not only interested to meet all these beautiful people, but also eager to see how our modest undertaking of a year ago at Freedom House would look, or would evolve on the broader, international stage. I did not doubt for a moment that this invitation to a conference under the odd name of Congress for Cultural Freedom (which made one think of the American Congress of Industrial Organizations and its bushy-browed boss, John L.

Lewis, Mr. Roosevelt's antagonist) was the result, the logical continuation of the Hookish protest action of 1949 and the *ad hoc* committee of American Intellectuals for Freedom.

But Chip Bohlen and other friends argued differently. "You should go," said Bohlen, "if only to tell your *Kulturnye* colleagues that it is a mistake not to invite artists. They've been the most persistent whipping boys of both the Soviets and the Nazis."

Of the tumultuous Berlin affair only very few images remain in memory. The one worth recalling took place on the plane that flew me and twenty-odd guests of Mayor Reuter from Orly to Berlin.

David Rousset, a roly-poly, amiable Frenchman, introduced me to a young woman. Her name was Elinor Lipper. I had just read her book, which was an account of several years in Stalinist concentration camps. To meet her was worth the journey. Elinor Lipper was extraordinarily beautiful. She had dark, sad, and tender eyes set in a very pale, diaphanously transparent face crowned by wavy black hair. Her smile was gentle and her voice soft. She exuded a frightened, infinitely vulnerable warmth and a suspicious caution.

It was my first encounter with a victim of the Soviet penal system. I did not dare ask her questions about it, yet I wanted to hear her confirm what I had read in her book. Fortunately the Russian language established a bond between us.

In the course of the next month we became close friends. Rarely have I met a human being endowed with so much quiet courage and intelligence, so much gentleness and integrity. We met in Paris, in Switzerland, as often as possible. I would have continued to see her had she not decided fairly soon to marry a French or a Swiss M.D. and disappear with him to Madagascar. She had a small child, born in one of the concentration camps. She felt that her child needed a father and a proper family life. She also felt that she had completed her duty by writing down and bringing to public attention her camp experiences. She did not want to become an anti-Stalinist propaganda showpiece. Many people and organizations tried to exploit her. But she balked. She fled the klieg lights of public exposure at the first opportunity. She had earned her privacy a thousand times. After September of 1950 I never saw her again.

The Berlin conference established a Continuation Committee to which I was elected. At its meeting in the autumn of 1950 in Brussels it was decided to establish a permanent organization with the same odd title as the Berlin conference. It seemed logical, because the money for the Continuation Committee and for the future organization was supposed to come from the American labor unions. Its representative in Europe, a gay, cheerful, and very, very bright fellow called Irving Brown, whom I met for the first time in Brussels, confirmed this. "How much it will be, I can't tell," he said, "but we'll see what we can do."

It was at this Continuation Committee meeting in Brussels that I was proposed as the future head of the future organization. I agreed to serve, but only for a while and not before the end of the school year at the Peabody Conservatory in May 1951.

Thus in 1951 I was to fly again to Europe to a new adventure.

In 1945 the adventure had seemed comparatively simple. I had taken off as a hired employee of the War Department. Now I was to go to Paris to head something that did not yet exist and for which there were no modern precedents, no models in the Western world. No one before had tried to mobilize intellectuals and artists on a worldwide scale in order to fight an ideological war against oppressors of the mind, or to defend what one called by the hackneyed term "our cultural heritage." This kind of ideological war had so far been the appanage of Stalinists and of Nazis.

Patricia had been most ardent about going to Paris. She left ahead of me and found a furnished flat near the Luxembourg Gardens, around the corner from Albert Camus, whom she had met in America.

Not very willingly, I was to follow her on May 23, 1951.

Unwillingly? Not really. True enough, I did not look forward to settling in Paris. Nor did I like the idea of turning away from musical composition once again (I knew, of course, that to start and shape a nonexistent organization would require, at least for several years, all of my time), or mingling with politicos, socio-, econo-, and other -ologists and establishing with them human (or pseudo-human) relationships.

On the other hand, I knew that this was a unique challenge, an opportunity not to be missed. I could perhaps accomplish a few constructive things—things that had to be done, provided there would be the necessary funds and the will to do them.

To lead a rational, ice-cold, determinedly intellectual war against Stalinism without falling into the easy Manichean trap of phony righteousness seemed essential to me, especially at a time when in

America that ideological war was getting histrionically hysterical and crusaderishly paranoiac.

While on the plane—a smooth, comfortable Pan Am stratocruiser with berths and an eleven-hour ride suitable for repose and reflection—I started formulating my first proposal to the cultural committee. I wanted to start off its activities with a big bang and in the field of twentieth-century arts. At that time contemporary art and music were the butts and the victims of Stalin's and Zhdanov's most odious repression, just as they had been a decade earlier in Hitler's Germany.

I felt that we had to reaffirm our belief in their values and that the time had come to draw an inventory of their achievements in the first fifty years of this century.

Thus, during that nightless night of May 23 was born the general outline of my first and so far most exciting festival, Masterpieces of the Twentieth Century, held in Paris from April 1 to April 30, 1952.

Curiously enough, not for a moment did the question of money cross my mind. It probably should have, because it was hard to imagine the American labor unions subsidizing a grandiosely expensive modern-arts festival and not in America, but in Paris, of all places.

For no apparent reason, perhaps because of my innate optimistic insouciance, I assumed that money for my festival would somehow come my way. After all, America was the capital of capitalism and of capitalist foundations. Wasn't there a chance to raise the money among public and private foundations for such a glamorous, unusual, and artistically *political* enterprise?

I knew America well enough to realize that we could not expect much from the Federal government and its agencies. I knew how punily and unwillingly (at that time) these agencies supported the arts. Besides, their support could only come on a national, not on an international, scale. And yet it was international support that I needed most.

Not in my wildest dreams could I have expected that my "dream festival" would be supported by America's spying establishment, nor did I know that the fare for my delightful first-class flight to Paris was being paid by the CIA via the labor union's European representative, the cheerful Mr. Brown. And soon, very soon, that same spy mill of the American government would be establishing a network of "consenting" or "passing" foundations to pump money to such groups as our Cultural Committee, to American colleges, to refugee orchestras, and whatnot.

In retrospect, it is very funny to remember, for instance, the silhouettes of two Russians, a thin, long one and a short, stocky one. The thin one was the Secretary General of the Union of Soviet Writers, the short one an odious SOB called Yermilov, a nasty little party hack. They were standing, both of them, in line to receive their *per diem* and travel allowance from my secretary, or rather the administrative secretary of the Congress for Cultural Freedom. They had come, or rather had been sent, to attend a conference commemorating the fiftieth anniversary of the death of Tolstoy, organized by me in Venice in 1960 in collaboration with the Cini Foundation. (Mr. Yermilov, turn in your grave: *you have taken CIA money!*) Or to think of the trip to America of a leftist French journalist who was paid by the CCF. Or of the subsidizing of an art student's travel to Moscow with the connivance of a personal friend of mine, a Soviet academician, for the purpose of photographing hidden treasures of abstract Russian art.

If only I had known about it at the time, I would have had my laugh much earlier. Or would I?

The history of the Congress of Cultural Freedom waits to be written. Why no one has done it so far is beyond my understanding.

Is it because of the general *gène*, the *malaise* that now surrounds most undertakings of the historical period referred to as the Cold War? Or maybe because the Cold War has turned into something stinkingly sour for which there is so far no appropriate term? The whole period and its term "Cold War," when mentioned or remembered, provokes a rash of pink cheeks, necks, and ears and a nearly audible tremor of cold feet. For some congenitally poltroonish reason, people do not want to hear about the record of any of the Cold War enterprises. Nor do they seem to wish those records published to speak for themselves.

There is, for example, no mention of the CCF in either of the two American encyclopedias I usually consult, whereas the unhappy conglomerate called United Nations, with all of its appendages, gets six columns of minuscule print in one of them. And yet the CCF functioned for over twelve years as a kind of Cold War United Nations of liberal, civilized intelligentsia. It published dozens of journals, reviews, had as its honorary chairmen and its collaborators ladies and gentlemen whose names are prominently displayed in those same two encyclopedias. One is tempted to draw a reverse analogy with the Soviet encyclopedia of 1934 or 1936 in which "Trotskyism" was mentioned but "Trotsky" not. It borders on a kind of *opera-buffa* sabotage.

And yet, to cite but one example, with what painstaking care, earnestness, and thoughtfulness (far greater than in most UNESCO enterprises) a group of fifteen to eighteen European and American scholars drew up the program of one of the CCF's earliest conferences called *Science and Freedom*. It was held in Hamburg in the summer of 1953. I still remember my preparatory trips and discussions of the conference's program with Lise Meitner, Werner Heisenberg, and Homi Bhabba, the nuclear physicists; with Michael Polanyi, the nuclear chemist turned sociologist and philosopher; and with Hermann Muller, the American geneticist, to name but a few among many. And I remember Lise Meitner's post-conference remark about how useful this conference had been if only because so many scientists representing such varied disciplines of both exact and applied sciences had met for the first time to discuss one precise subject. "At first I feared that the term 'freedom' would lead to confusion," she said. "But, quite to the contrary, it turned out to be of everybody's very precise concern."

Or is the awkward silence that now surrounds the CCF enterprise due only to the absurd "secret" system of its financing—a system that testifies to the queer disarray that existed then and still exists in the folds, nooks, and crannies of American capitalist society and its governmental apparat?

Whatever it is, it cannot but be a nefarious silence. Memories are short. Documents get lost. People die. A biography is hard to write when silence has surrounded its protagonist for too long a time. The question that one may ask in retrospect is this:

Was it really impossible to find *open* channels of subsidizing the CCF or was it the result of the same kind of thoughtless poltroonery, a kind of bureaucratic indolence, that led to having our Cultural Committee pumped full of money through the various CIA pumps?

Could it not have been done imaginatively, courageously, through the establishment of a worldwide fund made up of those famous "counterpart funds" that in the late 1940s were spread all around the world? A kind of Marshall Plan in the domain of the intellect and the arts?

If it had been done honestly and publicly, the whole ugly mess of 1964 or 1965 would never have taken place. Many reputations would have been spared, thousands of lies would have remained untold, and the eminently decent, honest Cold War period—now absurdly condemned because of a thing euphemistically called *détente*—could have been fought out, at least in the world of the intellect and of culture, openly and frankly. Especially since the money was there, and only much later started to move from "counterpart funds" to unemployable Euro or nowadays petrodollars.

The abysmal and needless impropriety of the method of thinking (or absence of thinking) that preceded the decision to pass money through the CIA to cultural organizations is especially glaring when one thinks that the Cold War was the toughest, most complex ideological war since the early nineteenth century, and that this impropriety occurred in a country that used to have a century-old tradition of what Camus called "moral forms of political thinking."

It still hurts me to think of those "wanton bruises of immorality" and the fact that a marvelous structure built with love and care by brilliantly intelligent, dedicated, and profoundly incorruptible free-thinking men and women was dragged into the mud and destroyed because of the oldest and most persistent hubris: unreasoned action.

One spring day in 1954 I was invited to lunch by Gian Carlo Menotti and Sam Barber at their house at Mount Kisco. I took with me records and tapes (both "pirated") of my *Return of Pushkin* and of another piece, also for voice and orchestra, a vocal concerto for soprano and tenor on three sonnets from Dante's *La Vita Nuova* with their prose introduction. The sonnets were sung in their original Florentine and the introduction in English in a beautiful translation prepared for me by W. H. Auden.

Gian Carlo, Thomas Schippers, and Sam Barber listened to both pieces, and though the records and tapes were hideously scratchy, they seemed to like them.

At the end of the last tape Gian Carlo asked, "Did you ever write an opera?"

I told him that I had often wanted to, but could not find a proper libretto, and that *he* should write one for me.

Gian Carlo replied, "You know, if I were Russian, I would write an opera on Rasputin. I think only a Russian can do it. I thought of it at one time, but dropped the idea. Why don't you? It's *un livret donné*—Rasputin is an 'opera hero.' "

I was taken aback and did not answer. Then Sam drove me to the station. My head started swimming. "Rasputin?" I thought, "How odious! After all those filthy films! And the American lecture tours by Prince Yussupov with their unappetizing title: 'How I Killed Rasputin'!"

An hour later the train crashed down into the tunnel at 125th Street and I found myself mumbling to the rhythm of its wheels: *Ras*-pu-tin . . . *Raas*-pu-tin . . . *Raas*-pu-tin."

Early next morning I went to a secondhand bookstore in search of Rasputin. I found an excruciatingly lecherous and silly book about him in German. But it did it. All of that muddled past, transformed by eons of time into mythology, started coming back to me.

Several days later I flew to Europe. The Congress for Cultural Freedom had called me back. But I decided first to stop in London to see Stephen Spender, and then in Hamburg to see Rolf Liebermann.

When I first told Stephen at his London home that I wanted to write an opera with him on the subject of Rasputin, he thought I was joking. "You don't really mean it, Nicky, do you?" he laughed. "It's such a bore . . . and so vulgar."

"But, Stephen . . . actually," intervened his wife, Natasha, "why don't you read a book on Rasputin and then maybe, when Nicky and you go to visit Hansi Lambert in Gstaad, talk again about it?"

"Well . . . yes . . . I see. You may be right," said Stephen, unzipping a stream of "s's" at the end of his "yes's."

I left with Stephen a copy of *The Holy Devil* by Fülöp-Miller and caught the morning plane to Hamburg, where I was met at the airport by Rolf Liebermann. Rolf was not yet the famous director of one of Europe's most prodigious opera houses. He ran the music department of the North German Radio Station and was a leading opera composer. He had just written an opera, commissioned by the Louisville Opera Company, on an astute libretto by Heinrich Strobel woven out of threads and shreds of Molière's *School for Wives*.

My point in meeting Rolf in Hamburg was "carnivorous." I wanted, or rather needed, a commission to start working on my own opera. Rolf had always been helpful, not only to me but to many composers, in arranging commissions, performances, speaking engagements, first when he was head of the music department of the Zurich Radio, and then in a similar post at the much more enterprising NDR (*Norddeutsche Rundfunk*) in Hamburg. Knowing the weight he carried in musical circles in Germany, I wanted Rolf to intervene on my behalf with the director of the Louisville Opera Company, a person called Moritz von Bomhard whom I did not know.

Contrary to Spender, Rolf found Menotti's idea splendid, but he was worried about the libretto. "Really, Nicky," he said, "why don't you have the libretto written by a German? The opera market is here in Germany. In America you might get one or two performances, but here we have thirty-two opera houses. If a German with a 'name' would write the libretto for you and you got published by a German publisher, you could make a lot of money."

At the time I did not realize how shrewd his advice was, but, as things turned out, I would not have acted upon it anyway.

Rolf promised to do what he could and told me that Bomhard would be in Salzburg in the summer and that I should try and see him there.

Rolf Liebermann did what he had promised, and when I got in touch with Moritz von Bomhard he was very well "prepared." He seemed genuinely interested and suggested that Stephen and I write for him an outline of the libretto.

When I saw Stephen in May at the Swiss chalet of our late friend and ever so kind patron, Baroness Hansi Lambert, the general outline and mood of the opera plot were fairly clear in my head. Fortunately, Stephen liked them and in a few days we put together on paper a fragmentary outline of what was to become *Rasputin's End*, an opera in three acts and six scenes to a libretto in English by Stephen Spender and Nicolas Nabokov, so far better known as *Der Tod des Grigory Rasputin*, or *La Fin de Raspoutine*, or even *La Morte di Grigory Rasputin*.

The plot of the opera as Stephen and I saw it was to be an elaborate exercise in remembering. Stephen started to pull out of my memory tattered photographs of the past. He helped me to put heads on bodies and eyes into faces, to shape characters and dress them up as protagonists of an opera, and above all to endow them with the gift of lyrical speech.

We refrained intentionally (at least on my part) from studying other libretti, not because we wanted to produce something "original," but because we felt the need of being true to our own "vision" of the Rasputin story. Both Stephen and I knew enough about opera to be able to decide when prose lines should replace rhymed poetry and when one should have arias, trios, quartets or other ensembles, how to construct a scene and what kind of *recitativo* to use.

In a way, we acted in a manner opposite to the way Hofmann-sthal, Auden and Kallman, and many other librettists worked. We tried to do our work *dans le noir*, relying solely upon our imagination in order to get *that* particular Jack out of its rusty, broken-down box.

I saw Moritz von Bomhard in Salzburg and gave him our outline, which he liked. Yes, he had obtained the commission for me on the same terms Liebermann had had. Yes, they would produce the opera in Louisville in 1958 if Spender and I could deliver it in time. Yes, the committee (or board, or whoever it was) liked our outline, but had expressed some misgivings about the size of the opera and the demands it would make upon the Louisville Opera Company.

Thereupon I started to receive letters containing warnings.

I should keep in mind that Louisville had no proper opera house, but only a high-school auditorium with a small stage and no orchestra pit. Therefore the orchestration should be limited in size and should omit the use of too many brass instruments. I swallowed this advice and took notice of it.

Then I was informed that it would be difficult to get a chorus onto the stage and if I felt the need of one (which I did) it would either have to be taped beforehand or hidden somewhere backstage and couldn't possibly exceed twelve persons, preferably male.

Regretfully, I accepted this second warning.

Then I was told that I should not write difficult vocal parts. Though the main singers of the company were good (indeed they were), the bulk of them were amateurs or voice students of the Louisville University Music Department.

My eyebrows went up, but I had to agree.

Several weeks later came another avalanche of advice, information, and warnings: Please, not too many difficult changes of scenery and costumes; the auditorium lacked proper machinery and the opera company money to produce custom-made theater costumes. The last warning seemed quite ominous: the length of the opera should not exceed one hour, otherwise it could be neither produced nor recorded.

I replied to my dear Louisville co-plotter that I could, if he wished, write an opera for half a flute and a singing petroleum lamp. We would then divide the commission money among himself, Spender, and myself. But my publisher friend in Paris, the late Hervé Dugardin, persuaded me to go on writing the music and that we would later find a way out.

I couldn't help seeing the whole story as grotesque and funny and also typical of the American scene.

If it hadn't been for the zeal, the talent, the inventiveness, and the total dedication of Moritz von Bomhard and a small group of his collaborators, no opera could have possibly been produced in Louisville.

The place where I wrote most of *The Holy Devil*, as the Kentuckian version of *Rasputin* was to be known, was Gstaad in the Bernese Oberland. My friend Hansi Lambert found a room with a piano in a farmhouse close to her chalet. Through the window came sweet Swiss smells: fried onions and cow dung, with an occasional overtone of midsummer pine and cut grass. I have always loved those eminently comforting smells. They make me feel as secure as a cuckoo in its clock.

Stephen and Natasha came to stay at Hansi's chalet. We plotted the second part of Act I and Stephen wrote the text. By autumn 1956 most of the music of this act was composed, but, of course, only a sketch—that is, not orchestrated for the "petroleum-lamp" size orchestra Louisville required.

Moritz von Bomhard bombarded me with more worried letters and received in return "tranquilizers"—that is, promises to be a good boy and sheepish requests to be patient with me. The ominous deadline was approaching. The première was set for April 16, 1958. I was in a panic.

The first orchestra rehearsal in Louisville was a disaster. The parts and the conductor's score were flooded with mistakes. But the singing was well rehearsed, and the voices were good.

Several days before the première, Stephen arrived, as charming and as detached as ever. He enlivened our work team with funny remarks about the fauna and flora of Louisville's Sheraton Hotel lobby.

By sheer accident, I discovered (someone obviously forgot to tell me) that the party after the première was being given not for Moritz von Bomhard, the cast, and the orchestra, but for Aaron Copland and other American composers whose works were being played that same evening at another hall in Louisville. I was therefore warned not to expect important critics or personalities at the première, but to be prepared for a half-empty hall unless it was papered at the last minute.

And so it was. The hall was one-third empty, the public bewildered and tepid. Under the circumstances, the performance was a real achievement (and the second one even better), but few people seemed to like the opera, and the press (what there was of it) did not like it at all.

I left Louisville with a tape of *The Holy Devil* in my pocket. That was Louisville's main contribution.

Thanks to two international musical festivals I had organized in Europe in the early fifties for the CCF, I knew a few VIPs of the European opera world. I looked them up and played the Louisville tape for them. After months of receiving unkept promises and polite refusals, Professor O. F. Schuh, who had just been named director of Cologne's modern opera house, promised to produce my opera. Even more enticing was Schuh's offer to direct the opera himself, with stage sets and costumes designed by Caspar Neher. Both Schuh and Neher were famous people in Mitteleuropa, Schuh as the director of many modern operas and plays and Neher as the early collaborator of young Brecht.

But of course Schuh wanted the complete work, not the Kentuckian version. This meant a new deadline of tortures. A second act had to be composed. The whole opera had to be reorchestrated from the "petroleum-lamp" size orchestra to a large one.

I had to work again in snatches at friends' houses: at Alix Rothschild's cozy castle in Normandy, and in the wine-world splendors of Pauline and Philippe Rothschild at Mouton.

The Cologne performance took place in November 1959. Now the opera was called by its proper name, *Rasputin's End*, or, more grandiloquently in German, *Der Tod des Grigory Rasputin*. The performance was lavish. It had ingenious lighting effects, changes of scenery by means of silently rolling platforms, and proper period costumes. It was beautifully sung and acted. Josef Rosenstock took excellent care of the music. It was what one calls a "great success." In *Odekolon's* capital the remote Rasputin saga came to life. It acquired its Manichean dimensions. It was tender and gruesome, moving and macabre. The public liked it and the house was packed.

The opera went through twenty-five performances in Cologne

and lasted for two long seasons. Subsequently it was performed in French in concert form by the French Radio in Paris in 1961 under the masterful direction of Manuel Rosenthal, and in Italian at the opening of Catania's opera season in 1963 in the baroque Bellini Opera House under the direction of the late and glorious Hermann Scherchen.

Then, after 1963, the old "jack" Grigory Rasputin went back to his box with its rusty springs. For the time being, he is fast asleep, waiting for someone to wake him.

"Myister Nab-O-kov! . . . Kherr Nab-O-kov!" gargled a voice in the intercom. "Tooo . . . informashon . . . kountr . . . plizz! . . . *Bittey . . . tsu . . . informatsions . . . buro!*"

I went to the information counter. "Hey . . . Pst . . . Have you been calling me?" I asked in English. "I'm Nicolas Nabokov."

From behind, someone took me gently by the elbow. I turned around. A slight, asparagus-like man with blond-blue eyes was smiling at me officially.

"Sorry," he started in German, "are you Herr Nabokov?"

"*Da, da,* it's me," I replied in Russian.

"My German's bad," he explained, not noticing my shift in language. "I spik better English. You spik English?"

"But . . . but can't we speak Russian?" I asked.

"Oh, Gospodin Nabokov!" His face pinked up and his voice sounded relieved. "The Embassy neglected to let us know that you speak Russian. Please forgive us." He looked apologetic. "May I introduce myself? My name is . . ." and he mumbled a long name with a lot of m's. "I'm from the *Ministerstvo Kultury*, Music Section," and more ceremoniously: "Welcome to Moscow!"

He stepped aside and from behind him appeared a pale, dark-haired, somewhat exotic-looking woman in her mid-thirties.

"And this, Gospodin Nabokov, is your interpreter, Elveera Nikitishna Melkumyan."

"Aha!" I thought. "Armenian."

"*Guten tag,* Herr Professor Nabokov," said the Armenian lady in labored German. "We were not informed what language you would wish to speak." And she stretched out her hand.

I shook the hand and said, "*Guten tag,*" regretting not to be able to say it in Armenian.

"May I have your passport and your baggage coupons?" asked

Mr. Music Section. "And please, will you follow me?"

I did. We squeezed through a side gate of the Passport Control. A glum man tore off the "entry" side of my twofold visa. Then the three of us, side by side, marched to the "Arrivals" hall of the Sheremetyevo Airport.

There a comforting sight awaited me: in the middle of the hall was a messy mound of multi-colored baggage being pulled apart by an anxious crowd.

I smiled and, turning to the Armenian lady, said, "It looks like a piece of modern sculpture, doesn't it?"

"*Nein*," she replied sententiously, "*das ist bagage.*"

"Why don't you go with Mrs. Melkumyan to the car," intervened the Music Section, "while I take care of your luggage?"

I followed the Armenian lady outdoors. Leftward, in front of a row of buses, stood a dark Volga.

Mme. Elveera opened the door and said in German, "I'm sorry, but I must leave you to make an urgent phone call," and she disappeared.

The driver did not say a word, nor did he turn around to look at me.

I waited for half an hour. It was much hotter here than in Berlin. I perspired and felt sticky. Behind me middle-aged men and women in pajama-like clothes were being loaded into buses.

"How short and plump they all look," I thought.

"*Iz* Sukhumi [from Sukhumi, a Black Sea resort]," the driver volunteered unexpectedly.

Suddenly the Music Section was there again with a wan old man dragging my two-ton bags. "Your music is *vsya v sokhrannosti* [all safe]," he said, climbing into the seat next to the driver. Mme. Elveera joined me in the back seat.

"We were not informed," began the Music Section in the same apologetic tone as before, "what hotel you would have wished to stay in. At this time all hotels are crowded because of the Film Festival. It is very hard to get accommodations. As you probably know, we were only notified ten days ago about your arrival. But I am glad to inform you that our Ministry was able to secure a room for you in a first-class hotel right in the center of town, Hotel Pekin."

I replied that any hotel would do, but that my trip had been planned several months ago by the aides of Ambassador Abrassimov.

253

"I do not understand why they had not notified you earlier."

The Volga's motor started with a lot of coughs and slipped into a blue cloud of ill-refined diesel fumes emerging out of a bus's exhaust.

"Have you been to Moscow before?" asked Mme. Elveera, still in German.

"Forgive me," I replied, "but must we speak German? Don't you speak any Russian? Because if you don't, I'll have to speak German and you will be translating it into what? Into Armenian?" and I smiled. "And who's going to translate it back into Russian?"

Mme. Elveera looked aggrieved. She pursed her lips and replied, "Of course I speak Russian, but our Embassy in Berlin neglected to . . ." and she repeated the same sentence she had said before, this time in Russian. "At the interpreters' pool of the Ministry," she explained, "they decided that you must be an American only by passport and Russian only in name, because you live in Berlin, don't you?"

I nodded.

"Nobody told us that you speak Russian." And again, sententiously, "The knowledge of language facilitates human contact."

Now that the language curtain had lifted, she pulled out of her handbag a piece of paper and started reciting the schedule prepared for me by the Ministry's Music Section. "Tonight the Moscow Art Theater . . . tomorrow morning at nine, visit to the Lenin Mausoleum . . . followed by a meeting with Mr. Tikhon Khrennikov at the Composers' Union . . . dinner at two p.m." . . . with . . . and so on.

Meanwhile the Volga drove slowly onward toward Moscow, tailgating a pair of smelly buses.

"How did I ever get into this fix?" I thought, while the Volga rattled along and Elveera Nikitishna enumerated the variegated pleasures and entertainments that awaited me during my "official" —she said it twice—visit to Moscow and Leningrad.

Indeed, one may ask, how did it come about that a "fascist beast," a "lackey of American capitalism," had got himself so handsomely invited—travel, hotel, the Volga with driver and an interpreter-guide—to the Soviet Union by its Cultural Ministry and the Ministry's musical appendage, the Union of Soviet Composers?

However illogical it may appear on the surface, the answer was and is simple.

* * *

Late in 1962, in the wake of the construction of the Berlin Wall that sealed off East Berlin from West Berlin, I decided to move to West Berlin. Sometime that year, I do not remember exactly when, I was appointed by its Mayor as "Adviser on International Cultural Affairs to the Berlin Senate." The Mayor was, of course, Willy Brandt.

West Berlin was in trouble. From being a magnet stretched out from the West to the citizens of the German Democratic Republic and to Eastern Europe in general, it suddenly became an extravagantly expensive "prestige enclave." Over its future hung the Khrushchev ultimatum. Though widely believed to be a bluff, it made its inhabitants feel edgy and insecure, especially since the spectacular and to most Berliners dismaying lack of reaction on the part of the American establishment to the workers' uprising in East Berlin on June 17, 1953. In a way, Berliners were the first to learn that the American foreign-policy slogans of the Dulles period were empty rhetoric, fraudulently inciting people to revolt when the U.S. government was neither willing nor able to support them.

When I flew to Berlin in January or February 1962 to settle there, I was keenly aware that West Berlin should now play an important cultural game to regain some of its lost cosmopolitan glamour. Furthermore, it was clear to me that in such a game one should try to gain the support and participation of scholars and artists from the Soviet Union and from the so-called Socialist Block. In other words, it was my view that Berlin should stop attracting the *political* attention of the outside world and try for its *cultural* attention.

I had not the slightest idea of how to go about it, nor did I have any contact with Soviet representatives abroad, either in Berlin or elsewhere. I knew, of course, that I could not possibly achieve any kind of "cultural opening" to the East without a measure of their cooperation, yet I suspected that my name must stand high on their list of intransigent anti-Communist enemies of the U.S.S.R.

The West German aspect of the situation was equally tricky. I had to be circumspect in my actions, and this for obvious reasons: firstly, I was *not* a German; secondly, though known as an anti-Communist and an American by adoption, I was Russian by birth and could possibly be suspected of a nostalgic, sentimental bias toward my motherland.

Little did I know that in this endeavor I would soon gain two powerful allies—both of whom, for different if not opposite reasons, realized that the time was getting ripe to de-politicize Berlin.

While the American establishment was still centered on promoting the number of tunnels dug under the wall and the ever shrinking number of desperado escapees across the wall, these allies believed in fostering the internationalization of Berlin's cultural life, achieving limited accommodation with the East, and thus playing as ably and as peacefully as possible the cultural poker game in West Berlin's interest. One of these allies was Mayor Brandt, the future inventor of the policy of "opening to the East"; the other, the Soviet Ambassador to Berlin, Pyotr Andreyevitch Abrassimov.

I have always been fond of Berlin, and this fondness lingered even during the bitter Hitler years. But if I were asked why I prefer Berlin to other capitals of Europe, I would be at a loss to give an exhaustive and convincing answer.

Is it because I spent here a few happy and profitable years of my youth and formed lasting friendships? Or is it because of Berlin's physical beauty: its spaciousness, its leisurely, linden-bordered, broad streets and avenues, its quaint Jugendstil apartment houses and superb modern buildings, its admirable artistic institutions—the opera, the Philharmonic and Radio orchestras, the museums and lively theaters—its bracing dry and clean air, and the vast lakes that surround this charmed city? Or perhaps because of the humane quality of its citizenry, their genuine cosmopolitan hospitality, their respect for civil liberties and lack of any kind of bias or moral inhibitions, the unhurried and yet diligently civilized pace of their lives, and the grand Socialist Mayors—Ernst Reuter, Willy Brandt, and now Klaus Schutz—that have governed this genuinely egalitarian capital since the end of the war?

My reasons include all of these and yet something more, and the more is intangible, elusive. In any case, I have been *ein Berliner* at heart long before the late President Kennedy became one for quite different reasons.

Like everybody else, I had my love affair with Paris. But after World War II that old mistress of so many artists lost its charm for me. The charm dissolved gradually and is now reduced to a feeling of amused tenderness for the sweet little street in a provincial part of Paris where my wife and I keep a tiny flat. The rest of Paris has, alas, turned for me into a mnemonic cemetery, some of it tender, most of it sad and a bit bitter.

Late in 1961 I prepared a detailed paper concerning the unexpected plight of West Berlin and what could be done to counteract the effects of the Wall in the field of culture.

My paper contained several concrete proposals aimed at counteracting the flow of artists and intellectuals away from West Berlin. I thought that the time was ripe to play Berlin's cultural card, but play it ably and firmly on a broad, international scale.

It turned out that those proposals of mine were well received by the Ford Foundation, which gave the city of Berlin a handsome grant for the realization of some of my projects.

On February 14, 1963, in Berlin a friend of mine died, Gustav von Westermann. Like Grandmother Nabokova, he was a Russo-German Balt. By profession a composer, he was an eminently civilized, educated, and able person who shortly after the end of the war had been appointed general manager of the Berlin Philharmonic Orchestra. He was also, as of 1950, the founder and director of the yearly Berlin Arts Festival.

The Berlin Festival was started as a part of a cultural prestige enterprise by the Western Allies. It was to be for East Berliners a showcase of the arts in the Free World. In those pre-Adamic times —before the Wall—they could come in droves to West Berlin, get free tickets to various performances, and wander aimlessly along West Berlin's main arteries, window-shopping though unable to pay even for a beer in a West Berlin pub, for want of West German currency.

Westermann, a dedicated and imaginative person, soon transformed this dubious "showcase" of Western agitprop into one of Europe's most respected institutions. It became a European model of festival *savoir-faire*.

With the rise of German prosperity the Allied contribution shrank and the Festival was taken over entirely by the Berlin Municipality.

Now in 1962, after a hiatus of one year, I was to take over the Berlin Festival as its artistic director.

My first Festival season was to be in September 1964, but I started planning for it in the spring of 1963.

For a long time I had cherished the idea of organizing somewhere a festival on the theme "Black and White", or, more precisely, on the influence of the art of black people upon Western art of the twentieth century. Now, I thought, this was my chance to do it, and by the end of 1963 I had got its program well under way.

* * *

"Herr Professor! Herr Professor!" She had slipped into the room unnoticed and spoke in a stage whisper. *"Die Russen sind da!"*

My assistant at the Festival office, Frau Viola Hilpert, was frail, briskly bright, easily excitable, and had a gay, ever ready smile. I adored her.

My office was large and ugly. The blond table stood catty-corner to the window. The rest was bare. On this dark, wintry day all the lights were on.

Frau Hilpert handed me a visiting card. I read: *"Yuli A. Kvitsinski, Kulturattache der Botschaft der U.d.S.S.R., Berlin, Unter den Linden."*

I smiled and told Frau Hilpert to show the man in.

In came a pair. Perpendicularly, both were equal—the "Socialist Motherland's" average of five foot two or three inches. But while the first one was stocky and blond, with a flat, pancaky face, the second one was trim and had an inborn suntan. "Cossack," I thought, "or maybe Armenian."

They crossed the diagonal toward my desk rockingly, the way minor Soviet bureaucrats walk. The obviously senior—the blond-and-gray one—stretched out his long sleeved hand and said ceremoniously, "My name is Kvitsinski, Yuli Aleksandrovich, and this is my colleague," and he pronounced a name I did not understand. It sounded spittlish and rubbery.

I asked my visitors to sit down and proposed to speak Russian. The dark one smiled, the blond one did not.

"As you wish," he replied in Russian and looked at me suspiciously. His eyes were blue, steely. Then, equally ceremoniously, he said, still smileless: "I congratulate you on your new assignment as artistic director of the Berlin Festival. I wish you more success than your predecessors had."

"Yes," I said, thinking that he referred to Gustav von Westermann's death, "It is a pity that Herr von Westermann died. He was such an able man and such a charming friend."

"I did not mean that," said Mr. Kvitsinski.

"What did you mean?" I asked.

He fidgeted in his seat and asked if he could smoke. I offered a cigarette and lit it for him.

"In the last years both your predecessors," he started with a smirk in his voice, "were not very successful in attracting people from East Berlin."

"Yes, of course," I remarked, "how could they? With all those obstacles, the Wall and—"

"And yet it was their aim," he interrupted, "wasn't it?"

I did not reply. I leaned back in my chair, clasped my hands behind my neck, and waited. There was a moment of silence. "What a gloomy start," I thought, looking at my two visitors and trying to put myself into their skin.

"But there were in general fewer people that came to your Festival during those last years," said Mr. Kvitsinski. "I mean, you had many fewer visitors from abroad than in former times. Hadn't you?"

"I wouldn't know," I replied.

He looked astonished. "But surely your collaborators must have shown you statistics before they sent you to Berlin. Didn't they?"

"Who do you mean by 'they'?" I asked.

"How would I know?" he said with a grin. "I do not know which American agency sent you here to take over the Festival. There are so many of them."

"Things are not quite the way you think they are." I threw my head back and laughed.

"What do you mean?" he asked. "Americans must be really alarmed about the future of Berlin to . . ." and he seemed to search for the words he wanted, "to delegate here one of their . . ." and he smiled in a sarcastic way, "one of their most . . . experienced . . . technicians."

I waited for a moment, then said very calmly in mock-earnest, "Yes, of course Americans are alarmed. But so is everybody. Aren't you? It is all so unfortunate. This division . . . this Wall . . . all of it so needless. You must admit that it is absurd to have, right in the middle of Europe, a great city divided by an inpenetrable wall."

He looked at me with suspicion, then down at his matchbox. "I agree," he started as if reciting a lesson, "Berlin should not be divided. It should be one great city. The capital of the German Democratic Republic."

I did not argue. I smiled, got up, and offered a drink. "Cognac? Whiskey?" I asked.

Both declined.

I went to my liquor closet, poured myself a glass of whiskey, said "Cheers" in English, and drank it in one swallow. "You see I'm still Russian, I drank it neat. Won't you change your mind and have one?"

Both declined again.

Suddenly, in a more relaxed tone of voice, he asked me, "So you are going to have a festival for Negroes, Gospodin Nabokov?"

"Not 'Gospodin,' " I corrected him, slumping back into my seat. "Nikolai Dimitrievich."

"Okay, Nikolai Dimitrievich," and he left the question floating in the air.

"Well, it is not quite that way," I said. "Not the way you put it. It is going to be an experiment. You see, what interests me, and has interested me for quite some time, is to organize festivals on particular cultural themes. One of the important events of this century has been the reciprocal influences of black and white artistic traditions. To show this, to prove it to the public audibly and visually, is the central purpose of the 1964 Berlin Festival. We will therefore bring to Berlin a number of artistic groups from Africa, America, and South India. We will also organize a few art shows. But, of course," I added, "all of this is only a part of a much larger Festival. And in all of it my aim is to be as open and as international as possible."

While I spoke I watched my two visitors. The blond-and-gray one sat like a mummy—inpenetrable. But the one in blue seemed to listen attentively and occasionally would nod, as if approving of what I was saying.

"Yes, we read about your plans," Kvitsinski began, opening a walnut cigarette case. "It was in the papers a few days ago. But our press attaché and our Tass representative were not invited."

"I beg your pardon!" I remarked. "That's not true. Not only were they invited, but your Tass correspondent and someone from your Embassy came up to me. They introduced themselves and asked for an interview. They promised to call. I'm sure my assistant will know who they were."

Kvitsinski turned to his colleague and asked, "Who could it have been?"

The other one shrugged his shoulders and mumbled, "How could I know?"

I was beginning to get bored and looked pointedly at my watch. "I could ask my assistant to come in," I proposed.

"Well, no . . . it is really immaterial," said Kvitsinski and put his cigarette case back in his pocket. "What interests me, Gospodin . . . excuse me, Nikolai Dimitrievich, is your plan to get all those Negroes to Berlin. How many Negroes will come, do you think?"

I winced at the term, especially the way he pronounced it. "You mean black or colored people, I suppose," I replied curtly. "I couldn't tell you now how many of them will come to Berlin. A little later, perhaps."

But he was unrelenting. "You may not know how many Negroes will come," he said with the same smirk in his voice as earlier in the conversation, "but I am sure you have already reserved buses to take them to the Wall and show it to them."

I laughed, got up, and said very calmly, "No, Yuli Aleksandrovich. Believe it or not, I hadn't thought of it. But you give me an excellent suggestion. Thank you very much! Of course our black guests should be shown the Berlin Wall! And by the way," I continued, "I am told that we here in West Berlin lack excursion buses, but that there are plenty of them in East Berlin. Maybe we could borrow a few buses from you and show our colored visitors from Africa, America, and India both sides of your Wall. Wouldn't that be fine? Of course, we'll gladly pay rental for the buses."

"It is easy for you to joke," replied Kvitsinski in a boorish tone of voice. "But I bet someone in this office or at the American headquarters is already planning for these bus trips to the Wall, and this is why—"

"Look here, Yuli Aleksandrovich," I interrupted. "If we are to continue this talk, let's change the subject. Let us talk about Pushkin and the weather, and then let us part peacefully. This way, it is a waste of your time and mine. Don't you agree? But," and I raised my finger, "if you want to talk seriously about the Berlin Festival, then let us do it! But let us do it constructively. You see, I, on my part, was glad to see you come. There are many things I wanted to talk to you about peacefully and maybe, in the future, to your Ambassador," and I looked at him amiably. "But first may I make the following points?" and I started a ten-minute speech, counting each one of my "points" on my fingertips.

I told Kvitsinski that he was right insofar as the Berlin Festival had originally been started by the Western Allies without Soviet participation. It was to have been a cultural attraction for East Berliners. But then, I said, even before the Wall my predecessor had changed the nature of the Berlin Festival radically. It had become one of the most important festivals in Europe, with no political implications whatsoever. By now it was evident to anyone that it would be foolish to play politics with the arts in this hopelessly divided town. I told him that my aim was to defuse tensions, not to increase them. I explained as precisely as I could that, being myself a composer, I had always considered festivals as vehicles for the advancement of the arts and not for any other purpose.

I told him that I was not an American agent, but had been for ten years the secretary general of the International Congress for Cultural Freedom. "Precisely because of that I think you could deal with me frankly and openly. You will not make a Bolshevik out of me and I will not make a capitalist out of you. But I would like to deal with your Embassy, if it is possible. I would like to deal with it because I need your cooperation for the Festival.

"So long as I run this Festival, it will be a purely cultural, artistic enterprise. But if it is to be complete, I must have the participation not only of Russian virtuosos, composers, and poets, but also of Russian theater, ballet, and opera, Russian orchestras, and those many native ensembles of the Soviet Union."

I enumerated names and organizations I would like to invite to the Berlin Festival.

"And now, Yuli Aleksandrovich," I concluded, "let us have a cognac and part peacefully. You will think over what I have said. You will report it to your Ambassador, and if you decide to cooperate, give me a ring."

I went again to the liquor closet, poured three cognacs, and we gulped them down. For the first time since the pair came into the room I saw their faces smile. I was pleased.

A few days later, early on a Sunday morning, came a call to my hotel. Kvitsinski asked me if he could come and pick me up, the Ambassador would like to meet me at eleven a.m. I said that I would be glad to come.

What was it that brought back those memories of postwar years, the vision of streets clogged with rubble, of ruin and desolation, that Sunday morning of December 1963 as Yuli Aleksandrovich Kvitsinski and I crossed the Wall in a Soviet Embassy Volga? My nose, probably; that distinctive awful smell of East European gasoline. It was odd, all of it, I thought. First the aggressive visit, then the turnabout and the abrupt command-invitation. And now I, a seasoned cold warrior, was sitting next to a Soviet *apparatchik* on my way to see the Soviet Ambassador in East Berlin.

I had learned from American *apparatchiki* that Ambassador

Abrassimov was "a tough cookie," but that he had suave manners and could at times exhibit charm and amiability. I had also learned, but from other sources, that he was one of the most powerful Soviet diplomats abroad. He was Ambassador to the East German Democratic Republic; member of the Allied quadripartite council, which theoretically was responsible for the destinies of East and West Berlin; he was delegate of a sister party to the governing apparat of the East German Republic's party and also a permanent member of the Central Committee of the Communist Party of the U.S.S.R.

In other words, I was not going to meet a "small fry" Soviet functionary, not even a temporary boss, like my postwar Soviet cultural colleague Colonel Tulpanov, but a real big-time operator. This, for a neophyte like me, was indeed a novel experience.

"What will he be like?" I asked myself. "Could he be really interested in such trivia as festivals in West Berlin, with or without 'Negroes'? Surely he must have other, more urgent problems to worry about than festival frivolities? But then why did he give me an appointment? Surely not because he wants to 'size up' someone his underlings believe to be a fresh American agent of sorts? That could be left to those underlings. So, for reasons unknown, he is interested in meeting me. Why? But if perchance he were interested in the participation of Soviet artists in the Berlin Festival, what would be the price of such participation?"

Yes, Kvitsinski's tone and manner had changed radically. From bureaucratic aggressive they had turned to bureaucratic smooth. He was pointing out the tidiness of the streets, the new and old landmarks—the Comic Opera, the former Propaganda Ministry of Goebbels, the new glass-plastic-and-metal buildings on the Unter den Linden.

He even joked while the East German border guard checked his Embassy pass. "He thinks you're my boss," he said in Russian and smiled. "It's because of your fur cap—it looks so Russian."

The Volga stopped in front of the Embassy. Kvitsinski led me through a side entrance into a drab anteroom, then along a dark corridor to a grand, red-carpeted staircase. "Please take a seat," said Kvitsinski, ushering me into a sunny, neat-looking salon. He smiled and left the room.

No one had described to me the looks of Ambassador Abrassimov, so my surprise was complete when he appeared. I had imagined an average, squat Soviet citizen with a flat, round face, or else a face like Brezhnev's. Instead, the person who greeted me politely but un-smilingly and offered me a glass of cognac resembled none of my imagination's clichés.

He was handsome, trim, sportsman-like, and taller than the aver-age Soviet diplomat. His face was well cut in a plain Russian way, his hair graying blond, his cold blue eyes looked straight into mine. There was something frank and open and curiously engaging in their gaze. Intuitively I felt that he was, after all, sizing me up, but in a different and much more subtle way than I had expected. There was neither hostility nor aggressiveness in the way he looked at me. Only interest, and perhaps a bit of caution. I found him attractive and un-fearsome, yet at the same time strangely distant.

He started to ask me the usual questions: When had I left Russia? Had I ever been back? Where was I born, and where had my family lived? Had I studied in Russia or abroad? When had I come to Ber-lin? Had I known Berlin before the war—before the Nazis? What foreign tongues did I speak? When had I gone to America? What was my real profession and why had I accepted the job of Festival director in West Berlin?

It was like a multi-page questionnaire. I answered candidly and fully, trying to be concise and matter-of-fact. I noticed no malice or aggressiveness in his manner.

After a while he interrupted me and smiled. "How come," he said, "that you kept up your Russian so well through those long years abroad? Your Russian is flawless." And he turned to Kvitsin-ski. "Shouldn't we ask Nikolai Dimitrievich to give a few lessons to our people here at the Embassy? So that they could learn to speak a *kulturny, litteraturny* Russian language?" And he glanced at me with an amused smile. "We don't hear such Russian often nowadays. Congratulations!" He raised his glass. "To the Russian language of Gospodin Nabokov!"

Then suddenly he said with real interest, "You have just said that you were born in Belorussia, near the Lithuanian border. I myself come from Belorussia. Do you remember the name of the place?"

I replied that not only did I remember the place, but that it had remained the fondest memory of my childhood. "I was born in a place called Lubcza, on the shores of the Neman. The house stood on a mound high above the river. It was destroyed during the First World War."

"Oh, but I know Lubcza! You mean you were born in that old ruin above the river with the two medieval towers?"

I nodded.

"But then . . . in that case we are *zemlyaki* [compatriots]." He sounded pleased. "Because I was born not so far from Lubcza," and he named a village whose name rang a faint bell in my memory. "Have you ever been to my village? Probably you cannot remember. All our villages were alike." His face had lit up. I felt that something had clicked. Unexpected common ground—*zemlyaki*.

I asked him when he had last been in Belorussia.

"Oh, I go often. I go hunting and fishing. You may remember Lake Kroman—do you?"

"Yes, yes, of course I do," I replied eagerly. "When were you there?"

"Not so long ago . . . only a year or so. It is still as round and as beautiful as ever. Good fishing and lots of crayfish. Still surrounded by forests . . . as in a fairy-tale." And in a warm and friendly tone of voice, "You should go back, Nikolai Dimitrievich." He smiled engagingly. "I'll take you out for a night of crayfishing. I'm sure you'll love it!"

I did not answer. Instead I looked surreptitiously at my watch. It was close to noon. I thought I'd better take my leave, unless, of course, he started talking about Festival business and Berlin.

He noticed my maneuver. "I hope you aren't in any hurry," he said, "because I happen to be free today. It is a rare thing for me to have free time. So why don't you stay and have a bite with me and with my colleague here?" and without waiting for my answer he told Kvitsinski to go and tell them to bring something to eat.

"So this is your first visit to our Embassy, Nikolai Dimitrievich. You're, so to speak, on enemy territory!" he said, half-mockingly.

I replied that it was not only my first visit to this Embassy but my first visit to any Soviet Embassy. The last times I'd had to deal with Soviet representatives had been in 1945 and 1946, when I was stationed in Berlin with the American Information Control Division.

"But haven't you ever been at our Embassy in America, or in Paris, where you lived for a while, as you just said?"

"No, no, never," I replied. "I had no reason to."

Abrassimov looked at me in an astonished way. "But weren't you ever invited on our national holiday? Or on May first, when all our Embassies usually give receptions?"

I smiled. "You know, Pyotr Andreevich, there is no reason for me to hide it, but I would be the last person to get invited to any Soviet Embassy. Me, a seasoned *émigré* and an anti-Bolshevik . . . Besides, as you probably know, I have been for over ten years the head, the secretary general, of an anti-Communist organization, the Congress for Cultural Freedom. Not quite the proper credentials for being invited to a Soviet Embassy anywhere, you will agree?" And I laughed.

He laughed back. "In other words, you mean to say that instead of having a bite with me," he said in mock-earnest, "I should have you arrested, or at least thrown out of our Embassy?" And he looked at me with an amused glint in his eyes.

"Probably yes," I said. "Do you want me to leave?" and I made as if getting up.

He held me back. "No. Please keep your seat." His face changed and he said in earnest, "You know, I like frankness. It is so much easier to deal with people when they are frank, don't you agree? I know, for example, that I will never make out of *Dvoryanin* ("country squire") Nabokov a good Communist; nor will you ever make out of me, an old Bolshevik, a capitalist. And that's a good start." He poured each of us another glass of cognac and said, "To mutual frankness and respect."

Caviar, herring in cream, gherkins, smoked salmon, something trembling in aspic, bread, butter appeared. Abrassimov filled vodka glasses and passed them around on a silver platter. "Please, help yourself," he said, pointing to the dishes.

He raised his vodka glass and said, "To your first visit to our Embassy. I hope that it will the first of many."

"By the way," he added, "I now remember that one of my aides once told me that you cooperated very well with Colonel Tulpanov when he was chief of our Cultural Affairs here after the war. Well . . . I hope we can resume this kind of cooperation." And again he looked at me in a friendly, uninhibited way.

I thought that it was time to start talking about the Festival, but Abrassimov raised his hand and interrupted me. "You do not have to explain to me what you have told my colleague," he said. "He reported to me fully about your conversation. And I have spoken to our Minister of Culture on the telephone. In principle, I can tell you at once: I do not see any obstacles to the participation of Soviet artists in your Festival in West Berlin. But you'll have to accept

what we can offer you. Because," and he looked at me in a courteous way, "our artists, the top ones, are in very great demand, as
you no doubt know. We'll try to do our best for your next Festival.
And then plan perhaps something more important for the following years. This year we can only offer you one of our great artists,
who also happens to be a good friend of mine. I know that he is
coming here to East Berlin in September. He's our best cellist. His
name is Mstislav Rostropovich." And he turned to Kvitsinski. "Will
you work out the details with Nikolai Dimitrievich? And . . . and
maybe something else will turn up in the meantime."

This was all I wanted to know. It was all said calmly and obligingly. I felt content. I had never heard Rostropovich play, but my
friend Igor Markevich had told me about him. At that time Rostropovich was very little known outside of Russia.

A little while later it was time to go.

So I became an infrequent but fairly regular visitor to "enemy
territory," to the Stalinist temple in East Berlin.

First Kvitsinski and I started to work out the visit of Rostropovich and his wife, the Moscow opera singer Galina Vishnevskaya.
Next I began to urge Kvitsinski to provide my Festival with a Russian choir.

"There should be a Russian chorus at that opening ceremony,"
I insisted. I wanted in particular to have the Yurlov choir, the best
in the Soviet Union. It had a vast repertoire and could refrain from
singing the habitual trashy folklore. I knew that the Yurlov choir
dared to sing such prohibited works as Stravinsky's *Les Noces*.
Stravinsky was coming to the Festival, and I wanted him to hear
once (he never did) his most Russian work well sung by a Russian
chorus.

I also asked for a Soviet conductor and, if possible, Russia's best
orchestra, the Leningrad Philharmonic, with its aged conductor
Mravinsky. Instead I was offered Kyril Kondrashin, whom I had
never heard of and who then, like Rostropovich, was largely unknown outside the U.S.S.R.

Soon I began to like Kvitsinski. I knew, of course, that he was a
political *apparatchik* and that culture was, to say the least, peripheral
to his real interest. He was also a thoroughly trained Marxist-
Leninist. But he was not lazy or lax or intellectually vapid. I liked
his hard-working, cool intelligence. He was quick, efficient, and—

at least with me—forthright. I prefer him by far to the newer PR type of Soviet diplomat that I have since met in New York and elsewhere. There was no nonsense about Kvitsinski. If he promised something, he kept his promise, and he was always meticulously on time.

I think he, in turn, liked me. I never pretended to be anything but what I was. He knew well my irrevocable skepticism about the "Socialist Motherland" and its satellites. Though he treated me with respect, politeness, and in as friendly a manner as he could, I always sensed that in some essential way I remained an enigma for him. The hardest thing for a Soviet *apparatchik* to imagine is the workings of the mind and the emotional condition of someone "liberal."

Rostropovich came into my life in the fall of 1964, and with his coming many things changed. Rostropovich is a person *en dehors de toute mésure*, to whom no measures apply. He is not only one of the most skillful performers of our time, a man of extraordinary erudition and charm, but he carries with him a climate of friendship, of enthusiasm, of human warmth rarely equaled in my experience. He, his wife Galina, and I became friends at once. He started urging me to come to Russia, and he promised to have my music performed there.

After Rostropovich's visit in September 1964 my cordial relations with Abrassimov changed to friendly ones and I became a fixture at the Soviet Embassy. The Ambassador and his wife, whenever they had a concert at the Embassy, or any other performance in town, invited me and counted on my presence.

Now Abrassimov himself was urging me to go to Moscow and Leningrad at the earliest opportunity. "You must go and see for yourself," he'd say. "You will meet our people, they will play your music. You can discuss with them your plans directly."

Rostropovich, whom I started to see wherever and whenever I could and for whom I proposed to write a piece—a set of variations on a theme by Tchaikovsky—also urged me to come to Moscow and Leningrad.

I told Ambassador Abrassimov that I would go in June 1967.

Thus, in June 1967 a Soviet Embassy car took me to the airport in Schonefeld in East Berlin and off I went for my first return to the land of my ancestors.

* * *

268

"Have you ever been in Moscow?"

This time it is not my Armenian chaperone but "Music Section" asking the question.

[No . . . no, I have never been in the Mother of Socialism's capital . . . or have I?

Once upon a time, at a very tender age, I was whisked out of my lower bunk in the *vagon mikst,* huddled into woolens and furs, packed up in the center of an *izvozchik*'s sleigh, and driven from one Moscow railroad station to another one. But somehow I never liked to remember that ride through dark, wintry Moscow.]

"No," I reply, "I have never been in Moscow."

"Oh, but in that case," suggests the Armenian lady, "why don't we drive around a bit, show Mr. Nabokov some of the sights? We still have time before the theater starts."

"Yes, why not?" Music Section echoes meekly.

The car enters what seems to be a suburb and a traffic jam. The chauffeur curses and toots his horn savagely. Mme. Elveera perspires. Her downy upper lip and her forehead are pearled. And so from suburb to suburb until we reach or are suddenly confronted by all those famous postcards! All of them at once. And all of them fully three-dimensional.

"This, Mr. Nabokov," Mme. Elveera announces proudly, "is the Krasnaya Ploshchad. I believe you call it the Red Square in English. . . . And this," and she points more solemnly to a dark stone cube leaning against a bare brick wall, "this is our national shrine, the Mausoleum—Lenin's Tomb. No doubt you have seen reproductions of it."

[How could I have escaped them? Don't all of us know that cube with its perennial top growth? October Day, May Day, Army Day, and other ritual feasts . . . Ten or twelve years ago a special issue of *Life* carried lush color photographs of the outside and the inside of this greatest of all fetishist temples. Both idols still lay side by side then—waxen, nicely made up, floating in the bluish light of their glass cocoons like some strange, exotic fish. Now "The Founder" is alone.]

"We have special passes for the Mausoleum. Tomorrow morning at nine," says Mme. Elveera.

269

"Why special?" I ask. "I thought it was open to everyone?"

"*Vne ocheredi*—out of turn," she explains, "otherwise you'd have to queue up. And the queues are sometimes very long, especially now during the tourist season." And she adds, "You are a guest of the Ministry of Culture and the Ministry provides its guests with this special privilege."

I do not reply, but take note that special privileges exist in the Soviet Motherland, even for its national shrine.

"And what you see over there, at the other end of this place is—" Mme. Elveera starts again.

"I know, I know," I interrupt. "I have recognized it. It's St. Basil's Cathedral."

[Another famous postcard: the gingerbread toy church with its lacquered Kodachrome *onionry. Una fantasia molto barocca*. More suitable for an opera decor—Rimsky's *Tsar Saltan*, for example, or some other folklorish haberdashery—than for Christian meditation.]

"And on this side," and Mme. Elveera points to a quaint Victorian-looking brick building painted *sang-de-boeuf*, "is the GUM, the State General Store. You can buy there anything you want."

[Of the three monumental postcards, I prefer this one. It is homey, harmless and rather nice.]

The car has stopped. The three of us crawl out onto the bulging pavement. Mme. Elveera gesticulates, pointing to various "sights." All of them famous.

[The Kremlin . . . There they all sat, the *Kammenozadye*, the "stone-bottomed" ones, to use a popular dictum. One after the other, with their slowly . . . oh, so abysmally slowly changing team of fundamentalists, sat, ruled, feared, and . . . oppressed.]

Mme. Elveera points to the Kremlin walls and its sentinel towers, giving the name of each one. The old brick looks shabby and the architecture, though distinctly Italian, second-rate. These Bolognese architects were chiselers. They used cheap bricks and pocketed the Tsar's gold ones.

Behind the Kremlin walls looms more onionry . . . gilt, blue. . . . Mme. Elveera names the churches and cathedrals to which these onions belong.

270

[Russian church architecture is endemically alien to me—
Too much like fairy-tale, folklore stuff, and all of it exterior
decoration. My heart is supposed to swoon, but it doesn't.
"C'est bien pour des âmes simples," wrote Balzac to Countess
Hanska. Evidently mine isn't simple. To me it looks like
mosques gone wrong. My churches, the ones I love, are diminutive Athenian Byzantine, or full-grown Romanesque Byzantine of the French southwest. But not our Russian onionry,
despite all of its fabled symbolism of "a sky in a sky in a sky in
a sky" from Manichean or Gnostic tradition.]

"Weren't those walls and towers whitewashed once upon a time?"
I ask.

"N-no, I don't think so," replied Mme. Elveera.

"Not in our time," seconds her Music Section.

"But surely they must have been," I insist. "Otherwise the term
Moskva Belokamennaya—Moscow, the white-stoned one—could
never have arisen?"

"I wouldn't know," Mme. Elveera says despondently, ruffled by
my question.

"Or maybe it was called that because the churches and palaces
inside the Kremlin were built of white sandstone from quarries near
the Moskva and Oka Rivers?"

"You mean like this stone here," and Mme. Elveera points to a
low semicircular wall in front of the Kremlin's main gate. "This is
the Lobnoye Mesto—the place of praise. It is—"

"It is the place where Stepan Razin, Yemelyan Pugachov, and the
Streltsy," interrupts Music Section, "were—"

"Yes, I know, I know," I interrupt in my turn, "were beheaded,
quartered, exposed in a cage. but it is also the place where tsars
showed themselves to the people after being crowned." And, I ask,
"Wasn't Ivan III the first one to show himself to the people on the
Lobnoye Mesto?"

"Maybe . . . I wouldn't know," mumbles Music Section, and
he looks at his watch. "I think, Elveera Nikitishna, it is time for us
to get going," he says. "Nikolai Dimitrievich may want to wash up
and change before going to the theater." He smiles amiably. "And
I have to go to my office, I still have work to do."

We climb back into the car. The driver starts the motor with a
great deal of fumes and noises. I turn around for a last look at the
Kremlin towers.

[A verse of Anna Akhmatova's swims into the forefront of my memory:

Budu ya kak Streletskie zhonki
Pod Kremlyovskimi Bashnyami vyt . . .

Like the wives of the Sharpshooters Guard
I shall howl under the Kremlin Towers . . .

Did she write those lines here in Moscow after trying to pass under one of those hideous towers? To see whom? To ask for mercy from whom?]

When after theater and supper I returned to my room, the lights wouldn't work. The key keeper, a huge woman sitting like a potted plant at the other end of the corridor, did not even raise her head from whatever she was reading or knitting.

"*Zhdite do utra* [Wait until morning]," she barked, "the *montyor* [engineer] comes at seven."

What a strange day it had been—a curious un-homecoming, like a parable gone sour: The Prodigal Son returns, but to the wrong address. Instead of "father," he finds: Hotel Pekin, Mme. Melkumyan, Music Section, and official hospitality. In me there's not a shadow of a tremor, not a whiff of an emotion, or even the slightest nostalgia. Only irritation and impatience. A desire to get this "welcome" over with, start seeing the few friends I have here, and meet the people I am supposed to meet. But also try to escape some of those obligatory visits: the Mausoleum, the inside of the Kremlin, the museums, all, no doubt, in the company of Donna Elveera or some other "guide."

Why, for instance, should I go to see the exotic human fish in its glass cocoon? It isn't a shrine of mine! And why visit the Oruzheinaya Palata with its historic *bric-à-brac:* the boots of Peter I, the Romanovs' crown, their thrones, and those largely phony crown jewels?

The play Mme. Elveera and I went to that evening was called *Chekhov.* Slow, visually over-curtained, out of date, but well acted. Unfortunately, much too obvious a copy of an Anglo-American model, a play fabricated out of Bernard Shaw's correspondence. I had seen it recently in New York and had found it tedious. This one was nicer (because Chekhov was nicer than Shaw) but less skillfully compiled, and because of that more tenuous.

After Act I, timidly and politely, I suggested that perhaps we could leave. Mme. Elveera seemed relieved. She too had had a long, strenuous day. All morning at the university, then to the airport to meet me and show me around, and then—worst and longest of all —check me into the huge seraglio of the Hotel Pekin. After each of these stages she had had to make an "urgent" phone call, as if she were reporting to someone about the "pilgrim's progress."

Once I and my bags were reunited in the hotel room, all of which took at least an hour, and Music Section had disappeared, saying a hurried "*Dosvidanya*," she had smiled politely and said, "*Noo vot*, Mr. Nabokov, I hope you don't mind if I leave you for a few minutes. I've brought my evening clothes with me. I'll change in the ladies' rest room. I won't be long, because the play starts in half an hour and we must hurry up."

I decided not to change. I washed my hands, sat on the bed, and looked around. The room was drab, ill kept. But, fortunately, high up, and therefore there was a great deal of sky and light.

Less than ten minutes later there was a knock on the door and Mme. Elveera reappeared, transformed. She wore a smart, dark suit and looked surprisingly handsome. A well-bred Armenian beauty, a bit ample, in her mid-thirties. Pale skin, dark hair, Orientally somber eyes, and regular facial features. Obviously someone civilized, intelligent, a person evoking sympathy and exuding charm. Only the deep bluish rings under her eyes betrayed a hard life and overwork.

I had hoped that after the theater we'd part and go to bed. Nothing of the sort. Mme. Elveera insisted on supper.

"You are our guest," she said, "you've had nothing to eat since noon. You must have supper before you go to bed. It won't take long." Alas, it did.

I started mechanically to read the menu and made up a quatrain that—as I soon discovered—formed the culinary core of all hotel restaurants in the Soviet Union:

> Su-dak Or-loff
> Boeuf Stro-ga-noff
> Shashlyk Kar-ski
> Kot-let Po-zhar-ski *

---

* Sudak Orloff: bass-like fish, fried, with tomato sauce.
Boeuf Stroganoff: shredded beef in mushroom-cream-paprika sauce.
Shashlyk Karski: grilled rack of lamb, previously marinated.
Kotlet Pozharski: ground-veal hamburger.

Mme. Elveera, off to phone again, was taking longer than I had expected. Whom was she calling? Family? Or to report on her ward?

["No, we did not stay to the end at the theater. He said he was tired. . . . Yes, we are going to have supper. . . . Yes, here, at the hotel. . . . No, he did not contact anyone. . . . Yes, tomorrow at nine I'm taking him to the *Mavzolei*. . . ."]

"I'm sorry, Mr. Nabokov, it took so long," Mme. Elveera said when she reappeared, her face freshly powdered, rouged, and perfumed. She reeked of lilac. Her dark eyes were sad and gentle. "I had to wait in line. There was quite a crowd before me. Finally I got through to my mother." Her mother had been ill, she explained. Nothing serious, just flu with high fever. "But she is very old and she looks after the children when I'm at work."

The waiter would not come to our table. Mme. Elveera had to go to find the supervisor. The supervisor wrote down our order and sauntered away.

Mme. Elveera started at once to re-expose the program prepared by her Ministry for my fortnight's stay in the Soviet Union.

"*Noo vot*," she began, "as I have already told you, I will come and fetch you tomorrow," she looked at her watch, "excuse me, today—at eight thirty. We will drive to the Mausoleum. Then at ten thirty you are expected at the Composers' Union."

She went on and on, like a wound-up toy. It sounded like a litany, a Russian wake, toneless and hypnotic. I marveled at the alacrity and precision with which this wan, worn woman was reciting a cumbersomely detailed program, looking only now and then at a little notebook where all the hours and the events were marked.

Quite a few people must have been at work preparing this program. And it was done as carefully as the Japanese or the Germans would have done it. They must have phoned the Embassy in Berlin, various offices in Leningrad, contacted elusive people like Rostropovich and busy ones like Khrennikov, arranging for passes, tickets, and train, plane, and hotel reservations.

I felt as if I were a very delicate object, wrapped in cotton wool and packed in a soft cardboard box with a HANDLE WITH CARE label pasted on top. An object to be carefully unwrapped, and then genteelly but thoroughly processed, so that toward the end of its stay in Moscow and Leningrad, with a possible excursion to Suzdal and Vladimir, it would acquire a newly found gloss of Sovietophilia, based on a common native heritage. The object could then be rewrapped and shipped safely back to Berlin.

Mme. Elveera was interrupted by a waiter, who came to announce that the kitchen was closed and no hot food could be served.

"But what *can* you serve?" asked Mme. Elveera, perplexed.

"Wine, *konyak, chai,* or *kofe,*" answered the waiter.

"Excuse me, Mr. Nabokov," said Mme. Elveera, "I'll have to go and see what can be done." And before I could stop her, she leaped from her chair and disappeared toward the entrance door.

I sat and waited once more. When Mme. Elveera returned she grumbled, "A real scandal! I'll have to report it to the management. Please excuse me." The same waiter came trailing behind her and brought fish in aspic, stale-looking cold cuts, bread and butter.

"I am really sorry, Mr. Nabokov," Mme. Elveera started again, "your first meal in Moscow, and so awful—"

"Don't worry," I interrupted, "I'm not hungry. This is perfectly all right. And . . . and why don't you address me the proper Russian way—Nikolai Dimitrievich? What kind of 'Mister' am I, after all?" And I laughed.

"*Noo Khorosho.*" She smiled back. "So . . . so where were we, Nikolai Dimitrievich? *Akh*, yes! At the Tretyakov Gallery on Tuesday. Well, after the visit to the Tretyakovka, we go to . . ." and while we ate, she went on unrelentingly with the program. "We have left open quite a few hours for rest and . . . at your private disposal. But, please, be kind and advise us, I mean me, in advance what changes you wish and where you want to go. Because—"

Again I interrupted her. "Of course, of course I will," I said. "I will even ask you for help and advice. I am, after all, a stranger in this town. But thank you anyhow for all those admirable arrangements. I would, for example, like to see Ambassador Thompson and Mrs. Thompson. They are close personal friends. I also would like to have Lina Ivanovna Prokofieva's phone number. She, too, and her husband were close friends of mine long ago in Paris. And, as for a special wish, I would very much like to meet your compatriot Aram Khachaturian. I have never met him. Everybody says he's such a nice person. And also his son or nephew, whom Stravinsky

275

liked so much when he came here."

"Oh, Aram Ilyich!" exclaimed Elveera Nikitishna, and beamed. "We'll see him in Leningrad. He'll be conducting the Philharmonic while we'll be there. He's a wonderful person!"

She was about to rise, but I held her back.

"You said," I started, "that I can suggest changes in the program. I've got one minor request for a change—I hope you'll understand. You see, I am quite tired tonight. Just as you must be. It has been a very long day. And I'd like to sleep a bit late into the morning. So, if possible, could we refrain from that visit to the Mausoleum at eight thirty?"

Elveera looked startled and embarrassed. "As you wish." She said it coldly, and I felt that my impudent request had dissolved the apologetic and to a degree even affectionate warmth that had established itself between us in the course of that long day and evening.

I said "Thank you" and "*Dosvidanya*" and kissed Elveera Nikitishna's outstretched hand.

She smiled again, but a bit awkwardly. "*Okay* then," she said.

The bed had a loose spring and a hole in the middle. Every time I moved, a wire jangled and emitted a middle D. The room was sticky—the air did not move at all.

[I am seized by the feeling of the *déjà vu, déjà vécu*. It is familiar. I know that it comes when perception is disconnected —like slowed-up cinema, with stops in between.

But this time it feels different. As if there were something real, something concrete behind it. And *fearfully old* . . . as if, from the farthest recesses of memory, ancient photographs were forcing themselves to life, to existence . . . faded, blurred, yet strangely tangible. What are they about? Of whom? From when? From how far?

I force myself to remember, but nothing happens. I am about to give up when something clicks.

A very long, searching silence. Then all of a sudden, like an explosion in Cyrillic letters:

Ира...Ира... Шибаева....

Eera Shibaeva, a girl who is staying with us this year in Yalta, I do not know why. A creamy, plumpish girl . . . but, oh—so tempting.

One day late in May we walk high up the hill, beyond the

town's limits to the Armenian church. It is a weekday, the church and the cemetery around it are deserted. We hide in the entrance porch on a stone bench. We kiss and kiss and kiss— every pleat, every fold, every swelling. She is less impatient than I. Much subtler. Instinctively experienced.

She dresses slowly and asks me to button the front of her blouse. And while I do it, she tickles my mouth with the tip of her tongue.

Later on we walk slowly, side by side, holding hands down the steep, pebbly path. It has rained. The scent of Persian lilacs in bloom bathes our bodies.

We stop at a small open platform with a bench and a view. Down below, evening is settling on springy, misty Yalta, and the sky is leaving tendriled mother-of-pearl trails upon the still water of the harbor. And someone is banging at my door.]

"Just a minute," I shout in English, trying to get my bearings. Where am I? Who is it? What time is it?

A pale, thin, incredibly seedy-looking man stands at the door. He is carrying a tiny, beaten-up fiber overnight case.

"I am the electrician. Your lights," he explains in no-man's tongue.

"Come in, come in," I reply.

"*Akh!* You speak Russian," he exclaims. And I see my first Russian smile melt upon a Muscovite's face.

The *montyor* repaired the lights in a jiffy and left. I went to the bathroom, longing for a warm bath. This time the hot-water tap wouldn't even gargle or cough. It was mute and dry.

I had noticed the day before that next to mine was a door with a sign: "ENTRANCE PROHIBITED. REST ROOM FOR PERSONNEL." I thought I'd find someone in there to repair the hot-water tap.

In the corridor, a woman came toward me. As she passed, she said in a sullen monotone, "No hot water today. Boilers under repair."

I returned frustrated to my bathroom.

The floor was filthy. Dark-brown, chipped tiles. Some of them missing. Under the washbasin and around the john, stains of chewing gum, like squashed beetles. Soft music and voices coming from a ventilation hole in the ceiling. "How strange," I thought, "in a bathroom."

The shaver's socket wouldn't work. I shaved Gillettingly and washed up cold in a plugless tub. As I was finishing there was a hesitant knock at the door.

A diminutive charwoman with a shrunken face like a last-year's apple stood in front of me. She looked ancient, like someone out of a folk-tale.

"*Vann ikh komm sol,*" she mumbled stutteringly in no-man's German.

"When should you come to do what?" I asked.

As with the electrician, the face of the old woman melted, the wrinkles dissolved and turned into a broad, toothless beam.

"Oh, God bless you," she said very gently, "so you speak Russian! How very fine!" and she looked at me fondly. "I wanted to know when you would like me to come to tidy up your room."

"In about an hour," I replied, "if that is all right with you?"

"Oh, but of course it is, of course it is," she muttered hurriedly. "And would you have anything to wash up? Shirts, handkerchiefs? Because if you give it to me now, I'll get it back to you before four—before the night shift comes."

"I don't have much. Except perhaps this shirt. Could you do it?" And not knowing how to address her, I said *Sudarynya* (ma'am), which I knew was wrong.

She laughed in a tiny, high-pitched laughter, showing once more her toothless gums. "What kind of ma'am am I?" she exclaimed. "Call me simply Tanya, or Tatyana. And what's your name, sir, if I may ask?"

I told her my name, then spelled it out, letter by letter and repeated it slowly: "Ni-ko-lai Di-mi-tri-e-vich Na-bo-kov."

"Aha!" she exclaimed again and beamed. "Sounds like a Russian name. And you speak like we do, only *pokulturneye*—more civilized." Her gentle voice sounded full of pleasure. "You're, as it were, *sovsem svoi chelovek*—completely our own man?"

And suddenly her face became wrinkled again.

"But why did they tell us," and she frowned, "that you are some sort of a German? They are such liars. I mean those supervisors. Here you are with a Russian name and speaking like we do and they call you a German!" She shook her head. "Don't you trust them, *Barin mily*. I mean Nikolai Dimitrievich . . . my head is a sieve, I forget everything right away. I'm worn out like a rotten cabbage. . . . What was I saying? *Akh*, yes," and she came close to me and started whispering in my ear. "Better close that door." She pointed to the bathroom door.

"But why?" I asked.

"Don't ask why. Just close it," and she went and closed the door noiselessly. "When you speak in here," she continued in a half-whisper, "you better keep this door shut. Believe me, Nikolai Dimitrievich, it is safer this way. Especially when you are a stranger who speaks our language."

"You were saying something about the supervisors," I intervened. "Do you mean the woman who sits near the lift, at the end of this corridor?"

"*Akh!* Yes. What is there to say about them?" she said with disgust. "You can see for yourself, can't you? The day one is a bitch—she growls and bites. And the night one is a fat mare, stupid but nasty. That's all. But don't you trust them, *Barin mily*. And don't give them any tips. They're not worth it. They're a devil's brood! All of them here at this hotel are a pack of wolves. The Lord is witness I'm saying the truth," and she made a broad sign of the cross and muttered something.

"From whereabouts are you, Tanya?" I asked, to change the subject.

"Who? Me?" she asked, perplexed by my question. "We're from those who belonged to the Shcherbatov estates, not far from Moscow. My father was gardener there. But that was long, very long ago." She waved her arms. "I barely remember when our last landlords were chased away. My father's been dead now for many years, bless his soul," and she crossed herself again, "and so's my mother. We were their only two children, my sister and I, and neither of us married. So we're quite alone. My sister, bless her soul, is older than me and nearly blind. When she was young, she wanted to be a nun. But those godless ones, you know whom I mean," and she pointed at the open window, "they closed the nunneries. So my sister and I worked as charwomen—near our village —at a sanatorium. Then came the war and the Germans burned our village. So we moved nearer to Moscow. My sister can't work any longer. She's old and, as I said, she doesn't see well. But we live very far out of town—three kilometers to the bus stop. Sometimes I think I can't make it any longer . . . but what can I do?" She picked up my soiled shirt, looked at it with a connoisseur's eye, and said in a matter-of-fact voice, "This one should never be boiled,

Nikolai Dimitrievich. I'll do it by hand. It dries fast—good *Amerikanski* material—I'll have it all ready for you before dinner." And she glanced at me again with tender, beaming eyes.

She was about to leave, but I stopped her and led her into the bathroom. "Could you explain to me, Tanya, why this floor is so worn and filthy?"

Suddenly the tiny old woman was transformed. She looked furious. "What can I do, sir?" she shrieked. "Every day I report it to the management. But that devil's brood downstairs, those hooligans only say, 'Mind your own business, go on, wash!' "

"But at least one could wash that floor properly," I said amiably, as if I had not noticed the change in her tone of voice.

"What do you mean, properly?" she exclaimed indignantly. "I rub it every day. I rub thirty-two bathroom floors on these two corridors, my dear sir! One after the other! I'll show you how I do it. I'll show you!" And she ran out of the room.

A moment later she reappeared holding a battered bucket full of ink-black water.

"Here's how I do it," and she pulled out of the bucket a torn rag as black as the water.

"Don't . . . don't do it now," I interrupted her. "You can do it when I'm gone."

"But I wanted to show you that I—"

"Yes, of course, of course, I see," I interrupted again. "But if you wash the floors of those thirty-two bathrooms with that kind of water and that kind of rag, you'll never get them clean. They'll only get dirtier."

She looked at me bewildered and replied stodgily, her arms akimbo, "I wash with what I'm given!"

"Yes, Tanya, of course you do. I understand. But can't you *change* the water, use warm water and have the management give you soap?"

"*Akh, Barin mily*, you don't know anything about us people here. Just go and try to talk to these . . . these birds downstairs! I've been clamoring for a new rag and for soap for years! And for hot water! Even you don't get hot water every day. Every week one of their boilers goes *kaput* and there's no hot water in the whole of the Pekin. 'Go, mind your business, old hag,' they say. 'Do what you're ordered and do it with what you're given!' Yes, dear sir, that's what they tell me! You should see how clean I can keep a floor. There, in our little room, the *Kamorka*—where we live—my sister and I. It's spick and span—like a mirror."

"I believe you, Tanya. I believe you," I said, trying to soothe her. I smiled at her. "I'm not reproaching you. But there is one thing, Tanya, I believe you could do." I took her by the arm and pointed to the chewing-gum stains on the floor. "Couldn't you get those off?"

Tanya's face got crimson. "Look here, *Barin mily*," she exclaimed, exasperated, "I've been rubbing those filthy stains for the last two years! They simply won't go off! They only get darker every month! I've told the management a hundred times to put spittoons in these bathrooms! Because when some of those godforsaken delegates come, they're not neat like you. They're filthy dirty! They spit this American rubber candy all over the place! Soon these bathrooms will be pigsties!"

"But did you ever try to use a knife?" I suggested.

"And where, my dear sir, shall I get a knife? Now look here, *Barin*, if I go downstairs to those bastards and ask for a knife to clean bathroom floors, they'll think I've gone berserk. And . . . and I'll lose my job! How would you like that? They'll kick me out!"

"I know where to find a knife, Tanya," I said. "Come with me," and I took her gently by the arm. "Come, I'll show you where there are plenty of knives."

I went next door to the room reserved for the personnel. The door was ajar. Two charwomen younger and plumper than Tanya were eating and drinking tea.

Tanya pulled me by the sleeve. "You're not supposed to go in here, *Barin*," she whispered.

I went straight to the table with silverware, said "Hello" to the breakfasting pair, and asked if I might borrow a knife. One of them started to mumble something about the sign on the door. "I know, I know," I interrupted. "It won't take more than a few minutes." I picked up a knife and left.

Tanya was speechless as she watched every one of my movements. When we came back to my room I easily scraped off two of the chewing-gum stains and had started scraping a third one when I heard Tanya's tiny little voice.

"*Smotrite skhodit!* It comes off!" She looked at me in amazement. "*Noo, Barin mily*, you're a real wizard, a magician!"

281

"Now you see, dear Tanya, it can be done," and I laughed. "But I had better take that knife back before we get into trouble." I went to the personnel room and returned the knife.

Tanya was waiting for me, her smile sweeter than ever. "*Noo*, Nikolai Dimitrievich . . . I can only say live and learn. Thank you, thank you, *Barin mily*."

When I came back to the hotel in the evening, all the chewing-gum stains were gone and the tiles of the bathroom floor looked much lighter.

On my night table, in a tiny vodka glass, stood a sprig of wilted forget-me-nots.

EPILOGUE

A Postscript to Russia

A letter to a friendly ambassador

Dear friend,

After my return from the Soviet Union you asked me point blank to tell you: How did it feel to be back home? What did I like? What went against my grain? What went wrong? Did I have a good time?

"And, please, Nikolai Dimitrievich," you added, "don't lie! Don't be afraid to tell me the truth. I am an old mule. I can take it. And I promise not to hold it against you. Especially since it comes from an innocent capitalist underdog like you."

I told you *all*, as frankly and as honestly as I possibly could. I described in detail my sojourn in Moscow and in Leningrad. I told you how warm the welcome had been, how wonderful it was to meet Slava and Galya Rostropovich in Moscow and later on at their *dacha*, to have a huge birthday feast with them for their two daughters with the Shostakoviches and Rozhdestvenskys, Slava's mother and sister, and other neighbors of theirs. I told you how much I liked Aram and Nina Khachaturian, their son, and their nephew, and how nice to me were many other colleagues, young and old, among Soviet composers.

I also told you that one of the sweetest things that happened to me in Moscow was the luncheon to which your former colleague Y. A. Kvitsinski invited me at his home. I felt so comfortable with him, his wife, and another couple at their new flat on Moscow's outer ring. It was in fact very much like my own little flat in Paris, to which you came one day with your wife when you were Ambassador in France. Remember?

I liked some of the theater I saw in Moscow, and the music I heard at concerts or on tape, music by young Soviet composers, so far unknown abroad—Tishchenko, Denisov, Silvestrov, Shnittke, and quite a few others.

I fell in love with Russian portrait painting and returned several times to the Tretyakov Gallery to see those three or four rooms filled with portraits. I discovered by myself, and perhaps for myself, that the Russian gift for portrait painting is unique and consistent. From the Novgorod School of identifiable icons through the exuberant nineteenth century up to our time, it is one of the few art continuums Russia ever had. And I suppose it has to do with Russia's ingrained sense for the hieratic, deep-set, instinctive realism.

I urged you to impress upon your Ministry and the Union of Soviet Composers how important, if not indispensable, it is for young Soviet composers to travel abroad, to learn what their contemporaries are doing all over the world, and not leave the travel abroad only to those few who have acquired what one calls status.

You received my critical views with grace and magnanimity and seemed grateful to me for being scrupulously candid.

You even invited me to return the next year to Belorussia. You said you'd come with me and we'd visit together Minsk, Novogrudok, and my native Lubcza, and go crayfishing in Lake Kroman.

But then the next year was 1968. And just at the time when my wife, Dominique, and I were about to fly to Russia the invasion of Czechoslovakia took place. So I had to decline your invitation. I know you were cross with me for what you thought was "getting cold feet." But later, the inimitably wonderful Slava Rostropovich, the devoted, warmhearted, and faithful friend, soothed your anger. We became friends anew and . . . and I suspect that somewhere deep in your Russian heart—below the conventions of partisanship and rank—you respected my "cold feet."

I told you that what moved me most during my trip to Russia was my visit to Zagorsk and, of course, my visit to Leningrad.

There in Zagorsk, in the dark chapel of St. Sergei's Tomb, I heard, as if coming from very, very far, like the remote sound of a harp string, the quiet beating of the Russian heart. Unextinguishable, inexorable, like the ticking of a clock. The place was crowded. Not with old women, mind you, but with people of all ages, some of them in Red Army uniform. And the faces were earnest, handsome, and strangely solemn.

I fretted to go to Leningrad. I told you I would fret. You cannot possibly understand why, my friend. You have a land to which you belong. A piece—and a very large one—of our earth. You fought for it and regained all of it by the skin of your teeth, with valor and courage.

But I? I have nothing. I'm like a Jew in the early Diaspora, praying for "next year in Jerusalem." My Jerusalem is St. Petersburg. And I know it will never happen, it cannot possibly happen, and yet I pray for it deep down in my unconscious.

Because . . . because, as you yourself once said in your direct, pragmatic way, this is the culture to which I and my whole family, with all of its atavisms, belong. This is the culture that nurtured us and the likes of us in our Russian Diaspora.

And, yes, St. Petersburg did turn out to be a traumatic experience.

There it was, all of it, intact or reconstructed with infinite love and care by its inhabitants: The "Queen of the North" standing proudly on the shores of the Neva and the Neva's many confluents and those canals dug by Czar Peter to make it look like another Amsterdam. Splendid, spacious, airy, curiously absent-minded, yet the most extraordinary city human beings have ever conceived and built! Parallel only, but on a much grander scale, to such jewels as Venice before its present decline, or to Pekin, I suppose, at the time of the Ming Empire.

How could Pushkin have compared it with and called it by the name of the Hellenistic caravan town? Was it because in his time Palmyra was a myth of the literary imagination?

Dear friend, there is little new I can add to what I have already told you about what to you is the "heroic city of Leningrad" and to me will forever remain my childhood's St. Petersburg.

I did tell you that it appeared to me as if it were a shell. The content of that shell—its spirit, its soul (forgive me for using unMarxist terms)—was gone, gone forever. I felt like an explorer discovering and entering an inviolate Pharaonic tomb, with all of its beauty intact but with a hopelessly dead Pharaoh and grains of wheat that will never grow again.

285

I think I did tell you all of this. But I did not tell you, nor would you understand my gnawing sadness, that my own Jerusalem, my St. Petersburg in all of its reconstructed splendor, has since my visit become even more of a never-never land than it ever was, thoroughly unattainable but ever present. Like all myths, it is cruelly real, embedded in the depths of my psyche and connected by a myriad of blood vessels to the very essence of my Diasporatic life.

Touching its pure and perfect glory with my eyes, I felt like the gardener in Strindberg's *Dream Play*. "Yes, it is green," says the gardener, looking at a butterfly box he has wanted all his life and has finally received, "but it is not the kind of green I had imagined." And so it was with St. Petersburg, with all its glamorous yet soulless body.

Still there is one final episode, my dear friend, that I want to recall for you. The episode concerns my departure from St. Petersburg for Moscow. Here it is:

It was carefully planned by my Armenian Mother Goose, Elveera Nikitishna Melkumyan, that I should take the famous luxury train, the Red Star, back to Moscow.

Well . . . at the last minute something went awfully wrong. My chaperone kept my railroad tickets in her possession. She was to give them to me at the time of my departure. But instead of meeting me at the railroad station, she was waiting for me at my hotel. Smoothly and noiselessly the blue Red Star moved into the pale night of Leningrad's suburbia, but without me.

The next train was due to leave at 23:30. When it stopped in front of the platform, something like panic seized the crowd. They assaulted the train precisely the way trains used to be assaulted in 1917 and 1918. Even before it had stopped, people started to climb through windows, throwing their *chemodany* and *baooly* over the heads of the climbers, pressing and mauling one another in an unbelievable frenzy at both entrances of the soft-berth railroad carriage that had stopped in front of the bench where a friend and I were waiting.

"It is always that way," my friend, Igor Ivanovich, remarked morosely. "When shall we learn to be a bit more civilized?"

Suddenly I saw my guide running toward me, shouting something. "I got you a lower," he blurted, out of breath. "That stupid bitch sat on her arse at the hotel waiting for us, instead of coming here! Well, let's go!" The guide picked up my cases and pressed through the crowd that corked up the corridor of the railroad carriage. I followed in his tracks.

"This is your berth," he said, pointing to the lower in a compartment full of people. I saw a Caucasian-looking man pick up his belongings from what I was told was my berth and move out of the compartment with a despondent smile.

"I hope you did not kick out this man on my account," I said to the guide.

"What do you mean, 'kick out'?" he replied indignantly. "He had no right to be here anyway. I know him well. He's a black-marketeer. Wait till we catch him!"

Meanwhile the crowd in the corridor got settled for the night. I said goodbye to my friend through the open window and sat down on my berth. The train started with a jolt.

I shared the compartment with a young couple and two boys of seven or eight who looked like twins. Once the train had started, the male half of the couple turned to me and said, "Under your and my wife's berths are wicker baskets with chicks fresh from the incubator. They belong to the Armenian gentleman whose berth you have taken away from him. They are cheaper here in Leningrad than in Yerevan. So don't be astonished if during the night you hear peeping noises come from under your berth."

Then the four of them undressed, the father and the two boys on the two uppers, the mother on her lower, hiding behind a shawl she had asked her husband to hold for her. I took off my shoes, covered myself with a raincoat, and lay down on my back.

The train rolled smoothly on those arrow-straight tracks Nicolas I had drawn with a ruler on a map of Russia in 1848 or 1849. The sweet peep of the chicks made soothing music.

But I could not sleep, nor did I want to. I daydreamed.

I daydreamed about my Northern Queen, the jewel that I was leaving behind me—or rather the jewel's case. The jewel itself was buried away somewhere deep in memory.

Because, believe it or not, it was on June 30, the same date in 1917, that Valentin Pavlovich Diaghilev, Sergei P. Diaghilev's brother, and two of his sons took me, Aunt Caroline, my sister Lida, and her governess to the same train at the same station. And the night was as pale then as it was now, and the morning would come as early as it did precisely fifty years ago.

This is the episode I wanted to tell you, dear friend. Maybe somewhere, some time, in some language, you will read it.

And if you should read it, do remember (*please do!*) that I will remain forever grateful to you and to Slava Rostropovich for bringing about the homecoming of an old *Peterburzhets.*

And maybe someday we will go crayfishing in Lake Kroman. Could I bring my three sons—Ivan, the Russian; Peter, the American; and Alexander, the Frenchman? Notice that all of them have good old Russian tsarist names. But then you yourself bear the name of not just the most fearsome tsar of Russia, but the inventor of my northern capital.

Index

INDEX

INDEX

INDEX

INDEX

INDEX

INDEX

Born in Russia in 1903, Nicolas Nabokov emigrated first to Germany, then to France, and became an American citizen in 1939. He studied music in Stuttgart and Berlin, and acquired a degree in Humanities from the Sorbonne, Paris, in 1926.

At the close of World War II he became chief cultural assistant to the American Military Government in Berlin, and subsequently the cultural advisor to the American ambassador there.

After the war he returned to writing music and teaching, and in 1951 was elected secretary general of the Congress for Cultural Freedom, in which capacity he organized conferences and art festivals in Berlin, Paris, Rome, Tokyo, and New Delhi. Between 1963 and 1966 he was director of the yearly arts festival in West Berlin, and advisor for international cultural affairs to Willy Brandt, then mayor of West Berlin. He was composer in residence at the Aspen Institute for Humanistic Studies between 1970 and 1973.

Mr. Nabokov is a member of the National Institute of Arts and Letters, the Berlin Academy of Arts and Letters, and the French Society of Composers. He is also Commander of the Grand Cross of Merit of the German Federal Republic. His wide musical output includes two operas, two oratorios, symphonic works, ballets, and chamber music, all of which have been performed in America and Europe by leading orchestras under the direction of eminent conductors.

He has lectured widely in colleges and universities in this country as well as in Europe, Asia, and Latin America. His one previous autobiographical book, entitled Old Friends and New Music, *was published in 1951.*

Married to the photographer, Dominique Cibiel, Mr. Nabokov divides his time between Paris, Berlin, and New York, where he is currently a visiting professor at New York University.